EQUITABLE ADULT LEARNING

This book provides case studies written by practitioners from four organizations serving diverse adult learners in equitable, inclusive, and just ways. Their work employs an adapted version of the Education Deans for Justice and Equity Framework for Assessment and Transformation, a comprehensive tool grounded in research on equity and justice. This is one of the first published uses of that framework.

The editors situate this book in the history and need for increased equity and justice in adult education. They apply participatory action research to assist the four organizations in telling their stories. Authors of the organization chapters highlight their history and context in relation to their organizational structures, systems, policies, and procedures. Editors provide a cross-case analysis of the four case studies.

This book will appeal to academics in adult education, social justice education, qualitative research methods, and organizational development. Organizations and practitioners will find exemplars of how to live into their intentions to be equitable and just.

Bob Hughes is a Professor Emeritus of Adult Education at Seattle University, U.S.A.

Deanna Iceman Sands is a Professor Emeritus of Leadership and Teacher Education at Seattle University, U.S.A.

Ted Kalmus is the Director of Educational Administration at Seattle University, U.S.A.

American Association for Adult and Continuing Education Co-Publications

Adult Learning in a Migration Society
Edited by Chad Hoggan and Tetyana Hoggan-Kloubert

Equitable Adult Learning
Four Transformative Organizations Serving Diverse Communities
Edited by Bob Hughes, Deanna Iceman Sands and Ted Kalmus

EQUITABLE ADULT LEARNING

Four Transformative Organizations Serving Diverse Communities

Edited by: Bob Hughes, Deanna Iceman Sands, and Ted Kalmus

NEW YORK AND LONDON

Cover image: wildpixel / Getty Images

First published 2023
by Routledge
605 Third Avenue, New York, NY 10158

and by Routledge
4 Park Square, Milton Park, Abingdon, Oxon, OX14 4RN

Routledge is an imprint of the Taylor & Francis Group, an informa business

British Library Cataloguing-in-Publication Data
A catalogue record for this book is available from the British Library

ISBN: 978-1-032-26189-8 (hbk)
ISBN: 978-1-032-26188-1 (pbk)
ISBN: 978-1-003-28699-8 (ebk)

DOI: 10.4324/9781003286998

Typeset in Bembo
by KnowledgeWorks Global Ltd.

CONTENTS

MEET THE EDITORS

Bob Hughes, Ed.D., is an African American, cisgender male. He is a professor emeritus at Seattle University where he served as an associate professor of adult education and administrator. Prior to that, he held academic positions as a community college faculty member and dean at two colleges in the Seattle area, and as an associate professor of education at California State University Monterey Bay where he also directed one of four regional centers of a teacher certification program within the California State University system. He began in education as a secondary English teacher for 11 years. His current research and evaluation projects focus on models of equity-based effective practices in higher education and non-profit organizations, college faculty development, equitable instruction, and post-secondary transitions. He holds a doctorate in Teaching, Curriculum, and Learning Environments from Harvard University.

Deanna Iceman Sands, Ed.D., is a professor emerita at Seattle University. She currently works part-time as an advisor for the doctoral program in the College of Education at Johns Hopkins University. Her professional experiences included serving as a K-12 teacher, university faculty member, director, associate dean, and dean. Her work in education embodies values for equity, access, inclusion, and social justice. Deanna's academic and research experiences have been situated in the areas of special/general teacher education and leadership preparation. Her areas of interest included self-determination, student engagement, curriculum, instruction, and student-engaged formative assessment practices. Current research initiatives involve examining structures, systems, policies, and procedures to transform organizational leadership for justice and equity and advancing structures, routine, and norms for supporting student-engaged formative assessment in K-12 classrooms.

Ted Kalmus, M.P.A., is the director of Educational Administration programs at Seattle University where he serves as an instructor in the College of Education. Prior to his time at SU, Ted served for twenty years as a K-8 principal and Head of School in Seattle. Ted also works as a consultant, coaching principals, non-profit leaders and boards of trustees around organizational alignment, successful co-governance, and strategy making. His current research focuses on school incubation and design. Ted holds a Masters in Public Administration from the Daniel J. Evans School at University of Washington and most of a fine arts degree from the New College of California's Poetics Program.

CONTRIBUTORS

Dawn Hannah
Beyond Literacy
Philadelphia, U.S.A.

Bob Hughes
Seattle University
Seattle, U.S.A.

Ted Kalmus
Seattle University
Seattle, U.S.A.

Heather Lechner
Technology Access Foundation
Seattle, U.S.A.

Laura Medina
Building Skills Partnership
Los Angeles, CA

Kimmell Proctor
Beyond Literacy
Philadelphia, U.S.A.

Stacey Robbins
St. Mary's College
Moraga, U.S.A.

Luis Sandoval
Building Skills Partnership
Los Angeles, CA

Deanna Iceman Sands
Seattle University
Seattle, U.S.A.

Christina Taylor
Technology Access Foundation
Seattle, U.S.A.

Christian Valdez
Building Skills Partnership
Los Angeles, CA

Marguerite Welch
St. Mary's College
Moraga, U.S.A.

1

FOUNDATIONS OF EQUITY

*Bob Hughes, Deanna Iceman Sands,
and Ted Kalmus*

Adult Education Beginnings

If you work as an adult educator, you are constantly explaining to others what you do. When someone says they are a teacher, people quickly form a mental image. Their picture adjusts to their own experiences with elementary, middle, or high school teachers. Those same people typically do not adjust their mental depiction to experiences of being taught or trained as adults, even though these are likely more recent encounters with being educated. Education, as popularly understood, is for children. That understanding suggests that education ends at some defined moment that occurs as we become adults. That all makes "adult education" seem unusual. It actually is not. In this book that provides current models of equitable participation in adult education, it is important to look back and see the activities that brought us into the current context – especially in a field of study which few understand.

Societies have been educating adults throughout time. Much of what happened historically was informal and focused on providing skills training and community cohesion. Skills evolved as artisans or crafts makers perfected a technique and then others would adapt to and adopt the new technique. In the early 1800s, tin plating revolutionized food packaging to make tin cans possible after Englishman Peter Durand first patented the idea. Twenty years later, fellow Englishman Robert Clarke, a farmhand, saw the then newly developed tin plating process and adapted it to the musical pipes that had been made with other materials for millennia. Clarke went on to mass manufacture his tin whistles, which became and remain popular because of their cost and ease of use. The instrument was then copied by dozens of other makers. It is that informal adaptation and copying that marked how adults

DOI: 10.4324/9781003286998-1

learned most commonly and how skills and knowledge were disseminated throughout most of history.

In addition to the informal processes of skills development, societies maintained cultural cohesion by informally educating adults through maintaining ongoing religious practices, oral histories, and rituals. The Hopi Tribe in the southwest U.S. relies on rituals that begin at birth and encompass every part of life to include how dwellings and community life are structured. Adults learn to create Kachina dolls that they use to instruct younger members of the community. Hopi rituals allow adults to instruct other adults and youth to ensure that everything from history to language is preserved. All societies and cultures have similar practices that engage adults as keepers and builders of tradition.

While the participation of adults in learning is not a new idea, the structured and formal education of adults, however, is relatively new in the U.S. Schooling for children existed in the country for 400 years, but thinking about educating adults with similar formal structures became more common in the late 1800s. As new immigrants arrived, there were demands for their adherence to expected societal norms and concurrent demands that they master English quickly. As new and often controversial ideas formed during the Industrial Age, there was a need to debate and spread those ideas. As millions of people were freed from slavery, there was a need to educate the adults in that population, as well as a need for the larger society to have discussions about how to incorporate the recently freed; there was a concurrent need among the recently freed to organize and advocate for freedoms, participation, and opportunities. By the late 1870s, the attempted reforms of Reconstruction were waning, immigration was rising, and the nation felt the impacts of large numbers of diverse people moving into urban centers. These changes came as the majority population struggled with its relation to new immigrants and newly freed people. The demographic shifts strained the capacity of informal education processes to help adults develop the skills they needed in an industrial society. Additionally, informal education was wholly inadequate to support community and societal cohesion needed for a growing and increasingly diverse population. As a result, more formal systems began to appear (Stubblefield & Keane, 1994).

Traditional adult education historians (e.g., Knowles, 1962; Stubblefield & Keane, 1994) identify the beginnings of structured, formal adult, U.S. education in discussions that grew from the New York Chautauqua Assembly, coordinated by John Hay Vincent in 1874 in upstate New York State. That assembly was a summer camp experience intended to train Sunday School teachers, at a time when Protestant churches were major forces of cultural cohesion in the growing nation. With the success of that assembly, the Chautauqua movement expanded to other sites nationally and soon outgrew its original religious intent and became multiple venues for knowledge dissemination. By the early 1900s, a Chautauqua "circuit" developed that took the nation's major mainstream voices like William Jennings Bryant, Jane Addams, and Samuel Clemens to cities around the country to lecture (Scott, 1999).

For adults with reading skills, the Chautauqua lectures were supplemented by "reading circles" that arose from the Chautauqua movement. While reading circles have been common in recent years, they were uncommon in the early 1900s. Groups of adult readers requested a reading packet from a publisher or a third party. The packet included a study guide, and members of the reading circle would use that guide to read and learn about the material in the book. For a period prior to the expansion of telephones, when even national newspapers were uncommon in much of the nation, gathering together in a reading circle was a way for some groups of adults to interact with the emerging ideas of the day (Scott, 1999). These progenitors to the modern book club became more than discussion venues, though. The reading could lead to engagement and action, and the circle members' education could lead to community engagement. One example of the impact is in Bastrop, Texas, where circle members developed the town's first lending library, fought to preserve safety in city streets, led the efforts to build a town park, and established the county's historical society (Lewis, 2018).

It is important to note that these recognized antecedents to today's adult education efforts inequitably served only a small segment of the nation's overall population. Significant numbers of adults could not read the content sent to reading circles at a time when the nation was still wrestling with the structural and societal impacts from the Civil War and Reconstruction. While only 10.1% of the population was considered illiterate by 1900, adults were declared literate if they could read and write their name. Even at that very low bar, members of marginalized communities often did not meet the definition of "literate." For example, only 44.5% of African American adults met that definition. A better gauge of adults' functional literacy during that period is educational attainment. By 1910, the median grade completion of the overall U.S. adult population was grade 8.1, a level that suggests functional literacy, i.e., to be able to read directions and understand basic concepts. While there are no data kept for African American adults in 1910, the median grade completion rate for the first year that the census records it in 1940 was grade 5.4 for males and 6.1 for females – well below the levels of grade completion for the nation 30 years before. So, while what are considered the early efforts of formal adult education reached the already educated, there were adults whom formal adult education did not reach (Snyder, 1993). In effect the early focus on serving educated populations bifurcated the population for generations so that some people were educated for participation and leadership in the society and economy and others were not.

That failure was clearly not the result of education being unimportant to the impacted communities. Beginning in the Reconstruction era, it was often the African American community that provided the resources to build its own schools for its children, who advocated for their equal education or who moved to an area where their children could be educated (Irvin Painter, 1992). That emphasis on education did not end with care for children. Butchart explains how Black veterans hungered for literacy at the end of the war:

> ... black adult learners bought spellers and primers, cajoled literate white soldiers to tutor them or chaplains to set up classes for them, and subscribed funds to pay teachers for their services. One black regiment raised $700 in four months for its own education and donated another $60 to maintain a school for the black children of a nearby town.
>
> *Butchart, 1990, p. 5*

This desire for literacy and education was evident throughout the African American community through Reconstruction. It eventually grew into limited formal education opportunities for some freed adults. Some African American adults insisted on attending schools with the children in the community. Night schools were developed for African American soldiers and eventually for others in some areas. Adult community members were identified for their potential to be teachers and provided with advanced training so they could teach children (Butchart, 1990). Many of these efforts were curtailed as the larger mandates of the Reconstruction era were undermined through political compromises that effectively ended federal support for Reconstruction (Foner, 2014). However, the African American community continued its efforts in adult education. In 1892, Booker T. Washington sponsored the first Tuskegee Negro Conference that became an annual event which brought together leading African American educators and advocates to discuss, among other needs, the support for adult education. From these discussions came a Bible training school, a series of two-week seminars for farmers, a teacher professional development effort, the National Negro Business League, and National Negro Health Week. Washington brought together many of the African American leaders of the day, such as George Washington Carver and W.E.B. DuBois, for these efforts, all of which contributed to the educational needs of the African American adult community (James, 1990). These efforts struggled against the larger issues in the society as African Americans were systematically denied basic rights and opportunities. Throughout the late 19th and early 20th centuries, education for children and adults became one of those stolen rights.

During that time, the large numbers of immigrants who arrived during the late 1800s and early 1900s also needed education. The Settlement House movement and other charitable-based efforts sought to provide social support to immigrant adults and their families as they settled in their new country.

These organizations, often created and managed by women, offered advocacy, shelter, food, and education to adults and their children at a time where poor families lacked even the meager the resources provided by social programs in more modern times. Some were faith-based, and others came from secular and humanistic perspectives. Adult education was a relatively small component of these charitable missions (Berry, 1986; Horowitz, 1974).

As people moved away from rural areas and into cities, the nation's growing need for mass-produced food expanded. Farmers and ranchers needed to produce larger quantities of food to meet the demand. That required them to employ skills for which subsistence farming did not prepare them. States began hosting farmers' institutes to help land-based producers improve their methods. These institutes provided support for the challenges of production farming, and they also disseminated new knowledge. By 1880, 26 states developed these institutes to educate farmers on everything from seed storage to how to battle blights. The creation of these institutes eventually led to the development of the Grange and the Farmer's Union – cooperative efforts which provided education and advocacy for farming. Eventually, these organizations' efforts became a foundation for the founding of the Federal Extension Service that itself evolved into the extension programs that are still partnerships between land grant research institutions and state and federal departments of agriculture (Knowles, 1962).

The rise of unionism in the late 19th and early 20th century also had an impact on adult education. As Knowles notes, "These early labor unions had been very active in advancing the cause of public schools, public libraries, mechanics' libraries, mechanics' institutes, and lyceums [a model of study groups that preceded the Chautauqua]" (Knowles, 1962, p. 44). While the modern idea of unions is often understood to be a focus on wage, benefits, and working conditions, that is an incomplete picture of unions, either today or in the past. Despite some distrust of academics and intellectuals in the early union movements, there were efforts to see the broad needs that members needed to be trained and educated for their work, and beyond their work. This was paired with movements that sought to formalize training into systems of apprenticeship and career progression within the skilled trades (Knowles, 1962).

Evolving beyond Early Efforts

While the Chautauqua, unions, apprenticeships, reading circles, settlement houses, and community-based literacy projects were all beginning to create formalized processes to educate adults, it was not until the 1920s when adult education itself became a topic for research and rigorous development. At that time, the field of adult education began to emerge as something that needed to be studied in ways that the education of children had been studied and developed into systems and processes. In 1926, the philanthropic Carnegie Corporation funded a series of meetings that resulted in the creation of the American Association for Adult Education (A^{3}E), an organization that survives today through mergers that created the American Association of Adult and Continuing Education (Schmidt, 2013). A^{3}E brought together leading practitioners and early scholars of adult learning to discuss models and theories of adult learning. Through A^{3}E's gatherings for the 20 years following its founding, a field of adult education emerged with trained practitioners, models of practice, and definitions and theories of adult learning. It is of note that much of A^{3}E's focus was on supporting the development of an intellectual elite, rather than on the needs for employment training or literacy.

As the nation's economy expanded during and after World War II, and as there was a need for workers who had more than functional literacy skills, there was a need to increase adults' skills. The General Educational Development (GED) exam was developed in 1942 as a way to measure skills and knowledge of adults who had interrupted their education before completing high school. Together, the GED and high school diploma became demarcations of being educated. These were certifications that allowed employers to make hiring decisions. Within three decades after the GED was introduced, a high school diploma or a GED certificate became a foundational requirement for employment in jobs with wages that would support a family. By 1970, 55.2% of adults 25 years and older had attained a high school diploma (U.S. Bureau of the Census, 2021a). Moreover, many of these jobs needed special skills that required specialty training certificates beyond secondary education. Trade schools, structured apprenticeships, and junior college programs formed or grew, as did college and university attendance (U.S. Bureau of the Census, 2021b). Additionally, basic skills programs in adult literacy and English language development expanded as basic skills became foundational for economic stability.

In the period from the 1940s to the 1970s, adult education needed to take an active role in supporting the significant numbers of adults who needed to achieve the increased educational requirements. During this period, the development of adults' skills and employment-focused training began to take more of a prominent role in the field. Findings or recommendations from the Truman Commission Report in 1946 (President's Commission on Higher Education, 1947) advocated for community colleges to serve previously unserved populations. The establishment of the National Education Association's National Association for Public School Adult Education in 1952, and the passage of the Economic Opportunity Act of 1964 (U.S. Department of Education Office of Vocational and Adult Education, 2013), all brought an expanding definition for what adult learning encompasses. An evolution in the definition of adult education is still happening today. Adult education in all its forms – from adult basic education through technical training and universities and into the workplace – has become a widely encompassing endeavor that attempts to provide for the needs of adults from all parts of the society.

However, almost 60 years after the passage of the Economic Opportunity Act of 1964, which sought to create equal opportunities for all, there are still those for whom the adult education experience is inaccessible or non-responsive to the individual or collective needs of prospective learners. The systems, structures, policies, or procedures of models in which the education is offered, where and when it is offered, the costs, or the suitability to needs – these all can make educational experiences unavailable. Even though there is increased access, that has not translated to success for all as barriers still exist for some populations; and many educational organizations that serve adults are challenged to be successful in serving all populations they could serve. It has not been enough to open the door to educational opportunities equally to all. These systems and programs need to find ways to equitably support all learners. In more recent years, adult education has sought to be more than just equally available to all as it reacts to social pressures, legislative mandates, and funding issues that keep it from serving all learners equitably (Becker Patterson, 2014; Katz & Geiger, 2019; Ross-Gordon, 2011; Skobba et al., 2018). Successfully serving a diverse population of adults is challenging.

Equity and Justice: What Are the Barriers?

Adult education has evolved during its history as it shifted to accommodate larger societal needs. It is critical to understand that the served populations were not monolithic. The histories of different groups impacted their needs for adult education and the ways in which adult education can serve them. For example, the arrival of large numbers of Southeast Asian refugees that began in the mid-1970s is tied to the end of the war in that region. As these people arrived, and continue to arrive, they needed educational support to speak, read, and write English; they also needed citizenship classes and assistance in understanding the schools their children attended; and they needed to address the traumas of having lived through war. In the 1980s and 1990s, these refugees were joined by Eastern European immigrants, who left the former Soviet Bloc countries, and by East African refugees fleeing war and famine. This rich mixture of immigrants was further enhanced by Central American immigrants and refugees fleeing violence, persecution, and economic deprivation. As a result, adult literacy that had previously focused on undereducated, English-speaking adults found itself in need of developing much more robust and comprehensive offerings that could provide support for highly educated immigrants and refugees, as well as those who had interrupted or no education in their country of birth (Choi & Morrison, 2014; Li, 2012; Zakaluk & Wynes, 1995).

The historic inequities that exist in the U.S. also impact adult education significantly. For example, because of the legacy of separate educational systems that provide lower qualities of K-12 education for marginalized groups, African American, Latinx, Native American, and some Asian American adults begin adulthood with different post-secondary educational needs than their White counterparts (Darling-Hammond, 2007). Since it started looking closely at these issues, the adult education community has understood that a contest where some starters begin ahead of others is an unequal contest. Early responses within adult education attempted to move people of color forward in the contest. These efforts did not see how the impacts of that poor starting position impacted not just their position in the contest but also their ability to compete. For example, a 30-year-old woman refugee arriving with two children does not have the same educational and career opportunities as her native-born counterpart. However, much of the social safety system provides her with few more supports than someone who speaks English fluently and has already had some education in the U.S. As with all other aspects of inequities in the nation, adult education has needed to develop approaches beyond equality and into equity and justice.

Historic legislation and societal practices created barriers in employment, housing, education, and economic opportunities that continue to impact adult learners. Women earn less than men for the same work (Bureau of Labor Statistics, 2021a). People of color and immigrants work in lower-paying occupations than their White counterparts (Bureau of Labor Statistics, 2021b). People of color are more likely to be jailed and for longer sentences than White people who commit the same crimes (U.S. Sentencing Commission, 2017). These are all legacies of a history that goes back 400 years. These issues continue to influence how adult education is delivered as the nation often assumes that these critical factors have negligible importance. Adult basic education programs throughout the nation, for example, are mostly funded through the Workforce Innovation and Opportunities Act (WIOA). This act's progenitor is the 1966 Adult Education Act and a series of reauthorizations. Through federal legislation, adult basic education has increasingly focused on adult basic education for employment. In contrast, leaders in adult basic education went through an inclusive, six-year process to develop the Equipped for the Future Standards in 2000. Those standards proposed looking at adult learning needs comprehensively, and they saw employment as one aspect of adults' need for education. However, the federal focus has been on getting people employed to exclusion of all other needs (Hughes & Knighton, 2020). In practice, then, the larger societal demands, and the funding which shape how those demands are implemented, assure that the complexities of historical impacts of race, gender, and linguistic diversity are de-emphasized instead of addressed. Similarly, narrow focuses exist in all aspects of adult education as adult education in all its forms can easily lose sight of the complicated issues created by a historically inequitable society, issues that impact the two questions of equity: who is excluded from what is provided and who is not served well by what is provided.

The needs of an industrial society and now an information-based society have required increased levels of basic literacy for adults to participate economically and even politically. Women were not allowed to vote until 1920 and were limited after that, and were not encouraged to pursue any education and training. They were often barred from occupations. The legacy of that continues to impact women's opportunities. Societal educational imitations were extended to racial and ethnic groups, those with learning differences and people in poverty. All of those inequalities created generational cycles of under-educated children who became under-educated adults. Federal and state laws and court rulings opened the doors for more children to be educated after the Supreme Court's Brown v. Board of Education ruling in 1954. These laws and rulings ensured children's access to the schoolroom. They demanded equal treatment for historically ill-served groups, and they had some impact. From 1954 onward, the schools saw steady increases in the number of children completing increasingly higher levels of education, and the tide of increase affected all groups (U.S. Bureau of the Census, 2021b).

However, these increased levels of education did not proportionally increase educational success among all groups. The political response to Brown was ferocious and amplified a racialized set of *de jure* policies and *de facto* practices that inhibited access to capital, real estate, and job opportunities for people of color. African American, Latinx, and some Asian groups still do not complete high school at the rate of their White counterparts, often because of the continued segregation of the nation's schools where wealthier White communities offer a well-resourced education to children, and communities of color lack those resources (Orfield, 2005; Semega et al., 2020; Turner et al., 2007). The children of immigrants find themselves in those same schools with fewer resources, and they struggle within the intersection of linguistic development and an under-resourced education system (Zhang & Han, 2017). Women are hampered and still funneled away from traditionally male occupations and professions, which offer higher pay (Pedulla & Thébaud, 2015). Students with learning differences find themselves shut out of post-secondary educational opportunities or relegated to occupations with minimal or no preparation requirements (Hughes et al., 2018). All of these inequities eventually impact adult education as children become adults. Often, the issues get magnified in adult education as adults bring all of that to their experiences as adult learners.

In many ways, adult education faces many of the issues that the K-12 system struggles to overcome. Additionally, though, adult education must tackle the complex socio-economic worlds in which the adult population lives since the people seeking education in adult settings bring their complex lives with them (Boyadjieva & Ilieva-Trichkova, 2017). Most obviously, adults need to manage their own food, clothing, and shelter – and often for their children, also. The daily responsibilities of life mean that educational opportunities need to be shaped around those responsibilities. When those responsibilities include multiple jobs or the care of extended family members, educational opportunities are often further limited. This becomes even more complex when considering the ways in which racial, ethnic, gender, economic, and other biases create a host of barriers for adults who could benefit from the opportunities of adult education. At times, the delivery of adult education is, itself, the barrier as the delivered model may remain blind to these needs (Hughes, 2007).

These barriers get extended by propagandized labels put on different groups. These, often, gender, race, and ethnicity-based perceptions, have generated a political climate which has created policies, practices, and laws for serving adult learners. A good example is the Personal Responsibility and Work Opportunity Reconciliation Act of 1996, often identified as the Welfare Reform Act of 1996 (U.S. Department of Health and Human Services, 1996) which was passed in the U.S. Congress with strong support from both parties. That act came after two decades of politicization of social safety net programs that disparaged "welfare queens" who were, as the rhetoric suggested, unwilling to support themselves. Despite social safety programs overwhelmingly serving White families, the propaganda of the period suggested these "queens" were mostly people of color who lived well off from their public assistance. That act used a behavioristic approach of rewards and punishments to get people to work and off public assistance. This spawned a workforce development industry that gave people as few as 12 hours of training to begin a new career. It limited the benefits they received and eliminated those benefits as soon as they went to work. Its true impact, however, was to create a permanent underclass of adults who were given training to be hired into low-wage jobs where they had no opportunities for occupational or educational advancement, a change that has disproportionally impacted women (Edin & Shaefer, 2016). That has led to disproportionate impact on these populations. Organizations that seek to provide adult education to them struggle with the impacts of this history, a history that compounds any challenges of just providing instruction.

Equity and Justice: The Need for Examples of Success

The challenge of addressing the historical accumulation of disadvantage energizes many of those committed to adult learning. Adult educators begin with a passion for equity and justice that leads them to create and work within organizations that allow them to live that passion. Caffarella (1996) described that commitment over 25 years ago, and that same commitment remains central to the people and work described in this book. The ways in which people's commitments lead to action is also why the work is so diverse. As Chapters 3–6 of this book show, people with commitment see the need and they work to address that need. As a result, organizations have emerged which are designed or adapted to supplement the gaps in literacy, technological fluency, workforce training, college access, and legal and political advocacy, among many others (Fleinming & Nelson, 2007; Hemphill, 1996; Knox, 2002; Pekow, 2006).

At the same time, the bar set for "minimum qualifications" across a wide range of professions is rising steadily across U.S. job sectors. According to the Pew Research Center, U.S. manufacturing and jobs which only require physical and manual skills have decreased by a third since 1990 while "knowledge-intensive and service-oriented sectors, such as education, health, and professional and business services have doubled" in size over the same time period (Pew Research Center, 2016).

With these challenges in mind, access to (and success in) two- and four-year college programs and high-quality vocational programs has become paramount to the pursuit of employment opportunities that support and sustain families. There are also pre-college-level programs that serve adult learners as they gain literacy skills, workforce readiness skills, and workplace skills. Additionally, there are organizations and programs that offer enrichment and personal development for adults. For those who are college educated, there is a need to be able to navigate the diversity represented by their co-workers and the clients they serve. New teachers, for example, need skills in working with a variety or cultural groups; and as the education profession seeks to diversify itself, the newly certified diverse teachers need to have significant support in negotiating the system while advocating for its change.

It is this wide array of organizations that make it their business to calibrate Horace Mann's "balance-wheel of social machinery" that he used to describe education's central role in making a society function (Kendall Edgerton, 2009). However, while the size and scope of educational efforts vary dramatically, they almost universally face a daunting task. Structural, cultural, and resource challenges await adult learning organizations seeking to bridge opportunity gaps for their constituents. Fortunately, many of those committed to this work recognize both a moral and an economic imperative, despite the obstacles. As a result, many new organizations germinate from grassroots efforts or as a funded impulse initiated by a public grant, a political crisis, or the interest of a single donor. Such efforts have occurred throughout adult education history (Spence & Cass, 1950) from the Settlement Movement (Horowitz, 1974) to the Harlem Experiment (Nocera, 2018) to the current age. Infrastructure emerges, often hastily, with the understandable goal of directing the vast majority of resources toward direct service. These are origin stories full of hope and energy, but they contain the roots of many of the challenges faced by organizations as they mature and seek to sustain and expand their impact.

Institutions with long-established operational structures, such as colleges or universities, face additional challenges in confronting long-standing organizational practices and policies such as resource allocation or structures for promotion. Such habits create inertia against the need to create and maintain equitable systems for deciding who is educated, learner support, program alignment, establishment of community partnerships, or supporting program evaluation. Despite what is sometimes an established history, often these institutions are no less vulnerable to the fear of financial scrutiny, donor influence, or change. The resulting impact is often a pull against a focus on equity and justice as an established system often supports the established *status quo* (Dejean, 2015; Kayes, 2006; Lane, 2017; Meyers, 2015).

Adult learning organizations can present a paradox to those attempting to predict success. On the one hand, many organizations are supported by a deeply committed workforce who visibly share a foundational clarity of purpose, sense of mission, and a level of outrage energizing the work they do (Sergiovanni, 1992). Employees and volunteers carry powerful stories of success and failure and are driven to understand the impact of the organization's work (Schein, 2010). At the same time, several other factors commonly pose obstacles. Perhaps the most significant is the lack of (or perceived lack of) resources needed to meet the goals of the organization. In some cases, there are pressures created by external funders' philosophies and practices mixing with the bureaucracies and systems of funders and policy makers (Rose, 1994). In practice, grant funding, public contracts, and shifting political winds can leave revenue streams highly unpredictable, stranding unfinished projects and requiring layoffs or adjustments to the level and experience of the workforce (Daft, 2016). Understandably, many adult learning organizations self-describe a "scarcity mindset" as pervasive throughout (Mullainathan, 2013). In their article, "The Non-Profit Starvation Cycle," Gregory and Howard (2009) identify several trends that prevent organizations from seeking and maintaining the organizational habits that manifest the robust systems of data, time for strategy and reflection, and integrated systems for professional growth that result in cycles of sustained funding.

In particular, Gregory and Howard point to three habits common to scarcity cycles: the needs of funders, the endemic underfunding of "overhead costs," and the subsequent inaccuracies and misreporting of both financial and impact data. Adult learning organizations often exemplify the effort to funnel funding toward direct services and fail to build the administrative infrastructure they need to support and develop their staff, report on the work of the organization with fidelity, scale the organization when opportunities arise, or address complex problems when hard times hit.

Other factors can exacerbate an organization's sense of scarcity or emerge as symptoms. While the supply of clients far outweighs the demand for services, multiple organizations can assume competitive positions over limited grants or a small pool of funders. The influence of those funders in such an environment can be outsized, and the organization can drift toward services that are financially or politically motivated, and less aligned with its mission or desired outcomes. Many organizations straddle both public and private funding sources, amplifying the possibility of shifting priorities as those sources' priorities shift. These factors, coupled with typically low salaries at all levels of the organization, can commonly lead to a high degree of leadership and staff turnover, thus creating instability at all levels.

There exist additional forces at play here as well, and these can create significant hurdles. From their founding, many adult learning organizations are designed to operate within and against the currents of the systemic inequities inhibiting the clients they serve. Intersectional layers of racism, classism, gender bias, homophobia, and xenophobia are woven into the life experiences of both learners and the people who serve them. While these factors can function as an engine to fuel passion and purpose, they also manifest as organizational inertia because they can create a simulacrum of the system they were founded to confront.

For example, in his article "A Theory of Racialized Organizations," Victor Ray argues that it is imperative to reimagine the ways that organizations reproduce and challenge societal racialization processes (Ray, 2019). Regardless of their mission or purpose, organizations are constructed from the materials, resources, and narratives that inhabit racialized social systems (Bonilla-Silva, 1997). Constructed organizations, therefore, naturally develop a schematic system that is connected to and guides the acquisition and distribution of resources (Ray, 2019), in a way that often defaults to the power structure that shaped its raw materials. That is why, as Ray states, "incorporating organizations into a structural theory of racial inequality can help us better understand stability, change, and the institutionalization of racial inequality" (p. 1).

It is at this structural level that organizational designers and leaders can have the most influence in their effort to equitably serve diverse populations. If organizations embody or incorporate aspects of the environment in which they were designed and operate (Bonilla-Silva, 1997), it is easier to recognize the traces of those materials from which the environment is woven, including default systems of privilege and power and the disposition toward a scarcity mindset. Looking at the operational environment also raises the notion that the leadership of adult learning organizations can serve to perpetuate or disrupt the schema of such systems (Ray, 2019). As such, leadership behaviors inside adult learning organizations require a level of intentionality and interrogation. In this context, organizational leaders are themselves vulnerable, often defaulting to habits applied more in the service of maintaining a sense of control than toward the goal of increasing organizational effectiveness and capacity.

How then, do some organizations, despite these challenges, achieve such high levels of impact and success? What are the common structural elements, cultural indicators, and operating habits that distinguish thriving adult learning organizations? Because of the complexity and urgency of the work, it is difficult for even highly successful organizations in adult learning to have the time and capacity to document and reflect on what made them so effective, and thus to identify strategies for sustaining that success or to create visible models for other organizations in the field seeking to elevate their work or moderate the many obstacles that inhibit success. These challenges bring us to a significant reason for this book: to highlight successes and identify the reasons for those successes while understanding the challenges that also exist.

There are instances of how diverse adults are educated and supported through equitable models in adult education throughout the country. These successful organizations provide the support and systems that ensure access and success for the diverse needs of adult learners. In a historic moment when adult education needs to ask how it can be better, these programs provide concrete examples of what it takes to do better. This book highlights four of those organizations and allows them to tell their own stories as exemplars of equitable adult education that serves the diverse needs of adult learners.

As noted previously, equitably serving adult learners requires adult education providers to begin with two basic questions:

1. Who are we not serving, whom we could be serving?
2. Who are we currently serving unsuccessfully?

These two starting questions of equity and justice provide the direction for action. For example, an organization that realizes that it is mostly serving White members of a community that is racially and ethnically diversity needs to explore why it does not attract the diverse members of its community. Or an organization that attracts a diverse population to itself, yet sees certain groups not being successful, needs to explore the causes of that. It is by responding to these two questions that adult education begins to act equitably. The intent of this book is to highlight the ways in which organizations create and maintain equitable systems, structures, and practices. The chapters that follow highlight both the successes and challenges created when addressing these two questions of equity. Both the successes and challenges are complex, and each organization goes into detail to describe what they are for them. There are, however, some common factors that all organizations that educate adults must address as they serve adult learners. Those common factors are generated by historical context, demographics, economic factors, and social/political factors. As they address the two questions of equity, the organizations in this book offer solutions that other organizations should consider.

In the business world, models of innovation, start-up techniques, and radical impact are ubiquitous. In the domain of adult learning, models of organizational success can be hard to pin down. However, the unique combination of challenges faced by these organizations presents a clear and pressing need to shine a light on those that are thriving. As we interviewed candidate organizations for this project, the hunger for such models was repeatedly expressed. One of the leaders we interviewed expressed just such a sentiment:

> We need to see examples of leaders in our field who create systems that serve our clients, support our teachers, and make a lasting impact on our society. We need to better understand the complexity of how organizations like ours run equitably both externally and internally. Those are the voices and the stories that we need to consider, evaluate, and learn from.

Telling these stories serves another purpose as well. The skepticism and onerous demands for impact data on adult learning organizations are, at times, a reflection of a dominant and antiquated narrative about how such organizations are run – on a shoestring and with an immature understanding of financial and organizational leadership. We are in need of a countervailing narrative that places thriving adult learning organizations in the spotlight as examples of an organizational design that contributes directly to a community's economy, agency, and dignity. The four organizations we've chosen for this book do exactly that.

Participating Organizations

Our goal was to highlight stories from a national sample of four, exemplar organizations of the ways adult education can succeed with a broad range of communities that included race/ethnicity, disability, economic need, as well as geographic diversity. In the following chapters, you'll learn about four organizations:

• Beyond Literacy, Pennsylvania
• Technology Access Foundation's Network for Edwork and the Martinez Fellows Program, State of Washington
• Building Skills Partnership, California
• BA and MA in Leadership & Organizational Studies Programs in the School of Education at St. Mary's College, California

We selected these organizations for their characteristics as equity-focused adult education providers. However, we also selected these four because they serve a variety of adult learners and have a variety of purposes. The programs offer a picture of what a focus on equity looks like in different settings. Beyond Literacy is a recent merger of two of Philadelphia's longest-serving adult literacy and basic skills providers that reach low-skilled adults. Building Skills Partnership works as a bridge among employers, unions, and the communities they serve to bring those groups together; they provide skills development and advancement opportunities for property service workers who would otherwise be trapped in often low-paid work with no career progression. TAF's Martinez Fellows and EdEncounter programs provide mentoring and scholarships for pre-service teachers of color, and then the program transitions to a support system for these teachers as they enter and continue their careers and later, prepare for leadership positions. St. Mary's Kalmanovitz School of Education offers bachelor's and master's degrees in Leadership & Organizational Studies for working adults and has been successful in helping many people of color complete degrees that enhanced their employment and career opportunities. In subsequent chapters, you'll learn how these organizations overcome the barriers to equitable adult education. From the time we interviewed each of these organizations, and as we worked with them during their completion of their self-studies and chapters, the book editors found ourselves in awe of the work that each does.

The equity focus of these organizations has implications for their communities and the larger society. As adult education has evolved over the last 120 years, it has been inextricably linked to economic opportunity. However, the organizations that are in this book see and work within a much larger purpose. While the outcome of their work can be economic progression, they all work with an understanding that impacting the complexity and unique needs of each adult they serve is central to their mission. They developed integrated, whole systems of support that are based in an understanding of education as an act of justice. As illustrated in their chapters, these organizations understand and work within the much larger needs that adults bring to learning. These four organizations also provide the people they serve a step toward participation within their worlds beyond jobs. As we will discuss at length in the concluding chapter, each of these organizations offers more than just skills development or content knowledge. These successful adult education providers meet an ethical imperative to provide for the comprehensive needs that adult students bring to learning.

Each of the organizations also has a larger impact than the students it serves. While each organization's students can and do become leaders and advocates, these organizations are themselves becoming advocates within their spheres of influence. They regularly appear before state legislatures and policy makers, other organizations seek their models for guidance, and these are organizations that are called on to lead new efforts and engage in addressing new challenges. The editors believe that these leadership roles accrue to any adult education organization that equitably meets the needs of its community as well as these organizations do. These chapters provide evidence of the transformative impact of equity and justice work on organizations. It is our hope, as editors, that these organizations' stories help to highlight the value of serving historically marginalized adult learners.

Adapting the Education Deans for Justice
and Equity Framework

Education Deans for Justice and Equity (EDJE) is a national alliance of over 200 current and recent education deans and directors/chairs of education in institutions seeking to advance equity and justice in education by speaking and acting collectively and in solidarity with communities on policies, reform proposals, and public debates (https://educationdeans.org/). Conceptualized and facilitated by Dr. Kevin Kumashiro, the former dean of the School of Education at the University of San Francisco, the coalition was first convened in spring of 2016. The organization hosts semi-annual meetings and is governed by a steering committee. EDJE's work is premised on several foundational beliefs including that public education is a basic human right and an essential cornerstone of a democratic society; educators must dismantle the structures of poverty and inequality, which have a profound impact on educational attainment; and schools and colleges of education have a moral responsibility to listen to and learn from communities that have not been well-served by public education. EDJE members engage in both outward and inward facing actions and policy initiatives. Externally, the EDJE community has generated and co-sponsored education policy statements on principles of education and democracy, teacher education, and assessment, written op-ed pieces, and conducted presentations at national, state, and local levels.

Of particular importance to the work described in this book is an initiative aimed to provide a forum for the EDJE community members to interrogate their own professional work and contexts. Their effort was inspired by the conviction that educational inequities and broader social injustices harm children, particularly those from historically marginalized groups. Furthermore, they acknowledged these same inequities and injustices weaken democracy. Finally, as deans they recognized historical and current roles colleges and schools of education (COEs) can play, as educational institutions, in perpetuating or transforming such problems. Through several convenings, the EDJE community designed a collaborative framework, the *Framework for Assessment and Transformation* (Education Deans for Justice & Equity, 2019) to guide the work of building capacity within COEs to advance justice and education.

The *Framework for Assessment and Transformation* (*EDJE Framework*) provided a tool for COEs to engage in self-assessment using the categories, priority areas, and questions in the framework. This allowed COEs to identify how their structures, systems, policies, and procedures were aligned with or served as barriers to principles and values of equity, diversity, inclusion, and justice. The *EDJE Framework* outlines, 13 "Priority Areas of Work." The framework distributes those 13 areas into four, over-lapping thematic categories: (A) Governance and Finance, (B) Teaching and Learning, (C) Faculty and Staff, and (D) Partnerships and Public Impact. The respective areas of work included subsections such as strategic planning, democratizing governance, and leadership, strengthening curriculum, supporting students, increasing racial diversity of staff, deepening external partnerships, and managing crises within and beyond the organization. The *EDJE Framework* is a set of priorities and questions within the categories to prompt thought, conversation, data gathering, deliberation, and planning. The EDJE community expected that multiple stakeholders, internal and external to an organization, would participate in the self-assessment process as a COE employed the framework. Results could aid an organization in identifying its strengths, challenges, and opportunities to reflect and further develop efforts to advance equity and justice.

For this project, we elected to adapt *EDJE Framework* to guide the work reported in this book. We based this decision, in part, on the two themes that guided the *EDJE Framework's* development. First, the framework begins with a recognition that educational institutions, including organizations in which adult education is provided, have never been and cannot ever be neutral politically or ideologically. Within educational institutions, decisions, and policies about how to educate adults should be guided by a deep understanding of their future roles and the roles of adult educational institutions within a larger society that is remarkably unequal. As noted previously, adult education has perpetuated injustices against those who are marginalized; it is not immune to discrimination, prejudice, or forms of bias. A second guiding theme to the development of the *EDJE Framework* was the belief that injustices and inequities play out on at least three different levels in educational institutions: at the individual (including interpersonal interactions and internalized oppression), at the institutional level (including system, structural, and cultural dimensions), and at the ideological level (including the meta narratives that shape "common sense") (Education Deans for Justice and Equity 2019, p. 2; Kumashiro, 2020). Understanding how injustices and inequities play out in adult education organizations and understanding how to mitigate systems, structures, policies, and practices that contribute require attention at all three levels. As editors of this book, we began this project with the belief that a framework guided by these primary themes provides the basis for a comprehensive picture of the strengths, opportunities, and challenges of education organizations.

For this book, as we explain in more detail in Chapter 2, we found that adapting the *EDJE Framework* required little modification and that organizations readily applied the adapted framework to their needs.

Summary

Even though adults have been educated informally throughout history, the history of formal adult education in the U.S. is relatively new. As it emerged in the late 1800s and early 1900s, formal adult education served to expand new knowledge to those already educated, and, as it sought to provide services to adult learners in the early parts of the 20th century, it assumed a utilitarian approach tied to employment, a focus that continues to the current era. The bifurcation of services to the already educated and under-educated contributes to the larger inequities that exist in the society; however, there are some organizations that counteract that bifurcation. By examining their role within the larger society and examining the ways in which they operate, these organizations seek to provide the adults they serve with a fuller participation in the society. The four organizations whose cases are included in this book provide examples that show the complexity required to successfully serve the diverse communities they seek to impact. By conducting a self-analysis that uses an adapted version of the *EDJE Framework*, the four organizations show how they achieve that success.

References

Becker Patterson, M. (2014). Post-GED-credential college prospects for adults with special needs. *Journal of Research & Practice for Adult Literacy, Secondary & Basic Education, 3*(3), 22–35.

Berry, M. E. (1986). *One hundred years on urban frontiers: The settlement movement, 1886–1986.* United Neighborhood Centers of America.

Bonilla-Silva, E. (1997). Rethinking racism: Toward a structural interpretation. *American Sociological Review, 62*(3), 465–480.

Boyadjieva, P., & Ilieva-Trichkova, P. (2017). Between inclusion and fairness. *Adult Education Quarterly, 67*(2), 97–117. https://doi.org/10.1177/0741713616685398

Bureau of Labor Statistics. (2021a). *Usual Weekly Earnings of Wage and Salary Workers, First Quarter, 2021.* Washington, DC. Retrieved from bls.gov/news.release/pdf/wkyeng.pdf

Bureau of Labor Statistics. (2021b). *Labor Force Statistics from the Current Population Survey.* Washington, DC. Retrieved from https://www.bls.gov/cps/cpsaat11.htm

Butchart, R. E. (1990). *Schooling the freed people: Teaching, learning, and the struggle for Black freedom, 1861–1876.* The University of North Carolina Press.

Caffarella, R. S. (1996). Can I really do it all? *Adult Learning, 8*(1), 8. https://doi.org/10.1177/104515959600800105

Choi, D. S.-Y., & Morrison, P. (2014). Learning to get it right: Understanding change processes in professional development for teachers of English learners. *Professional Development in Education, 40*(3), 416–435. https://doi.org/10.1080/19415257.2013.806948

Daft, Richard L. (2016). *Organization theory & design.* 13th edition. Cengage Learning.

Darling-Hammond, L. (2007). Third annual Brown lecture in education research – the flat earth and education: How America's commitment to equity will determine our future. *Educational Researcher, 36*(6), 318–344.

Dejean, J. S. (2015). Synching the law to resolve the disconnection between awareness and action in legally mandated diversity hiring practices in higher education institutions. *Journal of Research Administration, 46*(2), 34–54.

Edin, K. J., & Shaefer, H. L. (2016, August 22, 2016). 20 years since welfare 'reform'. *The Atlantic.* Retrieved from https://www.theatlantic.com/business/archive/2016/08/20-years-welfare-reform/496730/

Education Deans for Justice & Equity. (2019). *Education deans for justice & equity: A framework for assessment and transformation.* Retrieved from https://drive.google.com/file/d/1AVVkmzPxEMAt_g-BPYyNVHgseylmREnN/view

Fleinming, M., & Nelson, B. M. (2007). Mission possible: Transforming women and building communities. *Adult Learning, 18*(3/4), 20–24. https://doi.org/10.1177/104515950701800304

Foner, E. (2014). *Reconstruction: America's unfinished revolution, 1863-1877.* Harper Perennial Modern Classics.

Gregory, A., & Howard, D. (2009). The Non-Profit Starvation Cycle. *Stanford Social Innovation Review* (Fall, 2009). Retrieved from https://ssir.org/articles/entry/the_nonprofit_starvation_cycle#bio-footer

Hemphill, D. F. (1996). Flexibility, innovation, and collaboration. *Adult Learning, 7*(6), 21. https://doi.org/10.1177/104515959600700610

Horowitz, H. L. (1974). Varieties of cultural experience in Jane Addams' Chicago. *History of Education Quarterly, 14*(1), 69–86.

Hughes, B. (2007). *Technology and equity: Moving beyond access to addressing causal factors.* Paper presented at the Western Region Research Conference on the Education of Adults, Bellingham, WA. Conference Paper.

Hughes, B., & Knighton, C. (2020). Are transitions a sufficient goal for ABE students or programs? *Adult Literacy Education: The International Journal of Literacy, Language, and Numeracy, 2*(1), 66–72.

Hughes, B., Johnson, C., & Taga, B. (2018). Editors' notes. *New Directions for Adult & Continuing Education, 2018*(160), 5–7. https://doi.org/10.1002/ace.20295

Irvin Painter, N. (1992). *Exodusters: Black migration to Kansas after reconstruction.* W. W. Norton & Company.

James, F. (1990). Booker T. Washington and George Washington Carver: A tandem of adult educators at Tuskegee. In H. G. Neufeldt, & L. McGee (Eds.), *Education of the African American Adult.* Greenwood Publishing Group.

Katz, C. C., & Geiger, J. M. (2019). 'We need that person that doesn't give up on us': The role of social support in the pursuit of post-secondary education for youth with foster care experience who are transition-aged. *Child Welfare, 97*(6), 145–164.

Kayes, P. E. (2006). New paradigms for diversifying faculty and staff in higher education: Uncovering cultural biases in the search and hiring process. *Multicultural Education, 14*(2), 65–69.

Kendall Edgerton, K. (2009). Education as "the balance wheel of social machinery"; Horace Mann's arguments and proofs. *Quarterly Journal of Speech, 54*(1), 8.

Knowles, M. S. (1962). *A history of the adult education movement in the USA.* Krieger.

Knox, A. B. (2002). A field-wide vision. *Adult Learning, 13*(4), 2–3. https://doi.org/10.1177/104515950201300401

Kumashiro, K., (Producer). (2020). *Leading when faculty and students teach for justice.* [Webinar]. https://www.kevinkumashiro.com/webinarpushaug2020

Lane, T. Y. (2017). Tribulations and achievements: The lived experiences of African American college students formerly in foster care. *Journal of Human Behavior in the Social Environment, 27*(3), 141–150. https://doi.org/10.1080/10911359.2016.1262805

Lewis, J. (2018, September 22, 2018). 19th century reading circle helped shaped Bastrop. *Austin American-Statesman.* Retrieved from https://www.statesman.com/NEWS/20171026/19th-century-reading-circle-helped-shaped-Bastrop

Li, G. (2012). Literacy engagement through online and offline communities outside school: English language learners' development as readers and writers. *Theory Into Practice, 51*(4), 312–318. https://doi.org/10.1080/00405841.2012.726061

Meyers, H. (2015). Campus leadership challenges and changes. *University Business, 18*(1), 25–28.

Mullainathan, S., & Shafir, E. (2013). *Scarcity: Why having too little means so much.* Times Books/Henry Holt and Co.

Nocera, A. (2018). Negotiating the aims of African American adult education: Race and liberalism in the Harlem experiment, 1931–1935. *History of Education Quarterly, 58*(1), 1–32. https://doi.org/10.1017/heq.2017.47

Orfield, G. (2005). Why segregation is inherently unequal: The abandonment of Brown and the continuing failure of Plessy. *New York Law School Law Review, 49*(4), 1041–1052.

Pedulla, D. S., & Thébaud, S. (2015). Can we finish the revolution? Gender, work-family ideals, and institutional constraint. *American Sociological Review, 80*(1), 116–139. https://doi.org/10.1177/0003122414564008

Pekow, C. (2006). Working group and education department look at how to boost adult education. *Community College Week, 18*(14), 6–8.

Pew Research Center. (2016). *The State of American Jobs.* Washington, DC. Retrieved from https://www.pewresearch.org/social-trends/2016/10/06/the-state-of-american-jobs/

President's Commission on Higher Education. (1947). *Higher Education for American Democracy.* Washington, DC. Retrieved from https://www.aacu.org/sites/default/files/files/LEAP/he_for_democracy.pdf

Ray, V. (2019). A theory of racialized organizations. *American Sociological Review, 84*(1), 26–53. https://doi.org/10.1177/0003122418822335

Rose, A. D. (1994). Adult education as federal policy: The search for a literacy agenda. *PAACE Journal of Lifelong Learning, 3,* 4–13.

Ross-Gordon, J. M. (2011). Research on adult learners: Supporting the needs of a student population that is no longer nontraditional. *Peer Review, 13*(1), 26–29.

Schein, E. H. (2010). *Organizational culture and leadership.* Jossey-Bass.

Schmidt, S. W. (2013). Perspectives in adult education – the American Association for Adult and Continuing Education (AAACE): Its history, purpose, and activities. *New Horizons in Adult Education & Human Resource Development, 26*(1), 4.

Scott, J. C. (1999). The Chautauqua movement. *Journal of Higher Education, 70*(4), 389–412. https://doi.org/10.2307/2649308

Semega, J., Kollar, M., Shrider, E. A., & Creamer, J. (2020). *Income and Poverty in the United States: 2019.* Washington, DC. Retrieved from https://www.census.gov/library/publications/2020/demo/p60-270.html

Sergiovanni, T. J. (1992). *Moral leadership: Getting to the heart of school improvement.* Jossey-Bass.

Skobba, K., Meyers, D., & Tiller, L. (2018). Getting by and getting ahead: Social capital and transition to college among homeless and foster youth. *Children & Youth Services Review, 94,* 198–206. https://doi.org/10.1016/j.childyouth.2018.10.003

Snyder, T. D. (1993). *120 Years of American Education: A Statistical Portrait.* Washington, DC. Retrieved from https://nces.ed.gov/pubs93/93442.pdf

Spence, R. B., & Cass, A. W. (1950). The agencies of adult education. *Adult Education Quarterly, 20*(3), 230–246.

Stubblefield, H. W., & Keane, P. (1994). *Adult education in the American experience: From the colonial period to the present.* Jossey-Bass Publishers.

Turner, M. A., Woolley, M., Kingsley, G. T., Popkin, S. J., Levy, D., & Cove, E. (2007). *Severely distressed public housing: the costs of inaction.* Washington DC. Retrieved from https://www.urban.org/sites/default/files/publication/46416/411444-Severely-Distressed-Public-Housing-The-Costs-of-Inaction.PDF

U.S. Bureau of the Census. (2021a). *Table A-2. Percent of People 25 Years and Over Who Have Completed High School or College, by Race, Hispanic Origin and Sex: Selected Years 1940 to 2020.* Washington, DC. Retrieved from https://www2.census.gov/programs-surveys/demo/tables/educational-attainment/time-series/cps-historical-time-series/taba-2.xlsx

U.S. Bureau of the Census. (2021b). *Table A-1. Years of School Completed by People 25 Years and Over, by Age and Sex: Selected Years 1940 to 2020.* Washington, DC. Retrieved from https://www2.census.gov/programs-surveys/demo/tables/educational-attainment/time-series/cps-historical-time-series/taba-1.xlsx

U.S. Department of Education Office of Vocational and Adult Education. (2013). *Federal adult education: A legislative history 1964–2013.* Washington, DC. Retrieved from https://lincs.ed.gov/publications/pdf/Adult_Ed_History_Report.pdf.

U.S. Department of Health and Human Services. (1996). *The Personal Responsibility and Work Opportunity Reconciliation Act of 1996.* Washington, DC. Retrieved from https://aspe.hhs.gov/reports/personal-responsibility-work-opportunity-reconciliation-act-1996

U.S. Sentencing Commission. (2017). *Demographic Differences in Sentencing.* Washington, DC. Retrieved from https://www.ussc.gov/research/research-reports/demographic-differences-sentencing

Zakaluk, B. L., & Wynes, B. J. (1995). Book bridges: A family literacy program for immigrant women. *Journal of Reading, 38*(7), 550–557.

Zhang, L., & Han, W. J. (2017). Poverty dynamics and academic trajectories of children of immigrants. *International Journal of Environmental Research and Public Health, 14*(9), 1076. Retrieved from https://www.ncbi.nlm.nih.gov/pmc/articles/PMC5615613

2

METHODS

Case Studies from Insiders' Perspectives

Deanna Iceman Sands, Bob Hughes,
and Ted Kalmus

Introduction

As noted in previous chapter, the overall goal of this inquiry project was to understand how four, exemplar organizations (Denzin, 2001) support a broad range of diverse (e.g., race/ethnicity, disability, economic need, and geographic differences) adult learners and communities. We sought those organizations that strive to support success while having evidence of that success. More specifically, we were interested in organizations with intentional commitments to equity, diversity, and inclusion and the structures, systems, policies, and practices they employed to serve those diverse adult learners. We describe the rationale for our process more fully in Chapter 8, but at the center of our beliefs about telling these organizations' stories was that they should be the ones telling the story. Our job was to help them to frame and organize their analysis and story.

The project was carried out in multiple phases. The first required each organization to conduct a self-assessment. During the second phase, each organization wrote the story of their self-assessment and respective findings. The last phase involved the editorial team conducting within-case and cross-case analyses of all four, organizational stories.

Our Approach

Research Design

The editors approached this inquiry project with an eye toward employing case study, one of multiple qualitative research genres (Miles et al., 2020). According to Yin, case studies are "the preferred method when (a) 'how'

DOI: 10.4324/9781003286998-2

or 'why' questions are being posed, (b) investigators have little control over events, and (c) the focus is on contemporary phenomenon within a real-life context" (2009, p. 2). For this project, we asked how and why structures, systems, and policies and procedures allow organizations to serve diverse adult learners in just, equitable, accessible, and inclusive ways. As researchers, we had no control over the way these organizations operated, and we wanted to understand their operations from their perspectives. The editors believe that the best people to tell a story are those people who live that story. Therefore, we chose not to take the perspective that researchers often take in developing and reporting case studies. Instead of us conducting research into these four organizations and then reporting our findings, we chose to support the four organizations as they conducted a self-analysis, and then we supported them as they wrote their findings. As a result, each subsequent, organization-based chapter was written by people from the represented organization. Although each chapter has defined authors, the information that informed their writing comes from a broad selection of people and groups within the organization and connected as a stakeholder of the organization.

Our job as editors was first to help them define the information they needed for self-analysis. We adapted the *EDJE Framework* described in Chapter 1 and provided the organizations with the *Framework for Assessment and Transformation in Adult Education (FATAE)* for their analysis. We then assisted each organization as they narrowed their inquiry into elements of that framework. We also assisted each organization in creating data collection processes, further narrowing their scope of inquiry, and developing processes to analyze the data they collected. Finally, we helped them effectively tell their story by being critical readers and coaches during their writing process. In this way, we believe, the organization-based chapters represent as accurate a portrayal of these organizations as can be generated. Our model was informed deeply by the participatory research models advocated for by Fetterman et al. (2014), Greenwood and Levin (2006), Sleeter and Zavala (2020), and others. We sought to have the organizations see these chapters as fully reflective of their experience as an organization. The resulting chapters are evidence of how they mined the complexity of their experiences to produce an equally complex narrative that explains how they have become successful adult education providers.

Once the four organizations completed their chapters, the editors engaged Bartlett and Vavrus's (2017) comparative case study (CSS) approach, to compare the inter-workings of the four organizations. CSS is a heuristic that aids in the process of discovery or problem solving. Bartlett and Vavrus expanded upon more traditional applications of case study (Yin, 2009) by conceptualizing comparative research to involve three axes: vertical, horizontal, and transversal. This allows for understanding how "similar policies and practices unfold in distinct locations (horizontal), to and across scales (vertical), and historically (transversally)" (p. 3). As we explain more in Chapter 7, to conduct our own analyses that compared these cases, we had to become intimately aware of the inner workings of each organization so that we understood both their story and the reasons for how they told their story, and which experiences they emphasized in telling that story. This allowed us to understand how phenomena across these three axes unfold in social and cultural contexts over time. While this project primarily employed analyses at the horizontal axis level, it is the editors' intent that this project contributes to an expanding literature base at all three levels of how organizations serving diverse, adult learners can operate in ways that advance equity, justice, and inclusion.

Participating Organizations

After a purposeful nomination and selection process subsequently described below, four organizations participated in this project. The executive director of each organization appointed a coordinator as point person with whom the editors worked throughout the process. The editors and coordinators held monthly meetings. In addition, the three of us assigned one of us as editor to each organization as a primary contact, mentor, and supporter.

The organizations represented in this book have wrestled with equitably serving adults, and they found answers that have helped them to address the two questions of equity (i.e., who is not being served and who is not being served adequately). At the time of this writing, these organizations have existed between 22 and 54 years. Their work has been intentionally equitable, i.e., they have worked through the challenges and adopted practices that ensure equitable learning for all the people they serve and could serve. They wrestled with the challenges and found ways to do work that assured equitable access, engagement, and support for the adults they serve. They held discussions, they sought expertise to help them with the challenges, they willingly challenged their own work, and they generated models that fit their needs as organizations, and, more importantly, the needs of the adults they serve. They were included in this book because they continue to explore and grow into their intentions.

What Guided Data Collection

Since the original intent of the *EDJE Framework* described in the previous chapter was for application within schools and colleges of education (COEs), the editors adapted the tool for the purposes of this project. In reviewing that framework, we found many universalities that made the framework readily adaptable from colleges of education to organizations conducting adult learning. We also found that it was clearly based in the literature of equity and justice. That grounding helped us ensure that that organizations explored ideas in their self-studies that were research-based. We include a copy of the adapted tool, renamed the *Framework for Assessment and Transformation in Adult Education (FATAE)*, in Appendix A. The organization of the *FATAE* adheres to the same four categories as the original *EDJE Framework*. We asked each organization to use the *FATAE* to collect data across its four categories:

1. Governance and Finance
2. Teaching and Learning
3. Instructors and Staff
4. Partnerships and Public Impact

As illustrated in Appendix A, the *FATAE* has 13 priority areas distributed across these four categories, the same as contained in the original *EDJE Framework*, with associated questions for self-assessment and planning. We encouraged participating organizations to select the priority areas and questions that made most sense for them to explore, given the focus of their current initiatives, goals, or questions. Coordinators for each organization assembled a self-assessment team, and we asked that each team engage multiple stakeholders, internal and external (as appropriate), throughout their data collection initiatives.

We asked the organizations to document their process as well as to identify members of teams and stakeholders who participated.

We aimed our adaptations of the original *EDJE Framework* to apply more directly to educational organizations outside of Institutions of Higher Education (IHEs). We made four primary types of changes:

1. Language edits to address an audience beyond COEs.
2. Deletion of concepts that only apply to COEs (e.g., exploring the impacts of neoliberalism in education).
3. Clarifying language to explain some concepts (e.g., a definition of "leadership").
4. Adjustment of concepts that look different for organizations outside of COEs (e.g., replacing the focus on research with an emphasis on evaluation).

We added questions to prompt respondents to clarify the definitions they used within their organizations for certain concepts. For example, in the category on Governance and Finance, we posed the questions, "What is our definition of leadership? And "How might this advance and/or limit the diversity of candidates for leadership positions and/or the capacity of our instructors and staff to be leaders?"

We encouraged participants from the four organizations to suggest further adaptations to the framework beginning in the initial phases of the project. Through meetings with individual organizations and during coordinator

meetings that included all four organizations, they offered additional recommendations. We made some changes immediately; others were suggested
for the editors to attend to through their ongoing work with the original
and adapted versions of the framework or with our work through EDJE.
Suggestions ranged from ideas for simplifying language to prioritizing and/or
reducing the number of stem questions within each priority area to developing
implementation guidelines for use of the framework to assist organizations in
engaging with and applying the framework within their context.

For example, coordinators indicated that some stem questions were
"externally facing." These questions implied research external to their organizations was needed during the self-assessment process. For instance, one
question within the finance category was, "What are common models (and
less common but more promising models) for budgeting, and how does each
model advance and/or hinder justice and equity goals?" Their suggestion was
that if an organization identified issues with their financing model with regards
to equity, access, diversity, or justice, researching other models that would
advance these principles would be of use for future planning. Coordinators
indicated they rephrased the focus of some framework questions by posing
them as "How are we doing?" to move from a deficit-based to an asset-based
set of questions. They acknowledged that many questions posed by the framework prompted other questions, at times leaving them feel as though the
self-assessment process could easily become "cumbersome" and never-ending.
They described having to put "bumpers" or boundaries on questions to narrow and focus the information needed to provide a sufficient and useful set of
information. In the end, the application of the framework through this project
yielded a substantive set of information for the EDJE community to consider
in their efforts to refine and update the content and applications of the original
tool, as well as for future iterations of the FATAE.

Procedure

Prior to beginning our procedures, we submitted the project to the Institutional
Review Board at Seattle University for a review of our inclusion of human
subjects. We were notified that the project was exempt from full review.

Participant Selection Process

The editors of this book began planning the research for the book in 2019.
Just as we began our outreach to find participating organizations in 2020, the
worldwide COVID-19 pandemic struck. The pandemic, as it had in K-12 education, radically changed how adult education operated as face-to-face instruction closed everywhere. Adult education providers became quickly mired in the
process of shifting instruction to virtual models. Instructors needed to learn new

teaching methods; administrators needed to shift funding and staffing to support that teaching and to discern what kind of resources to use; and established patterns of student support and engagement had to change rapidly to address learners' needs. All adult education programs were overwhelmed. The book editors questioned whether 2020 was the right time for a project like this.

To gauge whether the project needed to be postponed, editors contacted colleagues who were directors or managers within adult education to hear what they thought. Their answers surprised us. Without exception, these organizational leaders explained that self-assessment was exactly the kind of activity their organization needed or planned to do at the time. Without prompting them, we found that each of these leaders saw times of challenge as the right moment for self-examination. We came to see that self-analysis is one of the hallmarks of strong adult education programs. As we screened applicants for the project, we looked for those organizations which had the capacity and eagerness for the detailed self-assessment that the project would demand of them. As a result, we selected organizations that would see self-assessment as a normal component of their growth and ability to meet their mission goals. Our selection process seems to have mostly worked. We began the project with five organizations, and we discovered that the changes one organization was undergoing were too much for them to complete the process; however, the other four successfully completed their analysis and the writing of their chapter.

Our primary recruitment strategy was to issue a nomination communication through multiple professional organizations that focused on adult learners, and we also sent the request to professional and personal contacts in our respective fields. For example, we reached out to organizations such as the Adult and Higher Education Alliance, American Educational Research Association, and the Association of Career and Technical Education. We also sent nomination invitations through our professional social media sites such as LinkedIn. We maintained a spreadsheet of names and organizations to whom we reached out or were nominated by others. We had several informal conversations with key leaders in organizations to provide additional information to help them decide whether they wished to apply for participation in the project. Then we sent an email invitation to participate to representatives from organizations ready to take the first step. The invitation described the purpose of the project, provided an overview of literature citing the need for this work, and outlined the general expectations for participating organizations as well as the editors' roles and responsibilities to support and coach the process. We emphasized the importance of each organization telling its own story since those involved in the work and those involved in being educated by the work could best describe what the work is like. When an organization expressed an interest in participating, we scheduled an interview between the organization and the three project editors.

We conducted interviews via video conferencing. Prior to the interview, editors provided interviewees with the *FATAE*. Interviewees were asked to include anyone in the interview who supervised or managed the areas identified in the *FATAE* since the interview focused on those domains. After review of the purpose and nature of the project, the interviews commenced as the three editors rotated through posing 13 questions. The questions queried participants about what they hoped to accomplish because of the self-assessment process, how their work helped the communities they served to experience justice, how their instruction connected to best practices and current research, how students reflected the highest needs in their community, the diversity of their staff and instructors, supports provided to instructors, and how the project fit into the work they were or had done. We then gave interviewees the opportunity to ask questions and convey other information about their organization.

Drawing from lessons learned from literature in the fields of leadership, adult education, participatory research, and organizational learning (Ajiboye et al., 2020; Cowan et al., 2010; Odor, 2018; Rodela & Bertrand, 2018; Takayama et al., 2017), the editors selected the five, initial participating organizations on these categories:

- Evidence of success with assisting diverse communities of learners succeed at the goals that learners establish.
- Intentional commitment to equity, diversity, and inclusion as identified in documents and in practice.
- Capacity and willingness to conduct a self-assessment.
- Capacity and willingness to write the results of a self-assessment.

We developed criteria for each category. Those criteria and any of the other materials we used in our process are available by contacting any of the editors. Once the selection process was finalized, each organization received a written participant agreement form for review and signatures. Though not a legal document, the agreement established the responsibilities of the assigned editors (and the participating organizations) so that everyone involved understood who was responsible for doing what. The editors first signed this document and asked that the most senior officer of the participating organization also sign it. Broadly, the editors' identified obligations were to provide initial training in responding to the *FATAE*, support the completion of an analysis using the *FATAE*, establish a timeline, provide ongoing check ins/consultation/feedback in completing the self-assessment, and assess progress of completion of self-assessment elements. The leadership and staff of each organization were responsible to commit to work with the editor, identify a primary contact for the editor to connect to on a scheduled basis, collect and review data required to complete relevant sections of the self-assessment framework, host discussions among key stakeholders to review and analyze the data, meet time-lines, and commit time and personnel to writing the case study, following a template provided by the editors.

Throughout the self-assessment and the development of the written case studies, the editors met as a group semi-monthly, and they met as a group with all the coordinators of the five organizations, typically every six weeks. The editors kept each other apprised of our respective organizations' progress, challenges, and needs. Meetings with all the coordinators were held at their request, and they often developed the agenda for those meetings. Over time, the editors' roles shifted from editorial to more of a consultative model. Increasingly, coordinators created something akin to a professional learning community and as Ted commented at one point, they became "stewards of inquiry." Participants openly shared their questions, opportunities, challenges, as well as strategies for organizing and managing their data collection, analysis, and writing development.

Data Collection and Analysis

Our process is more fully described in Chapter 7. However, generally, each organization mapped out their approach for collecting data by domain, priority area, and associated questions. It is in the data collection for the self-analysis that we decided to eliminate one of the original five organizations' chapters. While that organization began collecting information for their self-analysis, the two, lead staff in the project left employment and the person who picked up the responsibility was not able to resume where they stopped. Although this fifth organization submitted a draft chapter, it was not tied to the *FATAE* in a way that fits with the other chapters. When the remaining four organizations completed their self-analyses and respective chapters in this book, the editors analyzed data by organization and then conducted a cross-case analysis across all four. Here, we describe how information was collected and analyzed at these levels.

Organizational

Each organization designed individual processes for collecting data, aligned with the focus of the domain, their chosen categories, and respective questions of focus. Multiple forms of data collection were incorporated by each organization. For example, some reviewed respective records, policies, and documents. In other cases, coordinators interviewed past and current staff and instructors, board members, and adult learners individually or in focus groups. Some of the organizations employed survey research. Regardless of their instruments, the organizations then analyzed their collected data with approaches aligned to the way they were collected (e.g., employing quantitative and/or qualitative analyses). In brief, thorough self-analyses were conducted in a manner that helped the authors understand their organization more comprehensively beyond their own prior understandings. Additional details about each organization's data collection and analysis are included in subsequent, individual, organization-generated chapters. To aid in the process of writing up their findings and case studies, the editors provided authors with a style guide, a recommended outline for the chapter, ongoing draft reviews/feedback, and toward the end, final feedback from all three editors.

Editorial Team

In addition to biweekly meetings via videoconferencing, the editors remained in continual e-mail contact with each other and offered counsel and ideas to help keep the work on track. Our continued interactions allowed us to member-check each other in the process and to retain a constantly evolving understanding of what we were experiencing and learning. We each approach adult learning uniquely because of our backgrounds and experiences. Deanna approaches adult learning from teacher education and from having developed systems and processes for adult professionals in higher education. Ted comes to adult learning from having developed processes and systems for the teachers in the schools he has directed over the years. Bob has been working with developing learning environments for adult learners who are as diverse as Head Start parents, community college students, and graduate students. Our diverse experiences have enriched our conversations as this work has unfolded since we first recruited participants. Our backgrounds deeply shape what this book has become since we first envisioned it.

Of noteworthy value to us have been our biweekly meetings. We kept notes of those meetings, and our review of those notes shows our evolution. Those discussions show that we were exploring the themes of justice and equity alongside the organizations as we progressed. The notes show that we had extensive discussions about the ways in which larger systems of injustice impact these organizations' ability to effect justice. We also talked about the need to see this book as more than about adult learning since what the organizations were teaching us can apply to many social service organizations. We discussed the major themes that were emerging (discussed in more detail in Chapter 7), which showed the critical features of any organization seeking to live equitably and just. Early on, we discovered that one of those critical attributes is how much these organizations were constantly self-examining not just the work they perform but also how and why they perform it. And, of course, we discussed coordination, such as deadlines and how to support the organizations. All these conversations informed and shaped the work.

All three editors were involved in analyzing data from the self-studies developed by each organization. We used Excel to create an organizational display following the structure of the FATAE by which to enter data for analysis (Miles, Huberman, & Saldana, 2020). The first two columns represented information on the categories and respective domain areas, followed by the question areas associated by each. For example, the first column illustrated the four main categories (Governance and Finance, Teaching and Learning, Instructors and Staff, and Partnerships and Public Impact) and the respective priority areas of each. For example, Governance and Finance contained priority areas of "Centering Justice & Equity in Strategic Planning/Implementation," "Democratizing Governance and Leadership," etc. The second column illustrated the question areas associated with each priority area. Within the priority area, question areas included, Assumptions, Guiding Documents, Strategic Plan, and Resources. The subsequent four column headings represented each of the four organizations. Next a column was set up to capture common themes, and the final column was used to enter notes each editor could pose for later discussion and quotes to include as the findings were presented. Each editor had a unique tab with this structure by which to code the data independently. It is important to note, given each organization elected which categories, priority areas and questions were the focus of their self-analysis, accordingly there were no data to analyze for some cells in their respective data display. Table 2.1 shows the first category and criterion of the table that the editors completed in our analyses. The complete table includes all the categories and questions of the *FATAE*, and that complete table allowed us to conduct a thorough analysis of the findings in each chapter.

Each editor applied *in vivo,* or deductive, coding (Saldana, 2016) as a first cycle of data coding. After a thorough read of each organization-generated chapter (as many as four readings by each editor), we captured verbatim statements as they represented information by domain, priority area, and question area. For example, "decision-making" was one of the question areas associated to the priority area, Alignment of Budget/Budgeting within the category of Governance and Finance. From several of the self-analysis stories, the terms "Hierarchical" and "top-down" were used by representatives to describe how decisions about budgets and finances were made within their organization. Finally, we synthesized

TABLE 2.1 Analysis of Emerging Themes by Domains

Category/ Priority Areas	Question Areas	Themes – BSP	Themes – TAF	Themes – BeLit	Themes – St. Mary's	Common Themes	Notes
Governance and Finance Domain							
Centering Justice and Equity – Strategic Planning/ Implementation							

the resulting data and conducted thematic analyses across the four organizations to identify unique and common themes identified in Chapter 7.

Summary

In this chapter, we describe the approach used to guide the inquiry process followed by four organizations as they engaged in a self-study process and then described their results in the four subsequent chapters in this book. The structure we generated and the resulting work they undertook helped the four organizations identify and report on their strengths, opportunities, and the challenges they encounter. We expect that both the findings and the methods which we employed to uncover those findings to add to emerging literature in adult education and organizational development about how principles of justice, equity, access, and inclusion can serve as the basis of programming and support for diverse adult learners.

References

Ajiboye, A. O., Anderson-James, H. L., Fountain, J., & Vega- Gutiérrez, J. A. (2020). *Funnel vision: Through the looking glass of recruitment and admission practices.* https://scholarworks.seattleu.edu/

Bartlett, L., & Vavrus, F. (2017). *Rethinking case study research: A comparative approach.* Routledge.

Cowan, C., Goldman, E. F., & Hook, M. (2010). Flexible and inexpensive: Improving learning transfer and program evaluation through participant action plans. *Performance Improvement, 49*(5), 18–25.

Denzin, N. K. (2001). *Interpretive interactionism* (2nd ed.). SAGE.

Fetterman, D. M., Kaftarin, S. J., & Wandersman, A. (2014). *Empowerment evaluation* (2nd ed.). SAGE.

Greenwood, D. J., & Levin, M. (2006). *Introduction to action research: Social research for social change.* SAGE Publications.

Miles, H. B., Huberman, A. M., & Saldana, J. (2020). *Qualitative data analysis: A methods sourcebook* (4th ed.). SAGE.

Odor, H. (2018). A literature review on organizational learning and learning organizations. *International Journal of Economics & Management Sciences, 7*(1), 1–6.

Rodela, K. C., & Bertrand, M. (2018). Rethinking education leadership in the margins: Youth, parent and community leadership for equity and social justice. *Journal of Research on Leadership Education, 13*(1), 309.

Saldana, J. (2016). *The coding manual for qualitative researchers.* SAGE.

Sleeter, C. E., & Zavala, M. (2020). *Transformative ethnic studies in schools: Curriculum, pedagogy, and research.* Teachers College Press.

Takayama, K., Kaplan, M., & Cook-Sather, A. (Fall, 2017). Advancing diversity and inclusion. *Liberal Education, 103*(3–4), 23–29.

Yin, R. K. (2009). *Case study research: Design and methods* (4th ed.). SAGE.

3

BEYOND LITERACY

Greater Than the Sum of Its Parts

Kimmell Proctor and Dawn Hannah

Introduction

This is a story of how intentionally centering equity during a time of exponential growth can yield a whole whose sum is greater than its parts. In merging two, long-standing, Philadelphia-based adult education nonprofits with wildly different strategies for programmatic success, Beyond Literacy was able to break new ground as a newly imagined literacy agency in a city where 22% of adults lack reading proficiency above a third-grade level, nearly double the national average (National Center for Educational Statistics, 2022).

Although mergers may be common in the private sector, they remain atypical in the social change environment. This could be partly due to the nature of our funding. Our state and federal program contracts can stretch over several years, so decisions and strategic plans often reflect built-in inertia and focus on long-term impacts to the people we serve rather than the cumbersome process of organizational restructuring.

During the period of our merger, an exploration of our organizational histories through the lens of the *Framework for Assessment and Transformation in Adult Education (FATAE)* provided our staff and leadership opportunities to learn a great deal about who we were, are, and hope to be. In re-examining our mission and vision, we affirmed our belief that adult education presents a hopeful remedy for some of the most startling opportunity gaps in our city. Through a sequence of focus groups and strategic planning sessions, Beyond Literacy also explored ways that a commitment to equity is integrated or inhibited throughout our organizational structure and program implementation. In so doing, we expanded our understanding of the way power can be shared in supporting adult learners, reminding ourselves that a commitment

DOI: 10.4324/9781003286998-3

to equity requires that we give, receive, and relinquish power when it causes harm or diminishes the humanity of another. These are the conversations that grounded and guided the difficult work of our merger, as we sought to integrate the best qualities of our two organizations into a new, powerful center for adult literacy and learning in Philadelphia

Above all else, this chapter is a depiction of the many strategies required to manage and sustain transformational change. The *FATAE* proved to be a powerful tool in evaluating both our effective and default systems and processes that each former organization brought to the merger and helped to inspire the difficult task of integrating two organizational cultures in a way that galvanized our strengths and centered equity in our practices. To accomplish this, during a pandemic, within a city that struggles to overcome deep-rooted systemic structural inequality was by no means an easy feat.

The authors of this chapter bring distinct backgrounds and points of view to its writing. For each, the work is deeply personal, and amplifies the belief that addressing the "literacy gap" is central to the broad work of bringing opportunity and justice to the people of Philadelphia. Chapter author Kimmell Proctor grew up a "Navy brat" attending various schools across many different cities, developing a deep appreciation for the educators who helped her build community no matter where she landed. She identifies as a cisgender female who draws her commitment to education from her love of lifelong learning and its transformative power to help all succeed. Earning her B.A. in Government and Master of Teaching at the University of Virginia, she currently serves as the Chief Executive Officer at Beyond Literacy where she works closely with a wide range of partners to facilitate collective action and align impactful education solutions. Together with her extraordinarily dedicated staff, she seeks to narrow achievement gaps and empower learners of all ages and stages with the knowledge, tools, and resources essential for success.

Chapter author Dawn Hannah grew up in Philadelphia's "Black Bottom," born and raised by a 19-year-old single mother of two. According to stereotyped predictions, she should be receiving the services of the Beyond Literacy, rather than overseeing them. She identifies as a Black, cisgender female and grounds her commitment to adult education in her personal journey as one of the first in her family to attain a postsecondary credential, and the only one until recently to have earned an advanced degree. She attended Georgetown and Stanford and currently serves as the Chief Program Officer of Beyond Literacy where she works passionately to bridge the academic gaps that can limit one's life-chances.

Other contributors to this chapter included JoAnn Weinberger, long-time Executive Director and President of Center for Literacy, current Board President of Chester County Library System, and indefatigable adult education advocate and literacy cheerleader; and Rebecca Wagner, former Executive

Director of Community Learning Center, current Project Director at Tuscarora Intermediate Unit 11, and devoted mother and grandmother. Both former organizational leaders from the two merged organizations participated in extensive interviews, responding to questions based on the *FATAE* and providing extensive historical information to help guide the merger process. Additionally, Sheryl-Amber Edmondson, a Philadelphia native and trauma-informed educator grounded in equity and inclusion, conducted research that included staff interviews and a deep dive into the history of adult literacy in Philly.

Literacy Education in Philadelphia

The history of literacy education in Philadelphia is intrinsically linked to the city's long struggle against racial inequality and the resultant opportunity gaps that grew across its systems of education, employment, and criminal justice. Throughout18th and 19th century Philadelphia, education for both youth and adults (who had been failed by the system in their own youth), was widely seen as a public necessity. The purpose of public education was to equalize and civilize society. However, enslaved peoples had been historically barred from reading and writing and when the education system moved from the home to the schoolhouse, even free Black people in Philadelphia were restricted from participating in public schooling. By the end of the 19th century, the denial of access to both education and employment resulted in widespread poverty and idleness, which, in turn, gave way to historical levels of crime in the city (DuBois & Eaton, 1996).

Long before that time, many advocacy groups in Philadelphia recognized the critical importance of literacy education to advance and assimilate marginalized groups into American economic and social life. As far back as 1770, abolitionists established The African's School, a Quaker school within the city, where both children and adults could learn to read and write. Early private endeavors such as church schools, private schools, and literary societies became vital to the literacy development of Black Philadelphians at the time. However, it would be another hundred years before public efforts would expand to serve students of color. When they did expand, the efforts were created to prevent crime and establish civil order through education. In 1818, the Pennsylvania General Assembly established the First School District of Pennsylvania, a system for low-income White children to be taught for free. Still, 45% of adults in the city over the age of 20 could not read or write. It was not until the early 1900s, during the administration of Superintendent James MacAlister, who led the district to expand and diversify its curriculum, that the School District of Philadelphia took on the task of integrating adult education into the system and began to expand its curriculum to offer literacy classes in the evenings for Black Americans.

Over the course of the 20th century, numerous organizations, both public and private, emerged to try and mitigate the historical opportunity gaps through various forms of community education. However, even in the current day, Philadelphia remains a tale of two cities. Known for its vibrant communities and thriving economy, Philadelphia also holds the ignoble distinction of being one of the poorest and most segregated of our nation's largest cities. 25% of the population subsists below the poverty line (Pew, 2020, p. 4). Additionally, low adult literacy rates continue to plague the city. According to the Survey of Adult Skills, over 22% of Philadelphia's residents over the age of 18 lacks basic reading and numeracy skills (National Center for Educational Statistics, 2022).

After the decades of widening economic and racial disparity, addressing the opportunity gaps for Philadelphia residents with low English proficiency and limited schooling became imperative. Increasing publicity around the failures of the Philadelphia public school system prompted the call for a more comprehensive approach to adult education in the city. In 1968, the Center for Literacy, Inc. (CFL) was established as a volunteer tutoring program in West Philadelphia. By the 1990s, CFL had become the largest adult and family literacy provider in the nation, at its height serving more than 3000 learners per year.

Even while CFL grew, it could not reach all neighborhoods in urban Philadelphia. Two decades after CFL was established, another organization, the Community Learning Center (CLC), opened in Kensington, in lower northeast Philadelphia, with the goal of educating marginalized adults who had not been able to finish high school. Kensington's abandoned industrial buildings and convenient access to I-95 made it an East Coast epicenter of illegal drug trade, and high incidents of violent crime exacerbated the opportunity gaps in Philadelphia's poorest neighborhood. CLC quickly became a fixture in Kensington and its surrounding neighborhoods, complementing the work of CFL and establishing a reputation for high-quality literacy programs.

Each of these organizations, CLC and CFL, endeavored to understand and address adult learning needs in the region and provided important literacy and workforce training to thousands of marginalized Philadelphians. However, in recent years, political favor and funding for this work has waned. During the early 2010s, the Pennsylvania Department of Education (PDE) reduced the number of funded agencies in Philadelphia from 26 to 6. It became essential for adult learning organizations to manage scarcity, often through creative program design and the establishment of critical partnerships to share resources. It was this context that led CLC and CFL to merge in 2020, creating *Beyond Literacy*, now the largest literacy and adult learning organization in eastern Pennsylvania.

The merger has demanded intensive integrative work to meld two organizational cultures with distinct strengths and certain redundancies. Doing so effectively has required deep and objective reflection and planning, including the revision of our vision and values, the establishment of a new strategic plan, and the creation of a new organizational structure. These reflections opened critical questions about what it means to elevate our equity goals as a key metric for decision making and communications. The remainder of this chapter looks briefly at the history of our two organizations and then uses the *FATAE* to review our work in its relation to justice and equity. Our analysis helped us to highlight strategic opportunities that have emerged as a result of these efforts and to position Beyond Literacy as a powerful new force for literacy efforts in Philadelphia.

One City, Two Organizations

Like many cities in the industrialized Mid-Atlantic, Philadelphia's school age population grew rapidly in the period that followed World War II. The Urban History Association cites scholar Lisa Levenstein's observations that, building on decades of racialized resource allocation, "In the 1950's and 1960's, when the federal government allocated millions of dollars in urban renewal funds, school district officials in Philadelphia once again used most of those funds to build and remodel schools in majority-white communities, while Black youth attended school in toxic buildings with peeling paint, insufficient windows and inadequate heat" (Levenstein, 2009, p. 126).

As adult literacy rates in Philadelphia's poorest neighborhoods continued to decline, agencies such as CFL and the CLC organized to address the widening opportunity gaps through literacy education. Founded almost 20 years apart, both organizations found a way to thrive amidst sparse resources and the unpredictable ebbs and flows of Philadelphia's political climate. Indeed, more than 50 years after CFL's founding, it was the commonality of purpose and shared mission language that led the two organizations to consider the benefits of a merger.

Community Learning Center (CLC)

Founded in 1987 by Jean Fleschute, CLC met a dire need for adults whose formal education had not only been abbreviated but was further limited by Kensington's deep poverty and the poor quality of Philadelphia public schools. Starting with 67 students, Fleschute, along with a small team of volunteers, taught literacy classes in Kensington and soon expanded to open a second center in the high-need West Oak Lane neighborhood of Philadelphia. In 1996, CLC received its first contract from the PDE allowing for paid teachers to serve alongside the organization's dedicated volunteers. In 1999, the National Reporting System (NRS) was established as an outcome-based reporting system for state-administered, federally funded adult education programs. Over the fifteen years that followed, NRS regularly ranked CLC among the top performing PDE-funded agencies in the state, a reflection of their strong pedagogy and student-centered organizational design. Under Fleschute's leadership, CLC's reputation delivering cost-free, community-based education grew and the agency had attracted over 200 students annually by the time she handed over the reins of leadership to Rebecca Wagner in 2008.

Wagner expanded CLC's service community by 200% and maintained its strong, data-backed outcomes by being laser-focused on meeting and exceeding state standards. As the organization matured, it gained a reputation and developed practices that helped it to weather the difficult times for literacy organizations in the city. However, that success did not come without significant challenges. Despite its strong reputation, CLC felt itself slipping in the competition for shrinking Title II funding. Other organizations were proving more savvy at the storytelling and legislative advocacy needed to secure those funds. In the span of ten years, Philadelphia's number of state-funded agencies shrunk dramatically from 26 to 4. By 2016, the level of competition for and scarcity of Title II funds became a significant threat to CLC's sustainability. Uncertainty about how to best allocate resources and structure the organization going forward was exacerbated by waning staff morale and a series of leadership transitions. The pressure felt by CLC's leaders to perform in an increasingly restrictive and underfunded environment grew and three consecutive directors resigned over the three years that followed. By 2019, the need for new leadership to reimagine the organization had become urgent and immediate.

Center for Literacy, Inc (CFL)

Founded in 1968, CFL is among the oldest adult literacy organizations in Pennsylvania, striving from the start to understand adult learner needs and then work with partners at the local, state, and national level to develop the quality programs and services to narrow the city's opportunity gaps. From 1986 through 2015, CFL was led by JoAnn Weinberger, who helped grow the organization from a community-based tutoring organization located on the third floor of a church to the largest provider of adult education and family literacy in the nation. At its height, CFL served 3000 to 4000 learners per year, in nearly 100 sites throughout Philadelphia, with over 100 volunteer tutors and eventually a total budget of $5 million. During her tenure, Weinberger earned a reputation as the most influential advocate for adult education funding in Harrisburg, Pennsylvania's capital. Consistently positioning adult literacy as critical to alleviating poverty, Weinberger founded the Pennsylvania State Coalition for Adult Literacy, published an inventory of state resources available for adult literacy, and participated in regionwide rallies as a statewide spokesperson for adult education.

Until the mid-eighties, community-based organizations in Pennsylvania were ineligible for any federal funding for adult literacy allocated through the state, nor was there any direct state funding. At the time, all funding for education in Pennsylvania went directly to K-12 public school districts. That started to change in 1983, when the PDE granted other entities the eligibility for federal money with the approval of their local school district. At the time, CFL's budget was $300,000 which included minimal federal government funds. Corporate funding, motivated by Pennsylvania's Neighborhood Assistance Act tax credits, made up the majority of the revenue. However, with the passage of the Pennsylvania Adult and Family Literacy Act (1986), community-based organizations, as well as other non-profit entities, became eligible for state and federal funds. PA Act 143, which is still in force today, allocates 20% of the funds that organizations receive to tutoring costs. Notably, CFL played a major advocacy role in the passage of this act. Until 1986, Tutors of Literacy in the Commonwealth, a division of the statewide PA Association for Adult Continuing Education, had been pushing for years for the passage of this bill. When Weinberger became president of this division, she used her relationship with the Executive Director of the Senate Education Committee to convince her that this bill was critical. Thanks to Weinberger's advocacy, the bill was passed, and with it came the first state appropriation for adult literacy.

For its first three decades, CFL operated in a regulatory era when hard questions about return on investment (ROI) related to specific outcomes were not typically asked; there were no employment or High School Equivalency (HSE) or post-secondary (PSE) transition standards to attain; and educators who loved teaching and interacting with learners did not have to "prove" the value of their engagement in terms of average hours spent in instruction and gains. Agency reports and press releases would focus on the agency's long history and large numbers of students served; adults could stay in the program year after year, having personal agency to select and work toward goals that they chose, or none at all. For years, enrollment served as the primary metric for evaluating performance in Pennsylvania. However, as the climate for program assessment and accountability changed nationally and across the state in the early 2000s, the demands for additional metrics increased pressures on programs to show more than just enrollment numbers.

Upon Weinberger's retirement, CFL's Board of Trustees hired an executive director who was a state insider and who had led PDE's Adult Education division. CFL made this move to regain its standing in the city. Unfortunately, evaluative reports from PDE at this time noted several concerns including that CFL did not require advanced degrees for volunteers or paid teachers. Also, little was invested in teachers' professional development, and most teachers' salaries were quite low, particularly as compared to management. As state and federal funding sources required broader outcome metrics, CFL's state-contracted enrollment numbers fell from 1496 in 2011 to 785 in 2019, when CFL found itself again without an executive director. The need to conduct another leadership search brought the challenges to light and shaped CFL's most immediate needs. To continue to serve the potentially larger population of clients and to leverage its success as a leading advocate for literacy work, CFL would need to strengthen its resources and systems for instructional assessment and reporting.

A Strategic Alliance

With shrinking funds and an overstretched staff, CFL's board began to consider a new strategy for future sustainability, exploring the possibility of re-aligning resources and collaborating with a peer organization to increase efficiencies and create a strategic alliance. Seeking a bold change that could make substantial inroads into the intractable low-literacy rate of Philadelphia adults, the CFL board initiated confidential conversations with CLC's board about a potential merger of the two organizations.

In the midst of these talks, during December 2019, the CLC Board of Directors hired Kimmell Proctor as their executive director. Proctor had a background in education with years of experience leading strategic partnerships and nonprofit services. After a prolonged leadership search, CLC needed a leader who could evaluate and refine its operations and tell the organizations' powerful story in a way that translated to recognition and financial resources. For years, CLC's reputation among its supporters was that of a "best kept secret." It had consistently led the city in achievement of state outcomes yet remained a relatively small program that enrolled fewer than 500 students annually and was almost entirely reliant on PDE funding. In many ways, the small but mighty agency was focused on student success at the expense of its own. It needed to amplify its programmatic successes among potential funders as well as to raise name recognition among legislators in Harrisburg. In short, CLC had the substance but lacked visibility. Their website was dated and static, and they had no experience in the advocacy work that CFL had mastered under Weinberger. Despite the added complexity that a partnership promised, Proctor and the board quickly saw the advantages in the proposed partnership between CFL and CLC and the two organizations began to work toward their eventual merger.

The resulting vision was clear: bringing CFL and CLC together would be a critical step toward stability for both organizations and could advance the field of adult education for Philadelphia. As a merged agency with a combined 87 years of experience in the field, we saw the potential to expand opportunities and improve lives by unleashing the power of literacy through free, high-quality education services. Working alongside impacted residents to break the cycle of generational poverty, we could help unprecedented numbers of adults improve their academic and digital literacy skills, earn a High School Equivalency credential, develop English language proficiency, gain employment, and transition to postsecondary schools and job training programs. That vision became a reality in October of 2020, when Proctor was appointed as the chief executive officer of the new organization which would be renamed *Beyond Literacy* in the spring of 2021 (Figure 3.1).

FIGURE 3.1 Following the Merger, BeLit Rebranded with a New Name and Logo in the Summer of 2021

Leading the Merger

The charge to our newly merged organization was threefold: to integrate the two organizations as seamlessly as possible, to establish high performance expectations across the organization, and to position the organization for growth and long-term sustainability – all while navigating the lockdowns and health consequences of COVID-19.

The work ahead would demand transparency, engagement, and a shared vision among all constituencies. Proctor was eager to move the new organization quickly into a strategic planning process that would center equity and leverage the shared resources of the merged organizations. To do so, however, would require bringing the two organizational cultures together and establishing both a unified identity and trust in leadership. The *FATAE* astutely asks, "What conversations need to happen to build an organization-wide consensus of and commitment to democratic governance and collective leadership?" Working closely with program staff and the newly established culture committee, Chief Program Officer Dawn Hannah had observed inconsistencies in practices and also heard employee concerns about equity in pay and program expectations. Understanding the importance of elevating staff morale and the need to align internal systems with organizational values before launching a strategic planning effort, The Board of Directors agreed and approved investment in several important processes over the first year. First, a rebranding and revisioning exercise would help the members of the organization begin to articulate their shared purpose. Second, the organization would engage its internal constituents in evaluating its programs, operations and practices of data collection and analysis. Finally, our organizational chart and compensation structure would need to be revised to address role clarity and the pay equity concerns that employees expressed. With these foundational elements in place, the next strategic plan of the burgeoning agency could successfully chart an ambitious path forward.

Building Trust through Critical Conversations

To build trust and a sense of unity across teams, one of the first tasks was to establish an HR committee focused on organizational culture and comprised of multi-level staff from each of the initial two agencies' departments. The committee sought to engage and energize staff by establishing internal feedback loops that solicited and shared staff insights around identifying risks and opportunities to improve our newly integrated organization. The committee's initial post-merger survey on culture revealed that, while the majority of staff described our unified culture positively with descriptors such as "supportive" and "collaborative," there were others who felt our organization was "overworked" or "siloed." Clearly, we needed to continue refining our systems to better support, connect, and equip each of our team members to feel effective in their roles. We hope that as BeLit (the nickname we chose for ourselves – more on that below) evolves, our internal communication tools will serve the added benefits of actively encouraging staff to contribute ideas, share in decision-making, and develop a collective foundation of trust and accountability for BeLit's success. It was with this spirit that we launched focus groups to identify and explore key questions posed by the *FATAE*.

With all this, the merger provided an occasion for us to look collectively at our individual organizations and the ways in which we had historically successfully or unsuccessfully served our students. Furthermore, like many organizations challenged to continue providing services during COVID-19, adaptations in our modes of delivery and access forced us to reflect on the equity of our practices.

In this effort, the *FATAE* served to guide our inquiry throughout the merger's implementation. BeLit's full staff, board, and past leaders were invited to join collaborative conversions centered on the framework that examined existing internal and external organizational policies and explored possibilities for reform. Participants chose their preferred priority areas of work, posed questions, and provided insights. This approach allowed us to collectively raise awareness and develop a shared understanding of the complexity of operational and programmatic issues facing our merging agency. This preparation for action planning also provided a shared language for discussing equity and opportunities to embed equity in our strategic plan's initiatives, goals, and outcomes assessment. Surveys allowed us to engage the full board and staff in key questions about organizational climate, program, and strategic priorities and focus groups provided opportunities for small group discussions of our findings.

The entire *FATAE* provided a broad reminder to inquiry groups to center questions of equity in our assessment and goal setting around program, operations, outreach, and governance. That meant groups were empowered to identify areas of the framework that felt especially germane in supporting the strategic growth of our merged organizations. From those conversations, several themes emerged around organizational impact, equitable support of instructors and staff and the establishment of a powerful new public voice in support of the organization's goals.

Organizational Impact

The *FATAE*'s section on Teaching and Learning asks us to consider "[how] our organization situates its work in larger social movements for justice and equity?" As teachers and leaders of decades-old adult education organizations, we felt we needed to collaboratively extend the question by exploring *What have we done to address inequities in our city? In what ways have we attempted to dismantle failed systems? How have we inadvertently colluded to maintain systemic inequities?* We endeavored to develop a transparent understanding of our shared history in the region and ensure fidelity in establishing guidelines for our future work together. Ultimately, we seek to move to action by asking, *"What steps can we take to ensure that our mistakes are not repeated? How can we ensure that our combined future is even more accomplished than our separate past?"*

For decades, each of the merged organizations provided educational alternatives to adults in Philadelphia who, for whatever reason, had been unable to receive the education they needed. During its 53-year history, CFL served as a leading advocate for adult education, engaged hundreds of volunteer tutors, and served tens of thousands of learners, particularly within Philadelphia's robust immigrant communities seeking English language instruction. Prior to the merger, English to speakers of other languages (ESOL) comprised 70% of CFL's programming, In contrast, CLC had focused less on serving immigrant communities but had demonstrated strong success in helping its adult basic education learners achieve potentially life-changing core outcomes that met or exceeded state standards. Because ABE and ASE were their core programs, CLC hired subject-area specialists, and placed students in single-subject classes based on their assessed reading and math levels, making it easier to meet students' subject-specific needs, and to help students to achieve academic gains and graduate in greater numbers. These areas of focus presented as complementary strengths. CFL leveraged relationships in the state's capital that would help to keep adult education on the minds of legislators as a funding priority; while CLC pushed to ensure that the ROI on that funding was evident. As Beyond Literacy, immigrants seeking ESOL now comprise 30%

of our students. Also, since merging, the number of ESOL program graduates who stay on to earn their GED has doubled. Our strengths are proving to be complementary.

Externally, CFL served a substantial number of learners, prioritizing enrollment over the systems or supports for deeply impacting its learners as measured by NRS and Pennsylvania's four core state outcomes: educational skill gains, high school equivalency attainment, post-secondary enrollments, and living-wage employment. CFL also staffed more generalists to teach all subjects of the high school equivalency, making it harder to offer students classes specific to their level and subject needs because the generalists did not have the expertise to offer all of the subject-specific courses that students needed. As discussed earlier, although CFL's communications and development departments necessarily told compelling stories of high numbers and positive impact to the public, without attention to missed outcome targets, CFL's education and student support teams did not have sufficient information about areas for improvement and were, therefore, ill-prepared to address them. Meanwhile, CLC's vigilant focus on outcomes sometimes resulted in strident policies that required a demonstration of grit and responsibility from adults who had already proved their resilience by virtue of having returned to school at all. As a result, CLC turned away quite a few students whose struggles included barriers to punctuality or consistent attendance. The result in both cases mirrors what we see in failed K-12 systems where underfunded schools are able to do too little for too many, and/or find themselves pushing out learners in an effort to ensure making adequate yearly progress. In terms of the employment trajectory of students, neither organization historically focused sufficient attention – or much at all – on ensuring that students were connected to work that would raise their income to much above subsistence.

Our inquiry of historical operations revealed gaps in the practices and systems employed by both individual organizations. CLC and CFL leadership had each set the bar low in different ways for either staff or students. For example, CLC Leadership had, at times, struggled to include veteran staff and community members in decision-making. In its section on Governance, the Framework asks *What does it mean for decision-making processes to be "democratic" and for leading to be a "collective" responsibility?* For us at Beyond Literacy, the question posed an immediate design challenge, *"How can we raise the bar for faculty/staff performance so that it is consistently characterized by instructional excellence and stewardship of our organizational decision making?"*

Fair Compensation

In the section on Governance and Finance, the *FATAE* challenges us to align our budgets and budgeting processes with our equity goals, *"What are [our] common models for budgeting, and how does each model advance and/or hinder justice and equity goals? How often are we assessing and improving our budgeting structures, policies, and procedures?"* Our historical analysis of salaries revealed that CFL leadership had strained to compensate staff adequately and equitably and that significant gaps existed between the workloads and compensation scales of the two organizations. The group conducting the analysis recognized quickly that this issue was a threat to both staff morale and to the success of the merger, setting the stage for an immediate review of BeLit's compensation policies as a foundational element of organizational integration.

The efforts to increase faculty/staff voice in leadership and to develop a more equitable compensation structure were prioritized by the board, who contracted a benefits specialist to conduct for-profit and nonprofit education-sector wage surveys, and who established an ad hoc HR committee to lead an inquiry and make recommendations for improvement. This initiative built on work in process in each of the individual organizations in the years preceding the merger. CLC had begun efforts to increase staff salaries and to support the advancement and promotion of staff of color. CFL had been working to bring staff of varying levels (and alums) into executive decision-making processes that might have traditionally been limited to a governing board, as well as promoting from within as a standard operating procedure. Both organizations boasted a history of hiring program participants, including GED graduates Shaquanda and Tiffani Clemons, Niema Alfred and Clarece Hicks, and former ESOL students, Song Han and Leon Santos.

It is important to note an important change we are seeking as part of our efforts to be a more inclusive organization: While the diversity of staff was strong, our board was largely homogenous. At the time of the merger, the board predominantly identified as white (82%) and 100% identified as middle-upper class. The merged board prioritized increasing our intersectional representation and welcomed two new members from our service community, a recent graduate and a current learner, whose lived perspectives and insights would help to shape and advance our agency's strides toward excellence in diversity, equity, and inclusion. The effort has had immediate, visible demographic results. Beyond Literacy's board now identifies as 25% trustees of color with greater representation from the communities we serve.

It is no secret that nonprofits face challenges when it comes to balancing strategic priorities while keeping budgets and talent retention at the forefront. However, as a nonprofit whose mission is to provide opportunities and improve lives, we committed to starting with how we treat and pay staff. We found, when we looked comprehensively at our staff contracts, that there was often no logical justification for why two people in similar roles and titles were not being paid equitably. In some cases, lesser qualified employees were earning more than others with greater experience or qualification. The Board posed a strategic design question, *"How can we support high expectations for faculty and staff through a system of compensation, coaching and evaluation that is characterized by transparency and a shared sense of equity & value?"*

In response to this analysis, BeLit's board reviewed and reworked our entire compensation strategy through an equity lens, seeking to clarify responsibilities and salaries across the organization. Knowing that the organization could not thrive unless staff were thriving as well, the board allocated the bulk of funds freed up through merger efficiencies back into employee compensation. However, establishing an equitable system to guide implementation was easier said than done. Each merging agency had lacked a parity of compensation within and across their teams. Working through and creating that "equity lens" was challenging.

In doing this work, we started by conducting a comprehensive wage survey of both for-profit and nonprofit education organizations to determine fair market value of staff roles. Soon after, we took action to restructure salaries and to create a logical and equitable formula for how we pay our people. This required an adjustment to the organization's budget to allot more funds toward staff time and benefits. Thereafter, Beyond Literacy formally established a new standard for salary decisions to be made in the future that accounted for both professional experience and educational background. At the same time, we reviewed and adjusted salaries for all current employees to remedy our prior practices. By level-setting our lowest paying positions at $15 per hour, over Pennsylvania's 2021 minimum wage of $12 per hour, we hoped to signal to employees their value and critical contribution toward our mission. To further invest in our greatest asset, our staff, the board of directors approved quarterly 401k contributions for every full-time employee, without any match requirement. When budgeting for these contributions, the board chose equal distributions over a percentage model so that the least-compensated employees would benefit the most.

While establishing pay equity was an important first step, shaping a work culture that is equitable, transparent, and excellent requires more than high investment; it requires high expectations and a well-supported staff. Aligning with our agency's adopted value of "lifelong learning," BeLit's board approved a significant increase in the organization's professional development budget. Confronted with America's "great resignation" which compounded our organizational changes, staff and leadership development opportunities would not only be a way to address current needs but also would position BeLit as attractive to top talent and create a pipeline for leaders who could advance beyond direct-service roles. Committed to providing advancement pathways, BeLit ultimately filled all five new managerial and leadership positions internally with standout, frontline-staff candidates.

Although leadership had developed an effective plan to promote from within and compensate teams equitably, we did not fully take into account the cultural differences around workload expectations that existed between

CFL and CLC. While CFL had reduced their teachers' instructional hours at the pandemic's onset, CLC had maintained their teachers' pre-pandemic instructional assignments and invested in technology to support their staff in working from home. The new board policy had bridged the level of pay for similar job titles but had not yet taken into account the actual workload and responsibilities of each individual. Staff who were historically advantaged by lighter workloads were slow to support the efforts to shift the system. In some cases, CFL teachers resented the change to more demanding management expectations. While these concerns were eventually mitigated by a strong investment in instructional technology to allow for more flexible, hybrid schedules, in hindsight, creating pay equity before workload equity was the wrong order to act; and the resulting tensions among certain teams failed to fully capture early opportunities for cultural integration momentum.

Expanding Our Public Voice

The merger required us to think deeply about how we would present our combined organization to our critical external constituents – our clients, donors, and public funders. The work of honing our name and guiding language felt urgent, not only to provide an internal compass for planning and operations but also for elevating our reputation and strengthening our advocacy for much needed resources. Thus, the Framework's organizing inquiry around partnerships and public impact provided several critical questions that helped guide both our re-branding and the strategic planning processes.

- *What is the reputation of our organization?*
- *Whom should we prioritize as our target audiences right now? What are the venues for doing so?*
- *Who are potential partners for such educational efforts (e.g., advocacy groups; media)?*
- *What are the types of partnerships that best align with our justice and equity goals?*
- *Who else should we partnering with, and why?*

Our agency's rebranding campaign presented an opportunity to reimagine how we inspire, support, and forecast for the future. We needed to not only raise awareness of our expanding services, but also to compel each of our stakeholder groups – students, staff, program partners, funders, and donors – to remain invested in our new, evolving agency. Believing that the renaming and rebranding process would lay the groundwork for more extensive strategic planning, we gathered a working group comprised of both internal team leaders and external partners to consider these essential questions and to help rename the organization.

When two organizations merge, they often maintain the use of one or both names to help assert greater market dominance. "Market dominance" is traditionally a for-profit concept but, in Philadelphia, our "peers" are also our competitors for funding. Another school of thought around renaming recognizes that mergers combine different but compatible capabilities and, in doing so, make their sum greater than their parts, thereby requiring a distinctly new name. It was this latter perspective that ultimately prevailed. After several months of brainstorming, our board and staff were equally split between the name *Center for Literacy and Learning,* an homage to our past, and *Beyond Literacy,* a nod to our future. We had intentionally approached this process with the goal of "strengthening our ability to advocate for resources" and so turned to our major adult education philanthropists in the final round of name selection to ensure we would be able to build the strongest brand recognition for cultivation of funding opportunities. Noting that expanded capabilities were the key impetus of our union, our funders unanimously voted for *Beyond Literacy* noting that, by joining together, CFL and CLC were able to go "above and beyond" for our learners and become the leading advocate for adult education in the city and state. To keep our name relatable and easily recalled by those we served, our short-form nickname became *BeLit.*

It was that same thinking that extended our imagination for what the outcome of our merged organization could be. Eager to broaden our impact on civic policy surrounding housing and education and to extend our disruption of systemic poverty, our leadership approved a revised vision statement that energized the work ahead: *Adults empowered beyond literacy; children, youth, and families inspired; our communities thriving; our city transformed.*

Mapping the Path Ahead – Strategic Planning

Even while our staff worked to better align our operations and resources, we were moving quickly through the rebranding process, and our full staff and board next engaged in a seven-month strategic planning process of convening, conversing, and collaborating to establish initiatives, milestones, and tasks that would help us bring our vision to fruition. At our first convening, we had 20 of 21 board members present, alongside all 52 staff members. Broad representation across the organization was critical. Despite our best efforts to be inclusive, the merger had progressed quickly, and some members of the organization were feeling excluded from decision making. How we approached the work of strategic planning could certainly exacerbate those feelings or serve to further unify *Beyond Literacy* into who we hoped to become. The *FATAE* asks us to consider *What are ways the [strategic planning] processes can impede [or promote] justice and equity goals?* For our newly merged organization, the planning process needed to cultivate a shared sense of possibility, inclusion, and stewardship. Giving ample space and time for the process meant inviting a level of deep self-reflection that has been both healing and cathartic. Through focus groups and stakeholder surveys, staff who had felt excluded from merger negotiations were able to surface their frustrations and have a voice in shaping the more transparent culture they wished to see in our new organization. While at times the conversations were uncomfortable, including critics and challengers in the strategic planning process enabled us to build trust, exchange perspectives, and coordinate efforts as the systems-change process unfolded. In its consideration of what effective, equity-focused strategic planning looks like, the *FATAE* astutely asks, *Do our core values, program goals, and other guiding documents explicitly and fully reflect our commitment to justice and equity?* By collectively defining our short- and long-term goals, and aligning our goals with our core values, we fostered a sense of shared identity and encouraged even the merger's skeptics to contribute to the broader collective good.

Through our process, we generated these values:

Beyond Literacy Values

Belonging: We create a positive environment where all learners may experience a sense of belonging and worth.

Equity: We provide equal access to education to combat systemic injustices that lead to unequal opportunities.

Lifelong learning: We believe everyone can learn and grow throughout their lives.

Inclusion: We foster an inclusive space in which all cultures, traditions, and social identities are welcomed.

Transparency: We are sincere and accountable to each other and our community.

The *FATAE* further asks, *"To what extend does our strategic plan center on justice and equity goals? Does our plan require that all [of our] undertakings involve asking complex questions about diversity, equity and justice?"* Our strategic planning process invited our full staff and board to reimagine our organization and develop a shared vision for impact, set measurable goals, and track our progress. Building on the work of the organizational inquiry groups, we used the first three months as a "discovery phase," assessing our successes and failures on issues that matter on an intrinsic level to us, as an adult literacy organization, and as colleagues. Key outcomes and goals from the process reflected a new level of diligence in "asking complex questions about diversity, equity and justice." We committed to promoting inclusive prosperity through fair, competitive compensation and identified formal systems for identifying and implementing diversity, equity, and inclusion policies and practices going forward. We also attached specific initiatives and outcomes to these goals, including:

- Contracting with minority- and women-owned partners in our business activities.
- Providing free laptops to the 30% of our learners affected by the digital divide.
- Funding a mobile learning lab to bring classes into disconnected communities.
- Adding Juneteenth as an agency-wide holiday.

Our strategic plan centers on ensuring high quality and broad reach, expansion of apprenticeship and industry-focused opportunities, increased graduate support, and increasing advocacy and awareness to ensure continuing financial support for our programs.

As ambitious as our planning has been, the impact of the work will lie in its implementation and measurement. The *FATAE* asks *"To what extent does our strategic plan center on justice and equity goals? Does our plan include measurable outcomes, clear activities and timelines, adequate supports and resources, appropriate assessments, and opportunities to revise in the interim?"* As we expanded staff engagement and accountability, we sought to create meaningful feedback loops with our learners through weekly, small-group student workshops led by social support staff and peer mentors to inform programming and support, as well as to improve our data collection and analysis procedures to reflect racial equity goals. In expanding and updating our data collection tools, language, and processes, we realized that we also must check our assumptions and address inherent bias within our data collection and analysis.

Taking an iterative approach to gathering feedback through regular learner surveys has amplified our ability to learn and respond nimbly when needed. An example arose when a recent survey included concerns about our use of the term "ex-offender," a term our primary funder and evaluator, PDE, has used for more than a decade when referring to justice system-impacted program participants. Our Director of Workforce Development was able to use the feedback to develop real-time training to help our practitioners recognize the ways the term "ex-offender" is pejorative in its description of the over 20% of our learners who self-report as having prior convictions. A more accurate and humanizing term is "returning citizen" which BeLit subsequently lobbied PDE to rethink and revise on their forms, as well as in our shared data reporting system. In a rare instance of cutting away bureaucratic red tape, PDE agreed that the "ex-offender" label stereotypes and marginalizes adult learners rather than supports them in rebuilding their lives, and they have since revised their terminology. We agreed that living in a country with the world's largest incarceration rate, the words we use to reference people should reflect their full identities and acknowledge their capacity to change and grow. It is an example of the kind of lenses BeLit seeks to employ in the ongoing review of its policies, practices, and performance measures in the effort to operationalize our equity values.

Early Signs of Impact

The work that has gone into aligning our internal structures and establishing our strategic priorities has, at the time of this chapter's writing, created space for the development and emergence of exciting new areas of programmatic focus and partnership development. One such opportunity lies in the area of workforce development. Sixty percent of our students self-report being either unemployed or under-employed in one or multiple minimum-wage jobs. As an adult education agency that touts equipping our graduates to go from learning to earning, we must also prioritize connecting adult learners to sustainable, high-paying careers, in lieu of the low-wage jobs that typically follow even those who have earned their high school equivalency. Before merging, neither CLC nor CFL had capacity to develop an industry-focused workforce development program, yet our learners reported year over year that their primary reason for seeking our services was to qualify for a family-sustaining, living wage job. Our new strategic plan recognized this critical need for workforce development as a key priority for growth going forward; however, even our leadership was surprised by what an immediate game-changer our new career pipeline program would be. Our emerging workforce development efforts show some of that impact.

Empowered to consider innovative approaches to workforce programs, Beyond Literacy appointed CLC's longtime upskilling teacher, Marcus Hall, as its new workforce development director. In reflecting on the *FATAE*'s questions around the pipelines and pathways used to support our students and graduates, Hall envisioned launching a pre-apprenticeship program in partnership with Pennsylvania's utilities and green energy corporations. From line workers to solar panel installers, to readers who operate and maintain electric grids, to high-volume call center operators, these in-demand, high-paying roles do not require a high school diploma or equivalent, a lower-than-average threshold of education relative to other high-paying positions. An analysis by researchers at the Brookings Institution (Muro et al., 2019) finds that starting salaries in the energy sector are 19% higher than the national average, including for entry-level jobs which offer a pay premium. Experienced line workers in Philadelphia earn an average of $46 per hour which is 131% above the national average. This is remarkable considering that around 50% of entry-level line workers have completed only high school or less, and yet they earn higher wages than their counterparts in other industries.

Historically, Philadelphia's energy industry's workforce has not been representative of our city's communities. To potential employment partners looking for greater inclusion, Workforce Development Director Hall promoted the diversity of our learners: In our 2021 cohorts, 72% identified as women and 90% were people of color. By partnering with BeLit, our city's green energy companies would have a direct pipeline to recruitment of skilled, underrepresented, and economically disadvantaged groups who could fulfill their entry-level service needs. Within months of establishing BeLit as the academic preparation partner of PECO (Pennsylvania's largest electric and natural gas utility), Hall prepared 21 pre-apprentices, the majority being low-income with minimal work experience, by providing test-prep and career readiness, conflict resolution workshops, and financial literacy that explained credit management and investment accounts. Nearly 90% of the cohort passed their aptitude pre-training test, over 60% established financial accounts, and nearly all were placed in a paid trainee program that immediately provided the economic mobility to move into the middle class. At the graduation ceremony, earning a starting wage of $35 per hour, one of our former learners, now an energy tech trainee, remarked how he never imagined being 24 years old and earning more than his mother ever had in her lifetime.

Wanting to use this pre-apprenticeship model to break other systemic workforce barriers, Hall leveraged his corporate partnership success and proposed a cross-sector referral relationship with Philadelphia's District Attorney's Office. Now referred to as the DA's Emerging Adults Initiative, BeLit offers a programmatic option for young adults ages 18–24 with low-level misdemeanor or felony cases that can result in the elimination of charges. This pre-apprenticeship initiative provides returning citizens and system-involved individuals with the opportunity to avoid incarceration, obtain their high school equivalency credential, and complete a high-demand job training program to become a green energy technician. With this new focus, BeLit's pre-apprenticeship programs go beyond training marginalized workers to meet the skill needs of high-wage industries, to become powerful tools for building a more just society.

The Emerging Adults Initiative is one powerful example of the new partnerships and initiatives that have resulted from our inquiry using the *FATAE*. The Framework points us to these questions: *"What are different models and/or frameworks… for what our external partnerships can and should look like? How can a holistic and strategic approach to partnerships help us to meet our range of needs and goals? What are (and who should be) the types of partnerships that best align with our justice and equity goals?"* Our response to these questions has led BeLit to prioritize workforce development partnerships and to take advantage of new grants for which we would not have qualified previously. Hall's intentional relationship-building with employer partners hiring for in-demand sectors, such as energy and utilities, went hand-in-hand with our advocacy efforts to engage legislators by positioning adult literacy as a foundational building block for the city's innovation and its residents upward mobility. Publishing an Op-Ed in *The Philadelphia Citizen* entitled "The Real Opportunity Gap," Kimmell Proctor (2022) explained that the literacy divide is at the root of every opportunity gap – from the digital divide to housing insecurity to workforce readiness. She argued that these challenges will remain intractable unless we conquer reading and comprehension, writing and math, digital literacy, and workplace skills. In response, Comcast, the multinational telecommunications conglomerate headquartered in Philadelphia, awarded BeLit $15,000 and 500 brand new laptops to support our digital navigation services. With the infusion of new resources from Comcast, we grew our team of "Digital Navigators," and we trained tech support staff who provide tailored support for the full spectrum of our learners' digital inclusion needs, from internet and device access to digital skill building. This team helped the 30% of our service community without home connectivity to adopt no-cost, reliable internet through local and federal pandemic relief programs including PHLConnectED and the Affordable Connectivity Program.

BeLit's achievement in helping to bridge Philadelphia's digital divide via our public-private partnership with Comcast was hailed as a model success story in Boston Consulting Group's National Report, *A Human Approach to Closing the Digital Divide* (Kalmus et al., 2022). In turn, the report became a powerful advocacy piece for Kimmell Proctor to share with legislators and potential corporate partners alike. When it came to answering the framework's questions public voice and partnerships, advocacy served not only to educate and influence, it proved to be a powerful brand builder to attract and deepen relationships with external stakeholders. Exactly one year after the merger, Kimmell was appointed by the city's mayor to serve on the local workforce development board, Philadelphia Works, Inc. In this position, she is well-poised to strengthen coordination between the city's programs that receive federal funding (Title I workforce and Title II adult education providers), thereby increasing probability of positive outcomes in performance reporting, and more importantly, increasing likelihood that learners will succeed. Our scale of impact, data-driven ethos, and financial resilience to challenges regularly allow us new opportunities to go above and beyond in providing transformational impact through the breadth and depth of our robust adult education programs.

Conclusion

Following a complex and successful merger, Beyond Literacy is in a fortunate and powerful position to leverage its combined talent, capacity, and partnerships toward putting our priorities into action. In June 2022, thanks to the programmatic vision and evidence-based practices executed by Dawn Hannah and her team of instructors, the Philadelphia Department of Education (PDE) awarded BeLit a new 5-year contract that equips our agency with top-level validation and longevity funding to sustain our equity-informed services. While this contract, which comprises 50% of our overall budget, was awarded largely based on demonstrated effectiveness, our ultimate impact will be measured by the success of our students. Our Class of 2022 graduates included 12 new U.S. citizens, 25 proficient English language speakers, 28 new high school equivalency achievers, and 35 workforce trainees entering the energy and utilities industry. They were recognized in a widely attended event in front of City Hall that included the participation of news media, recording artist Montell Jordan, the iconic professional baseball mascot, the Phillie Phanatic, and leaders from Citizens Bank who generously donated a surprise gift of pairs of Philadelphia Phillies game tickets for each of our 100 program graduates. In bringing together our grads and their families, our community partners, legislative champions, volunteers and staff, the special celebration was a powerful demonstration of the value of our mission (Figures 3.2 and 3.3).

FIGURE 3.2 David Logan (left), 2022 BeLit Graduate, with Marcus Hall, Director of Workforce Development

FIGURE 3.3   BeLit's Class of 2022 Graduation Celebration, June 24, 2022 in Front of Philadelphia's City Hall

The following week, our HSE graduate David Logan, was selected by the Mayor's Office to deliver Philadelphia's Citywide Commencement speech. His inspiring words were a potent reminder of the life-changing effect of collaboration between adult education and workforce partners:

> I've dreamed of this moment for years. I dreamed of sitting in a classroom with teenaged high school students determined to finish what I started decades ago. The kids would mock me as I tried to pull off wearing skinny jeans hanging off my behind and sneakers that cost me a month's salary. Then I'd wake up, back where I started, in a different nightmare that I call *adulthood*.
>
> When I was younger, I convinced myself I didn't have time for this. College was a waste of money, and if I were to find success, I'd find it on my terms using the talents I was gifted with. I've picked up computer and business skills along the way. I've worked alongside of corporate employees learning what I could to keep up with my peers. After years of avoiding what was obviously holding me back, I realized that in the time I've spent teaching myself how to succeed - I could've used that time to have something to show for it.
>
> I've worked for what seems my entire life, thinking that as long as I got a paycheck and stayed out of trouble, I would be fine. I didn't

account for the stress of a dead-end job, not being able to advance in a career no matter how much I was qualified, and how fast every year went by the longer I deprived myself of this achievement.

I lived in New York when the pandemic hit. When I was displaced from my home, I had no choice but to come back here to Pennsylvania penniless, no place to stay. All I had was work experience and art talent. Eventually, I ended up getting a temp job making good money, but they couldn't hire me on after six months without a diploma. I was desperate to try to find a way out of this hole that I was in, so I was on a mission to make a significant change in my life.

That's when I found Beyond Literacy. I studied like my life depended on it. A few weeks in and I was introduced to the Energy Coordinating Association. It was the perfect opportunity to take up a trade and get my diploma/GED at the same time. This time, I was going to have something to show for the work I'd put in. Six months later, here I am.

Not only have I earned my diploma, I have earned multiple certifications to add to my resume. I've learned new skills I can use to make a real difference in my community. I've gained an extended family with my classmates and instructors. I've started a new career in mechanical engineering and start my first semester in college this fall. This was all possible by pure ambition, setting a goal, and a program with dedicated people who do all they can to ensure people in our communities succeed.

Most of us came into this saying we suck at Math. But Math is a lot easier than raising children on your own. I'll take Science over a complicated relationship any day. Don't let the little pride that we feel we have get in the way of your true purpose in life.

My advice to anyone who's held back by hardship, time management, childcare, disabilities, or any excuse to keep you from achieving your goals is: Things like this are possible. And it's closer than you think. All you have to do is reach out and grab it. It's like I told my classmates: the challenges we face every day are guaranteed; the easiest and most unexpected thing we can do for ourselves is fight back with an ambitious goal and a dream.

Those dreams I had of sitting in a classroom with people younger than me came true, but the difference is that we were all adults, and we became like family. No way I was fitting into skinny jeans, nor was I buying a pair of expensive sneakers.

I would like to thank the instructors from Beyond Literacy who helped me on this journey: Marcus, Dan, Joanne, Ivry, and Maryellen. To the instructors from the Energy Coordinating Agency: Mr. Jack, Jeff and Hugo, thank you.

> To my inspiring classmates- never have I've been a part of a group so
> cohesively positive and motivating: My brother James, Janay, Brianna,
> Shariff, Ivan, Keven, Kurt, Mann, Andre, Shawn. And to my friends
> and family who supported me through this whole process - thank you!
> *David Logan, 2022 BeLit Graduate and City-wide Commencement*
> *Keynote Speaker*

With the mechanics of the merger behind us, BeLit's next challenge is to evaluate and refine our new systems and continue implementing programs that build collaborative relationships, create high-functioning adult learning environments, and support the equity-based values of our combined organization now striving to serve 2000 learners annually from Philadelphia's diverse populations and most underserved communities. Having helped us navigate a prolonged period of complex change, the *FATAE*'s strategic exercises proved to be invaluable. The reflective process helped Beyond Literacy chart our evolving core purpose, competencies, values, and a vivid vision that is taking our organization to new heights of service and recognition.

References

DuBois, W. E. B., & Eaton, I. (1996). *The Philadelphia Negro: A social study.* University of Pennsylvania Press. http://www.jstor.org/stable/j.ctt3fhpfb

Kalmus, M., Hill, H., Lee, J., Goodchild, C., & Webb, D. (2022). A Human Approach to Closing the Digital Divide. Retrieved from: https://www.bcg.com/publications/2022/how-to-close-digital-divide-with-human-approach

Levenstein, L. (2009). *A movement without marches: African American Women and the politics of poverty in postwar Philadelphia.* University of North Carolina Press.

Logan, D. (2022, June 24). *Commencement Address.* Beyond Literacy Commencement Ceremony. Philadelphia, PA.

Muro, M., Tomer, A., Shivaram, R., & Kane, J. (2019). Advancing Inclusion through Clean Energy Jobs, Brookings Institute. Retrieved from: https://www.brookings.edu/research/advancing-inclusion-through-clean-energy-jobs/

National Center for Education Statistics (2022). U.S. PIAAC Skills Map. Retrieved from: https://nces.ed.gov/surveys/piaac/skillsmap/

Pennsylvania Adult & Family Literacy Act (1986 October 22). www.legis.state.pa.us Pub. L. No. P.L. 1452.

Pew Research Center (2020). Philadelphia 2020, State of the City. Retrieved from: https://www.pewtrusts.org/en/research-and-analysis/reports/2020/04/philadelphia-2020-state-of-the-city

Proctor, K. (2022). The Real Opportunity Gap. The Philadelphia Citizen. Retrieved from: https://thephiladelphiacitizen.org/real-opportunity-gap/

4

TECHNOLOGY ACCESS FOUNDATION

Building Healthy Ecosystems

Heather Lechner and Christina Taylor

Introduction

In this chapter, we share information about Technology Access Foundation (TAF) as well as our experience in engaging in a self-study focused on our equity and justice practices, using the Framework for Assessment and Transformation in Adult Education (FATAE). As authors, Dr. Lechner serves as TAF's Executive Director of Education. In this role, she is responsible for the strategic direction and oversight of the programming arm of TAF; which encompasses the work of the Network for EdWork (NWEW), as well as TransformED, STEMbyTAF Institute, and the Co-Managed Academies. Mrs. Taylor is the Director of the NWEW and is responsible for oversight of all programs and initiatives of the NWEW. She interfaces with deans from universities and superintendents from partner districts, as well as manages program managers. Currently, she is also leading Education Encounter efforts.

Participating in this self-study was an extremely daunting and rewarding experience. Daunting because the framework is extensive and asked us to not only explore our current practices but also those that brought us to this place and those that will carry us forward. When we initially interviewed for this opportunity, we did not understand the scope of the project and how intensive a review it would be. The opportunity to interact with so many of our stakeholders internally and externally was enlightening. This process uncovered that we have work to do organizationally. It provided an opportunity to understand all the complexities of the organization as well as the tapped and untapped opportunities to live and operate in a way that not only values stakeholders but also sees them as change agents in our equity and social justice work. This process illustrated that we and other like organizations have

DOI: 10.4324/9781003286998-4

a wealth of resources that we have not leveraged to move this work and our target communities forward. The self-study also gave us an opportunity to see what we are doing well and how we might learn from and apply those strengths in other areas. For those who are considering embarking on this journey, we offer that all things considered, you will undoubtedly believe you do not have the time to undergo this process. That may be true, and you may never, and yet it is still a valuable exercise to do. We encourage you to make the time as you will discover that self-assessment and associated discoveries are not an end point but a stop in the cycle of the ongoing development and transformation of your organization. If you genuinely want to thrive, represent your community, and center equity and social justice you, like us, have only just begun. We welcome you to learn, as we did about the internal and external workings of TAF, its strengths, challenges, and opportunities as we strive to serve adult learners in equitable and just ways.

History and Context of Organization

The Founding of Technology Access Foundation

To understand our organization's work with adults, it's important you understand how we were founded and eventually came to the point of working with adult learners. Fundamentally, the founding of and subsequent evolution of programs supported by TAF sought to consistently and unapologetically center BIPOC students while combating the historical models of schooling which relied on the standardization of curriculum and instruction that excluded most students from accessing authentic learning. Traditional models of education have not evolved over the course of 100 years, except to foster structures that impede meaningful learning including (but are not limited to) overloaded classrooms and ineffective methods of differentiation (Vetter et al., 2016). Students of color too often feel the brunt of these structures, and their inevitable outcomes have served to perpetuate inequities and race-based disparities socially, economically, and politically (TAF, 2020). The former Director of the NWEW, Dr. Cannie, stated, "Their exclusion from traditional models of education, including adult education, stem from leadership and institutions which upholds white supremacy, from the demographics of teachers to curricular content decisions which alienate learners of color to inequitable "reform" efforts which benefit white communities."

In 1996, TAF's co-founders Trish Millines Dziko and Jill Dziko founded TAF. Trish left her 17-year career in the technology industry to start the organization to ensure Black, Indigenous, People of Color (BIPOC) students had access to the skills needed to participate as inventors and creators in the growing field of technology. Jill worked at TAF as the Program Manager for a little over a year, then left in February of 1998 to have the couple's first child and be a stay-at-home mom. Jill became an adoption social worker in 2003. Though some did not understand Trish's decision to transition out of technology as the industry was taking off, she explains:

> At Microsoft in my role of Senior Diversity Administrator, I had the opportunity to see the potential of students of color when I ran the High School Internship Program for two years. That experience plus the realization the industry would continue to use the 'empty pipeline' as the excuse for lack of diversity in the tech field, led me to take the leap. I didn't see it as such a risk though because I knew I could always come back if things didn't work out. At every moment we struggled in our 25-year history, I stayed to fight for another day because our work is so important.

TAF's first programs launched in 1997 and were designed to prepare teenagers for tech-focused summer internships (programming, network engineering, web development, and media production) and college preparation. By 2001, TAF programs reached down through middle and elementary schools, thereby creating continuous year-over-year K-12 Science, Technology, and Engineering and Math (STEM) education.

Recognizing the limitations of programming outside of the school day, TAF built a five-year strategy in 2004 to reach as many students as possible by partnering with public school districts. After ten years of working in out of school spaces with great outcomes for students entering the STEM fields, TAF was approached by one of their funders who proposed TAF consider the small school model. TAF received funding to incubate and develop their STEMbyTAF model. In 2008, TAF created the only public school in Washington State co-managed by a nonprofit and a school district called TAF Academy, which would go on to be our flagship school.

TAF Academy used the STEMbyTAF model. The model was built upon a foundation of racial equity and the belief that every student is capable of being an agent of change; that they are deserving of a positive and rigorous learning experience; that those students have a right to be included in the direction of their education; and that an educator's primary responsibility is to support students' voice and choice. The STEMbyTAF model is comprised of four pillars; STEM integration, Interdisciplinary Project Based learning, Educational Technology, and College & Career Readiness, all of which are grounded in equity. The STEMbyTAF model can be distinguished from other models because we see each of these pillars as vehicles for equity, so equity is embedded in all aspects of the model and cannot be extrapolated. In a school embodying the STEMbyTAF model, both adults and students are expected to demonstrate character, civic responsibility, and respect for differences, and they are given multiple opportunities to demonstrate those values.

TAF Academy was designed based on the belief that every student in Washington's K-12 schools should be able to bring their authentic selves to the classroom and deserve access to highly qualified, excellent BIPOC teachers and education leaders, regardless of students' race, ethnicity, or socioeconomic status. Using the belief system and practices from the award-winning TAF Academy, TAF then established the STEMbyTAF Teacher Institute to prepare our public-school teachers to deliver an equitable student-centered 21st-century education in 2013. In 2014, TAF launched the STEMbyTAF School Transformation program, a system of structures, policies and procedures that would guide the full transformation of traditional public schools to operate like TAF Academy. Since conception, the Transformation program has worked in nine schools, with Boze Elementary of Tacoma Public Schools being the first to complete the five-year transformation process in the spring of 2020.

Following the success and expansion of TAF and its programming, TAF Academy merged with a middle school in Federal Way, Washington to form TAF@Saghalie in 2017, growing the middle school from 300 to 700 students. Consistently, this school made a significantly positive impact in student outcomes, including a 95% on-time graduation rate, 100% college acceptance rate, and recognition as a School of Distinction for seven years in a row by the Center for Educational Effectiveness (an achievement held only by TAF Academy/TAF@Saghalie). Drawing on these successes, TAF formally expanded its offerings and established a new arm of service through the Network for EdWork, establishing programs for adult learners across the K-12 educational system.

Network for EdWork

As TAF transformed network partner schools through the STEMbyTAF model (whether in an Academy or in a Transformation School), we recognized this was not enough. We knew we needed a broader reach. So, we asked ourselves, "What will it take to generate powerful outcomes and opportunities for underserved students in our K-12 public schools?" We determined the following conditions:

- BIPOC teachers and school leaders who have the mindset and support to disrupt the traditional content and pedagogy.
- BIPOC teachers and school leaders who are uniquely positioned and deeply connected to the success of underserved students.
- White leaders who are willing to adopt and consistently employ culturally responsive and antiracist practices.
- Schools where BIPOC teachers and school leaders can bring their authentic selves and ideas without being silenced or reprimanded.

Acknowledging that a small organization like TAF could not achieve this goal alone, TAF's leadership approached several community-based organizations about building expanded partnerships in which colleges of education, school districts, nonprofits, and government agencies would recruit, support, and retain BIPOC teachers while transforming the public education ecosystem to enable teachers to do their best work for students in Washington state.

We noted several efforts to recruit more BIPOC teachers into our colleges of education, then funneling them into public schools; but unfortunately, when they entered the profession, many BIPOC teachers were marginalized within their schools, which led many of them to leave the profession within three years (Mahatmya et al., 2022). We believed we could change those outcomes and under the guidance of the executive director, who adapted a method used to clean up the ecosystems of our waterways, such as ponds, to guide our work. That idea was to identify the issues within the pond, develop emerging solutions, inoculate the fish while implementing the solutions, believing the fish would begin to thrive as the pond was cleaned, and when the pond was fully cleaned, any new fish entering would have a much better chance of thriving. In Figure 4.1, this analogy substitutes the pond as the school environment, and the fish as BIPOC teachers.

What was missing was an opportunity to clean up the "pond" by transforming school environments into places where BIPOC teachers could thrive and eventually lead. These teachers needed a place where their voices were heard, their experiences valued, their professional expertise unquestioned, and they were not saddled with the responsibility for addressing all the school issues pertaining to students of color.

The NWEW programs and initiatives were designed to be a support and advocacy hub for BIPOC teachers needing a place of fellowship, guidance, and support as they navigated their majority white environments in which what they brought to the learning community was valued. Through TAF's efforts we sought to provide BIPOC teachers with tools and behaviors that help sustain inclusive and equitable schools and learning spaces. As a result, all students, but especially BIPOC students, will be able to learn in environments

FIGURE 4.1 Ecology of Creating a Healthy Pond

that are representative of who they are and help them value the cultures of the world around them. If we are successful, 5, 10, 50 years from now, the education debt owed to BIPOC students will decrease.

The NWEW is comprised of three programs:

- The Martinez Fellowship Program (MFP) – designed to recruit and support new BIPOC teachers.
- Education EnCounter – designed to support aspiring and current BIPOC leaders in education as they move through the leadership ranks.
- Ally Engagement Program – designed to support white leaders in traditional districts and university structures on their journey to redefine how they can create and sustain inclusive environments.

The Martinez Fellowship Program

In 2015, TAF was asked to assume leadership and management of the MFP, established in 2008 by Holli and Edgar Martinez. The MFP provides and supports multiple pathways to teaching, early career coaching, and ongoing professional development to improve teacher diversity and the retention of BIPOC teachers in Washington state and ensure there is more representation of the racial make-up of students among staff and leadership. The Fellowship's original mission was to have a significant impact on Washington's opportunity gap by improving teacher diversity and retaining BIPOC teachers. This was done through partnerships with colleges and universities' master's in teaching programs.

Since TAF assumed the Fellowship, the program has expanded and is now open to first-year undergraduates, graduate level students in teaching programs and alternative certification route programs. Over the course of the past 15 years, the MFP has developed partnerships with 11 colleges and universities and has grown to currently over 305 Fellows. The Martinez Fellowship has maintained 95% retention of BIPOC teachers beyond three years of service. Martinez Fellowship has also supported several teachers pursuing principal certifications and national board certifications. By 2036, the program aims to expand to reach 2400 Fellows.

The belief and drive for racial equity cannot be assumed to generalize across the world of education. Schools are often sites of oppression, marginalization, and microaggression for students of color. Various forms of racism and classism are entirely too common and to the learning experience for BIPOC students. Research (Egalite et al., 2015) suggests that in addition to providing social advantages for all students, increasing the racial diversity of the teaching workforce can help close the achievement gap (Dee, 2004). Both quantitative and qualitative studies find that BIPOC teachers can improve the school experiences of all students; furthermore, teachers of color contribute to improved academic outcomes while serving as strong role models for students (Goldhaber et al., 2019; Klopfenstein, 2005). Also, BIPOC people have a history of serving in education intentionally as activists for the advancement of marginalized groups.

The work of the MFP directly addresses the needs of BIPOC teachers through:

- Preparation: Trainings grounded in Liberation Pedagogy focused on the question, "What does it mean to teach and lead liberated?"
- Advocacy: Fostering the ability for Fellows to ask themselves, "What am I (as a Fellow) doing to help other teachers build their knowledge and capacity to teach and lead liberated?"
- Ongoing professional development: Through ongoing professional development, the challenging and emotionally draining work of liberated practices is supported and regularly connected back to the lived experiences of Fellows.

Table 4.1 illustrates the essences of programming targeted through the Martinez Fellow Program curriculum. This includes essential questions, outcomes, tools, and student deliverables.

TAF's most recent evolution and addition of programming was prompted as BIPOC teachers began matriculating thought the MFP; it became evident they needed an additional vehicle to cultivate and support their professional goals to transition into leadership positions. Working with emergent BIPOC

TABLE 4.1 Martinez Fellows Curricular Components

Essential Questions	Outcomes	Tools	Student Deliverables
What does it mean (in my own words) to lead liberated? Why is liberation pedagogy an essential tool for me as an educator? What am I doing to help other teachers build their knowledge and capacity to teach and lead liberated?	Fellows will understand broadly liberation pedagogy. Fellows can name the components and briefly explain each component of liberation pedagogy with fidelity. Fellows are confident to engage in conversation with others about their liberation process and help them think of their own.	List of questions to engage in self-reflection on each component of liberation pedagogy. Teaching resources for each component.	Successful demonstration of skills and competencies on the liberation pedagogy rubric. Action plan for engaging other teachers and students in liberation pedagogy.

leaders we found they encountered similar challenges to the teachers we were supporting. Regularly, they were either overlooked for administrative intern programs or they were pigeonholed in roles that focused on discipline and behavior management of students (often BIPOC students). Subsequently, Martinez Fellow Alumni were looking for the next level of development and support as they progressed in their careers, and Education EnCounter was created to do just that.

Education Encounter

Like many teachers, Martinez Fellows alum who had been teaching for at least five years were beginning to look for leadership opportunities as either instructional coaches, deans, or assistant principals, but many had no avenue, connections, or resources to pursue those options. In the fall of 2017, TAF convened leaders in education from across the Puget Sound to discuss how the Martinez Fellows could be supported and to brainstorm pathways for their success. Over a period of six months, 65 people attended one or more forums, representing over 25 different districts, universities, and community organizations. Over that period, it became clear that we needed to expand this network to more BIPOC educators, not just those who participated in the Fellowship.

After reflecting on the conversations that took place over those six months, we identified some important considerations for implementing a program to support current and aspiring BIPOC leaders in education. The program that emerged from those conversations was initially called the Network for EdWork which focused mostly on mentorship and informal networking in the community. This iteration of the program was inclusive of all leaders (BIPOC and White) and never really got any traction due to its integrated nature. As such, a decision was made to divide the programming in two, thereby creating Education Encounter and Ally Engagement; and the Network for EdWork became the umbrella for all programing This year was the pilot year with intentionally small cohorts to vet our curriculum and affinity spaces. Each group was limited to less than 15 participants. In the coming years, the number of cohorts available will expand to six to eight cohorts a year, per program.

We were motivated to establish Education EnCounter as a clear path from classroom to leadership for BIPOC teachers. We hoped to foster a steady increase in Education EnCounter members as well as Fellows and aspiring leaders to ascend to leadership roles. Finally, we want to maintain an 80% retention rate of BIPOC leaders at all levels of the education ladder.

Education Encounter has expanded and is comprised of mentorship support, bimonthly encounters (workshops), affinity groups, other resources for BIPOC leaders as well as an annual Convening. Much of the work was co-created with university partner programs, mission-aligned non-profits, district HR departments, and school principals. It was essential to work with school and district leaders to help them support leaders who participate in our Education EnCounter programming.

Ally Engagement

After establishing Education EnCounter, we began to strategize how to pull White allies into our ongoing work. We recognized that dismantling systems of oppression in education was not solely the responsibility of BIPOC educators.

Through the Ally Engagement program, we are providing learning opportunities for White university, school, and district leaders looking to transform their school environments to be antiracist, relevant, and responsive to BIPOC teachers, leaders, and students. We know how systemic racism engulfs systems (e.g., the education system), so this program provides space and guidance for White leaders to self-challenge and redefine those systems. Ally Engagement will work in tandem with Education EnCounter to enhance mentorship support, ongoing workshops, and other resources for White leaders and teachers across the state. We will look to university partner programs, mission-aligned non-profits, district HR departments, and school principals as partners in this work. Our hope is to establish Ally Engagement as the leader in school, district, and university leader transformation, with an annual 10% increase in BIPOC representation on leadership teams in schools, and an 80% retention rate amongst BIPOC teachers at educational institutions led by White leaders. At the time this chapter was written this work was in progress and too early to describe its impacts.

With the full spectrum of services that TAF offers we aim to ensure that the multi-faceted approach we are taking is articulated to provide adult learning that addresses the inequities that exist within the public education system. Through the evolution of TAF and our programming we have The STEMbyTAF Model and the work of the Network for EdWork to disrupt these narratives and achieve justice for BIPOC students and educators.

Introduction to Our Findings

Over the course of TAF's 25 years, there has been a firm commitment to supporting BIPOC students and communities. TAF has been unwavering in this commitment. When presented with the opportunity to participate in the self-study of equity and social justice, we saw writing this chapter as another opportunity to assess how equitable our practices are. Since we were also engaging in an external assessment of the organization with a researcher from the University of Washington, this seemed like an opportunity to have a holistic view of the organization and our practices.

In the next few pages, we look deeply into the practices of TAF through the lens of the FATAE. To illuminate the process, we incorporated a process for data collection, review, and reflection. We give a general overview of the entire process and then subsequently relay the independent findings for each of the four overarching domains.

Initially, when the NWEW team and Executive Director of Education received the FATAE we took time to review it and understand each of the four domains and respective priority areas within each category and how the priorities fit within a category. Since the framework is robust, this allowed us to unpack the components to explore its questions and begin to establish an idea of how the framework related to and could reveal the work in which we are engaged. Our next step was to collectively rate the priority areas within each domain according to our perceived level of need (i.e., whether that was based on it being central to our work or an area we felt we needed to improve). Our ratings revealed what will be explored further in the forthcoming analysis below.

Based on our initial assessment of the priority areas we would explore; we contemplated the questions provided within each priority area and determined questions we would pose during the self-inquiry process and areas or questions that we would not focus on based on our perceived level of need. Again, we considered our needs based on the indicators of the framework. Interestingly, as we considered the framework indicators by priority area, we realized we held assumptions about priority areas that were incomplete. For example, as the NWEW team examined the area of "Budgets and Budgeting," we realized we held a very narrow view of what that entailed: As authors, we saw it simply as being about money. We realized we knew nothing about budgeting structures, policies, and procedures, aligning budgeting to our vision, mission, and strategic plans or how decisions were made. This area then became a priority for us and the process of this self-assessment turned into a larger learning experience than we imagined.

Once we determined the questions for which we were most interested in addressing priority area and domain, we then identified the key stakeholders to involve in data collection. To ensure we would have a large cross section of participants, we reached out to current and past board members who held leadership roles on the board. We contacted staff from every area of TAF and ensured that a board member, a staff member, an executive team member, NWEW staff, and a community partner were contacted according to the aligned input area. Representatives of each group were interviewed or responded to questions through email. Once all responses were received and compiled, the resulting data were analyzed for trends and formal summaries were written for each priority area. The priority summaries were then compiled into categories with the intention of focusing on the following four questions.

- What was the critical/important information we gathered?
- What were the discussions we had?
- What have we concluded from the information and discussions?
- What were our plans for the future?

However, as we worked the framework and moved through the reflection process, we started to group content according to:

- What are the things that we learned about ourselves and our practices through this process?
- What are the things we do well?
- What are the things we need to grow in or change?
- What shifts will we make or are we making based on what we learned?

Though the questions above may not be specifically articulated as you read the remainder of our document and findings, we invite you to hold these questions as the lens through which you internalize our work.

Governance and Finance

Within the domain of Governance and Finance the FATAE provides four priority areas: Centering justice and equity in our organization's strategic planning and implementation, democratizing our governance and leadership, aligning our budgets, and budgeting, and increasing our fundraising and development. Based on the process described above, these priority areas ranked in the top four during collaborative conversations process. Thus, establishing from the outset that organizationally we saw the Governance and Finance category as core to the operation of TAF and subsequently the NWEW. To that end we spend time exploring our findings within each of these areas, beginning with TAF's foundational governing documents.

Foundational Governing Documents

TAF's foundational governing documents are comprised of three documents which we reference on a consistent basis to guide our work: our mission, our values, and the strategic plan. To speak to our current mission, it is important to review our former mission. The former mission was updated in 2018 in response to TAF expanding the scope of the work we were doing in schools in our partner district. It was crafted in a way that maintained BIPOC students at the center but gave a nod to project-based learning which incorporated STEM, grounded in relationships. This mission was able to speak to TAF's growing partnerships as well as our target audience.

TAF's former mission statement was as follows:

> TAF aims to equip students of color for success in college and in life through the power of an Interdisciplinary STEM education and supportive relationships.

However, as TAF's offerings grew to incorporate the training and support of BIPOC teachers through the Martinez Fellowship, it was evident that the mission needed to evolve as who and how we were serving in Washington was shifting. The needs of the adult learners that this shift represented, especially, required a revision that included that work. To help facilitate the process, we invited one of our board members with a background in human resources to guide us through a mission statement development process. The entire staff of TAF worked collaboratively in small groups to review our previous mission statement and determine if and how it still served as a north star. We then, as a whole group, unpacked each smaller group's findings and began to come to consensus about what needed to stay from the previous mission statement and what needed to be discarded, expanded, and/or replaced. After four working sessions over a month and a half we arrived at our current mission statement.

The Mission of TAF is as follows:

> We build collaborative relationships with public education to create access to transformative systems of learning for students and BIPOC teachers to eliminate race-based disparities in an increasingly diverse society.

The organization has a passion to ensure that racial equity is considered in all we do; therefore, it was logical that we would explicitly call out our focus on students and BIPOC teachers as well a focus on eliminating race-based disparities. Since TAF's inception there has been a focus on BIPOC students, but with our evolving programming we knew we needed to include BIPOC teachers as we now dedicate an entire arm of our work to them.

Organizational Values

It is often the case that as one aspect of an organization evolves, it affects others. As we were re-working on our mission statement, we found ourselves revisiting our values. One of the things we noticed as we considered them was that we did not speak to equity in any way. Subsequently, we found ourselves having to update our values statement along with our mission statement.

Former operational values statement:

- Commitment to Students: Our first priority is to provide the resources, support, and opportunities our students need to be successful individuals. Everything we do contributes to their success.
- Continuous Improvement and Learning: No matter how successful we may be, there is always room to learn more and improve. We actively and collectively improve our skills and share knowledge in an honest, respectful' professional way. We adjust our strategies based on the lessons learned and

performance data. We strive to continually improve our internal structure, staff experience, training methods, and curriculum to give our students the best educational experience possible.

- We strive to continually improve our internal structure, staff expertise, training methods, and curriculum to give our students the best educational experience possible.
- Collaborative Environment: We ask for support that is timely, respects individual responsibilities and deadlines and promotes the goals of the greater organization with enthusiasm and willingness.
- Leadership Development: We encourage and support each team member taking initiative that creates leadership opportunities and skill development and improves the capacity of the team.
- Fiscal Responsibility and sound Business Ethics: We conduct our business with integrity and fiscal responsibility. We actively provide our donors with current and reliable information on how their gifts are applied and exercise prudent judgment in our stewardship responsibilities.

As the staff reviewed our values, we continued to keep our students and adult learners first, and we knew that since we cannot do the work in isolation that collaboration had to remain. We went through a similar process with our values statement as we did with our mission statement, resulting in the values you see below. Notice they are much more concise, and we call out equity and the collective good.

TAF's Values Six values guide the work of TAF:

- Commitment to Students – TAF is committed to creating better outcomes for BIPOC students and adult learners so they may create the world they envision personally, locally, nationally, and globally.
- Equitable Practices – TAF fosters environments with structures and systems that are inclusive and ensure all employees have what they need to succeed while pursuing our mission.
- Continuous Improvement and Learning – We actively, collectively improve, share knowledge, and evolve.
- Integrity – Carry out all our work with the greatest responsibility and accountability.
- Authenticity – TAF operates from a place of being your authentic self with consideration for the good of the whole.
- Collaboration – Decisions are not made in silos. All aspects of our work involve collaboration for the good of the whole.

TAF's Strategic Plan

The final governing document is our strategic plan. The current strategic plan was updated in 2021 to articulate the objectives for the following four years (2021–2025). The strategic plan was also developed by the entire staff over the course of six months using a strategic plan planning framework provided by our board members. The strategic plan is updated every three to five years. The strategic plan has objective areas as well as tactics. This plan is intended to guide us toward the vision and goals we set on TAF's 20th Anniversary in 2018, which are intended to cover the next 20 years. The following four strategic goals set on TAF's 20th Anniversary guide our work to ensure we meet our vision:

- Develop TAF Academy into a national model of excellence in public education whose graduates are sought after by colleges nationwide.
- Build STEMbyTAF into a preferred public school academic model.
- Add 2400 BIPOC teachers to Washington State public schools.
- Influence public education policy in the areas of STEM education, school leadership, teacher diversity, quality pedagogy, multiple measures of achievement, and expanding the learning environment.

Reflection is an integral part of TAF's leadership process. To ensure that the executive team does this regularly we have built reflection time into our weekly executive meetings and created reflection tools to help guide us through a process such as our monthly team racial equity reflection form (in support of our racial equity rubric), quarterly updates, mid and end of year reports, and weekly staff one on one check-ins during which we ask, "what is something that is going well?" "What is an area of improvement or something you need support with?" "Where are we with our personal equity goals" Each of these items are used in correlation with our strategic plan and inform or align to our objectives.

The guidance, principles, and directions communicated through our governing documents mandate we consider everything we do from a place of justice and equity. We expect our mission statement, values, and strategic plan to focus on BIPOC students and teachers and be representative of the BIPOC communities we serve, always involving the voice of our stakeholders. In these documents, we work to implement support that interrupts the perpetuation of disparities with liberated, antiracist models. We do so in a way that considers the good of the whole through de-centering whiteness and White supremacy culture. Four years ago, we would not have been able to tell you what de-centering whiteness and White supremacy culture was. During one of our racial equity trainings, we were introduced to an article written by Tema Okun entitled White Supremacy Culture which has been since updated called White Supremacy Culture- Still Here (2021). This article explores the characteristics of white supremacy culture. As an organization and as individuals within the organizations we reflected on our practices and behaviors to determine which were connected to White supremacy culture. From there, we in teams and as individuals began to identify ways in which we could alter our practices and behaviors for the greater good of the whole. In doing so, we began to operate in ways that were counter intuitive to our socialization and thereby de-centered whiteness.

To write this chapter, in which we are evaluating how we as an organization actualize our commitment to racial equity and social justice, we spent a good deal of time over the course of the past year utilizing the framework to conduct an inventory of our practices, identifying gaps, and working collectively to rectify or address identified gaps we may not have been aware of without the tool. Upon review of the data garnered through interviews and our document review, we found that TAF's foundational documents propel us forward to meet our justice and equity goals rather than hold us back from them. They have helped us to ensure that we continue to drive toward our north star and not lose sight of our target audiences and the reason we serve them. From this foundation, the governance of the NWEW and its constituent programs were conceived.

Network for EdWork Governance

The framework suggests that an organization's foundational values and principles should guide its overall governance and operations. The Network for EdWork team has a strong leadership focus on justice and equity goals, as stated by the former director of the NWEW: "As the leader of this team, equity and social justice is who I am. It is what I live and breathe, and my team is aligned." The NWEW starts from a place of equity in our approach to our foundational documents, core programming, and plans. The NWEW operates from two main documents: our mission and core values – all built from and informed by TAF's governing documents. NWEW's mission statement reads as follows:

> We relentlessly support the sustainability of BIPOC educators by dismantling institutionalized and racist structures and practices within and around us; replacing them with tools and behaviors that help sustain inclusive and equitable schools and learning spaces.

Building from this mission, we strive to plan, facilitate, and reflect the following core values in all aspects of our programming:

- Decenter whiteness
- Honor this precious community
- Intentional in where we are, where we have been, and where we are going

For example, when we prepare for workshops, all facilitators are guided to include grounding activities that affirm the adult learners in the space, build community and be intentional with the learning outcomes in applying Liberation Pedagogy. In a subsequent section on teaching and learning, we expound upon examples of how our governing values and principles are reflected in our curricular and instructional activities.

Through our research and reflection during this project, we learned and affirmed our guiding documents were conceptualized and worded effectively to capture our core attitudes regarding our work of liberation. We define liberation as the "continual knowing of the whole self and living that way in an ongoing state of freedom from the limits of supremacist cultural expectations … plainly, being liberated is knowing you and doing you." Our inquiry process revealed the principles and values of justice and equity are reflected heavily in what we produce: 1) educational programming such as MFP Seminars, EnCounters for leaders of color, and Engagements for White allies; 2) the language we use in marketing materials; and 3) the resources we use to inform programming and during programming. Even our surveys, which all participants complete before and after attending any programming were developed based on our goals and demonstrate that commitment to equity.

We note that we will continue to refine the wording to ensure that it continues to articulate our beliefs concisely and clearly as our programming evolves. As such, in our efforts to continue to evolve, there are several points of growth we have targeted. We are looking at our agreements, contracts, reports, and evaluations to determine if they speak to equity or equitable practices. We want to ensure that internally and externally we are setting a standard that organizations articulate their beliefs and connection to racial equity work as a pre-screen to collaboration. There is a clear consensus that there must be shared missions, values, and goals with new partners like universities, districts, and other organizations. For example, our mission, values, and goals will guide us as we determine guests/instructors, grants, and partnerships. We are early in the developmental stages of getting to the point where we ask complex questions about new undertakings. Learning from our self-analysis marks a significant shift in how we think about the business contracts in which we engage.

Finance

TAF's budgeting process is a collaborative effort by all departments, program leaders, and staff. TAF does not employ a carry-forward budget process or a top-down approach. Instead, the budget is built based on proposed program-level action items for the upcoming fiscal year and the fiscal resources necessary to support those activities. TAF's Finance Director creates opportunities for every program team to meet with her to review the current year's spending and provides feedback and guidance on proposed initiatives for the new fiscal year. Each program manager and director are asked to revisit our mission and strategic plan to ensure that what they are doing programmatically and asking for financially are within scope of those documents. As diversity and equity are central to our mission, actions items aligned to those values are prioritized through budgeting within limitations of the overall budget cap. Moving forward a new, organizational equity rubric will be an important reference as we assess allocations in the future.

TAF has always focused on BIPOC students, but this does not guarantee that TAF has equitable practices. Since the work of TAF is multi-faceted we found that many equity inventories did not adequately speak to the whole of our organization and programing. We decided to undergo a one-year review with a researcher from the University of Washington. Following our assessment, they helped us to generate two equity rubrics (organizational and educational) to assess and monitor our equitable practices over time. Table 4.2 illustrates an example from the rubric specific to financial decisions.

TABLE 4.2 Sample of TAF's Organizational Racial Equity Rubric

Standard 1 – Organizational Leadership

Strand 4 – Allocation of Resources

Themes	Emerging	Progressing	Advancing	Transformative
1.4.A *Financial decision-making is grounded in racial equity*	TAF is aware that there are BIPOC businesses that are available to provide goods and services. TAF researches organizations that have a focus on advancing racial equity is a priority. TAF looks for BIPOC speakers and tries to find ways to diversity the volunteer and guest pool.	TAF has begun to send bids to BIPOC businesses and then compares bid to the rest of the general public. TAF Identifies BIPOC companies that offer services we are interested. TAF contracts with BIPOC speakers and tries to find ways to diversity the volunteer, families, and guest pool with a nominal stipend.	TAF sends most bids to BIPOC businesses first, and then compares bid to the rest of the general public. TAF requires organization to prove that they have a focus on advancing racial equity is a priority. TAF contracts with BIPOC speakers and ensures volunteer, families, and guest pool with a stipend or honorarium.	TAF sends all bids to BIPOC businesses first, and constantly signs contracts with BIPOC companies. TAF is actively investing financial resources in learning development, programming, partnerships, projects, and TAF staff that advances racial equity. TAF constantly contracts with BIPOC speakers and ensures volunteers, families, and guest pool with a stipend or honorarium.

In the Network for EdWork, funding goes toward programming costs, including guests/instructors/speakers, resources for furthering our learning about leadership and equity, and travel to partner sites. NWEW only works with people, programs, and organizations that are mission aligned, and budget is driven by connecting with those people, resources, programs, and organizations. Expounding upon this commitment, our data analyses pointed to work we still need to do; we are more aligned, on paper than in our practice. Current work and new undertakings push us to ask complex questions about equity and justice with regard to with whom we work and what we finance.

Fundraising

Using the framework, we explored our systems of fundraising to assess not only its efficacy and potential for growth but also for its alignment to our organizational values. Fundraising is vital to the existence and operations of TAF. As a non-profit organization, we also have earned income in addition to fundraising income. TAF receives limited state and federal funds and relies on our community for philanthropic support. Currently, fundraising initiatives are primarily focused on development at the organization level of TAF. NWEW does not have its own development arm. TAF has a development team, albeit one that is relatively small (i.e. four people) relative to funds that need to be raised (e.g., projections for 2023 are to raise $6 million), but is showing great promise to meet our goals. Through our inquiry for this chapter, we confirmed that the development team follows basic fundraising norms and ones that specifically align to TAF's values. According to our director of finance, "We follow Moves Management, a fundraising growth platform to encourage donation, and we employ some traditional roles: development officers, coordinators, etc. However, when considering sources for funding options, we place our values at the forefront of the decision." Since our values are central to funding conversation; we do not seek or accept funding if it is coming from an organization that or donor who does not honor our values. The Executive Director of Development and Operations stated, "We don't bend and form to what funders want," instead we stick to our goals and find funders who want to work with us as we are.

When interviewed, the Executive Director/Co-Founder confirmed and emphasized why our values are non-negotiable in fundraising initiatives. She shared, "We have been overlooked because our mission is to unapologetically serve BIPOC students and teachers, and we refuse to exploit those that we serve. We are not in the business of 'poverty pimping.' Instead, we highlight the positive things our students and teachers are creating and innovating." She then explained, "We seek funders who not only are funders but those who are truly interested in developing relationships." These funders must be aligned to our goals and willing to collaborate to help make us better.

As we build relationships, we encourage funders and corporations to see TAF through a different lens, not just through the mechanics of funding. As such, we create messaging around the amazing work students, teachers and the team are accomplishing when they have the necessary support, tools, and resources available to them. We stay loyal to our families, students, and teachers.

A big part of the fundraising for justice and equity is having the right fundraising team. Strengths revealed through our self-assessment process indicated TAF's development team collaboratively works among themselves to create strategies to increase the funding so that we can have the resources necessary to raise funds to scale. We also have a strong innovative communications team to market the work of our programs to donors who align with our values. Another potential strength was revealed regarding the role the Network for Edwork could play in the larger organization's fundraising efforts. Since the Network for Edwork is the newest arm of TAF, it has enormous potential to grow and have a broad impact, but it needs targeted fundraising as it is not readily recognized by usual funders, and it has not previously secured grants. Recently however, we have experienced that with an increasing awareness of blatant racism across our communities, cities, state, and nation, we see more donors prioritizing equity work. Donors are seeing our values and positive outcomes and are continuing to give or begin giving because of our commitment to racial equity. For example, recently the Network for EdWork received its first grant from a big company that wants to support educator diversity initiatives like ours.

As with everything, our inquiry pointed to areas in which TAF's fundraising initiatives can grow - it is a top priority for our organization. One area we found ripe for growth is training our board in fundraising. We should train the board not just on basic fundraising but opening their networks to our mission by speaking about TAF from the heart and from a place of racial equity. In addition, we found a need to bolster our fundraising efforts by revising internal processes and procedures, and to increase collaboration with external partners and potential donors. For example, we found evidence of conflicting messaging, approaches, beliefs, and understanding of how funds will be used both internally and externally. There is a strong need for a cohesive message and strategy to bring together coalitions of companies and individuals to pool their resources for change. By living out our value for collaboration, we combine resources, increase the power of pursuing collective goals and messaging, and avoid positioning one or more organizations to struggle individually. For example, by working with our higher education partners we could support their efforts in securing grants and philanthropic initiatives so addition funds could be directed to increase the number of BIPOC students into their preparation programs and subsequently partner with increase the power of the MFP. Creating cohesive messaging and supporting distinct partners to come together in our fundraising initiatives would benefit our individual and collective goals.

Teaching and Learning

The teaching and learning domain of the FATAE is organized around two priority areas: strengthening programs and curriculum, and supporting students. As we reflected on the evolution of TAF with a focus on how we teach and learn, we concentrated on getting data on two priority areas: our programs and curriculum directed to adult learners and how we support our adult learners. In this section, we address teaching and learning on two of the three NWEW programs, the Martinez Fellowship and Education EnCounter. As a new program, the Ally Engagement initiative is early in data collection processes. We asked key questions about how we situate our programs within the larger social justice movement, how and why we collectively approach the design and implementation of our programs, and the pipelines and pathways our adult learners use to join our programs and their experiences.

Programs and Curriculum Design

Salient questions about programs and curriculum design from the framework center values and principles for education for democracy, teaching collectively, engaging existing research and theory, and the use of collective resources to strengthen programs and curriculum. From its genesis, TAF leadership engaged our value for collaboration with the NWEW team and colleagues to design, implement, and assess programming based on TAF's trademarked Liberation Pedagogy framework, which happens to encompass the core values of the FATAE. Liberation Pedagogy roots all the programming of the NWEW and guides educators and leaders through a community process of recognizing racism and white supremacy while engaging in decolonizing pedagogies and tools to undo and replace those harmful elements. TAF's Liberation Pedagogy serves as a guide for all programs and focuses on internal work, professional development, and community engagement. Thus, teaching and learning for the MFP and Education Encounter programs are based on and reflect the foundational values and principles shared above.

In addition to the collaborative approach from key stakeholders, our organization drew on community expertise and literature on diverse models of education from Paulo Freire, Linda Tuhiwai Smith, and bell hooks to cite a few. Our work was built on scholarship and activism, and we invited scholar activists, educators, and leaders from all over for NWEW to contribute. The NWEW engages in expansive literatures and models about education that are anti-oppressive, asset-based, community engaged, critical, culturally affirming, responsive, inclusive, Indigenous-centered, and intersectional. The Liberation Pedagogy is rooted in this. Strengths of our programming design approach reflect alignment to our mission and values.

The summer Summit is highly anticipated by every Fellow: both while they are in the program as a student teacher, and once they advance in their teaching career and can come back year after year. The Summit allows participants to truly build authentic relationships and learn from one another in an environment set up just for that: learning and listening, personally and professionally. For example, during our orienting events, each Fellow and participant shared stories about their experience as a BIPOC student navigating the education system, whether it is in high school, an undergraduate degree, or even a graduate degree. These are everyday experiences their White peers and colleagues simply do not share and thus typically do not find themselves isolated from a single school campus or district

Each seminar and workshop begin with various grounding exercises to acknowledge the lived experiences of the participants and guide them to focus on the session ahead. The success of our program begins with welcoming all to be their authentic selves in that moment and provide a much-needed safe space that cultivates vulnerability, reflection, and community.

While there are areas of strength in TAF's programming, there were some lessons learned through our self-assessment indicating how we can improve and do things differently in learning and teaching. Key areas for improvement were: 1) Increasing collaboration with organizations that have shared values; 2) expanding the application of Liberation Pedagogy to leaders in education; and 3) increase participation to leaders in public schools and district offices, veteran teachers and educators, and college/university educators and leaders. Expanding the adult student participation in our programs aligns with transforming school environments to be places where BIPOC teachers can thrive as well as students as the leadership in those environments would have engaged in racial equity work provided by TAF.

As shared previously, we partner and collaborate with many community-based organizations. Recommendations from our self-assessment process revealed organizations with whom TAF can increase collaboration include school boards, teachers' unions, educational districts in which public schools are assigned to pool resources (such as the Puget Sound Education School District (PSESD) in Washington state that includes 35 school districts), community organizations that focus on equity in education, and non-profits with similar goals to TAF.

We learned, for example, the NWEW does not take full advantage of relationships reported earlier within our school-based programming and has missed opportunities to connect Martinez Fellows with networked schools for direct job placement, mentorship, and career growth. In addition, during the genesis of the MFP we initially focused on university partnerships but learned we can broaden our pipeline. Feedback through this self-assessment revealed we should reach out to local community colleges that have teacher preparation programs, Historically Black Colleges and Universities (HBCU's), and teacher preparation programs outside Washington to recruit new or welcome back home BIPOC teachers into Washington. Furthermore, we could tap into the AmeriCorps volunteer programs that exist at non-profits as well as Act Six Scholars. Troops to Teachers is another pipeline that school districts and HR departments should consider for diverse candidates (diverse ethnically/ racially, social-economically, ability, linguistically and diverse life experiences). Working with our district partners to advance these programs would in turn increase the potential applicant pool for our partner teacher education programs, and TAF's Martinez Fellows Program.

Additional feedback from our inquiry of programs and curriculum indicated a need to contextualize and expand our Liberation Pedagogy for a wider audience of adult learners, specifically those served through Education EnCounter and Ally Engagement. We realized Liberation Pedagogy taught during Martinez Fellowship seminars to BIPOC students entering the teaching profession is a great tool that can be applied to those in leadership. While maintaining the foundation and purpose of Liberation Pedagogy, it requires us to address the needs of diverse audiences, both BIPOC and White leaders and allies. New driving questions were formed as well as outcomes that specifically targeted the needs of white and BIPOC leaders in education. For example, students enrolled in Ally Engagement will be guided by a key question as they engage in Liberation Pedagogy: "What am I doing to create a space where BIPOC leaders, teachers, and students can thrive free from oppression?" Expanding essential questions and outcomes in the Liberation Pedagogy curriculum framework will strengthen the tool to address White supremacy in public education.

Finally, as we analyzed feedback and data about the experiences of students in our programs, we learned additional ways we could support students in our programs. One of our veteran Fellows spoke on a particular challenge for adult learners:

> Childcare has been a little tricky for my family in attending seminars. I felt comfortable enough and welcomed my daughter to meetings, although I know that it can be distracting to me (and others) as we try to focus our attention on the seminar's presenters.

To serve our adult learners more effectively, we were urged to consider the length of the retreats, seminars, and workshops as well as dates and times. For example, within the MFP, seminars only held on Saturdays were six hours long and multiple-day retreats during the same time every year place a heavy expectation on teacher candidates who are also balancing full academic demands and may only have weekends for rest. Remembering to incorporate the voices and needs of adult learners as we design, and schedule programming is in keeping with our values and core beliefs.

The Student Experience

In the NWEW, the MFP consists of a diverse group of adult learners. They are BIPOC teacher candidates and leaders. The intention of MFP is to mitigate the challenges of navigating culturally white schools and systems. Furthermore, we hope that graduates leave our MFP with the skills and knowledge to effectively teach students in their prospective grade level or content area in the K-12 education system. We wish to impart strong intellectual and academic skills that will enable them to succeed in their future endeavors, and that they maintain a joy for learning and a sense of pride in themselves. As well as growing BIPOC leadership and continue the strong retention of BIPOC teachers.

Within the NWEW, the Martinez Fellowship is the longest established program, so it is our most clarified pathway in which adult learners can participate. The pipeline includes marketing, informational sessions, an application process, interview process, new Fellow orientation, and quarterly partner check-ins that help all the pieces stay aligned. Application and acceptance into the MFP are currently through collaborative partnerships with teacher education programs.

The students are introduced to the MFP by their department leaders followed by an invitation to attend informational sessions from the Program Manager. It is during those info sessions that the adult learners get a taste of the communal values of our programs. The identities of each student are affirmed, and they are assured that within the Fellowship, their whole selves will be honored and supported. This continues through the application process that uses a group conversational interview style and welcomes alumni of the Martinez Fellowship to participate.

While Martinez Fellows are in their program, TAF provides all programming to them at no cost. We work with our coalition of university and district partners to help them fund student tuition, support internship placements, as well as cover preparation program travel and material costs. Additionally, we work with our partners to fundraise and access grants to ensure Martinez Fellows can access additional funding for other professional opportunities. For example, we support preparation for National Board certification and provide Fellows with access to training support when applying.

We hope that our Fellows have learned a keen sense of self awareness, and a deep connection to their personal race, culture, and voice. As they navigate education systems that were not set up for them from the start, we hope they will have an ethical and moral compass to identify and dismantle injustice. The practices explored through Liberation Pedagogy are a key takeaway for graduates; it actively pushes them to constantly reflect and challenge their complicity in maintaining white supremacy. Our hope is to have helped students cultivate the tools to live out liberatory practices and strengthen their ability to articulate needs and step up when necessary. After our time together, we aspire to prepare graduates to be willing and able to bring others along on this journey of growth and understanding.

Supporting adult learners is of importance for our Education EnCounter programming as well. As stated previously, Education EnCounter was developed initially to serve veteran Martinez Fellows who transition from early teacher to leader as well as BIPOC leaders currently in position at educational organizations, schools, districts, colleges, and universities. This has since been expanded to not only serve veteran Martinez Fellows, but current BIPOC veteran educators and leaders.

BIPOC leaders in schools, districts, colleges, and universities who have some relationship with TAF and aware of our programs are invited to learn more about the leadership professional development series that brings racial equity and racial awareness to organizational leadership. The adult learners in our leaders focused programs like Education EnCounter, provide a yearlong series of evening workshops, access to virtual affinity salons, and networking opportunities for a fee. The needs of the leader adult learners differ from those in the Martinez Fellowship.

Through this process we have learned the strengths and opportunities for growth lies in our programming and curriculum. Our Liberation Pedagogy affirms the adult learners who participate in our programs and strengthens the community of BIPOC educators and leaders. We welcome the challenges of expanding Liberation Pedagogy to better apply to organizational leaders and strengthen partnerships with other non-profits and schools.

Staff and Facilitators

To support quality teaching and learning, an organization needs quality staff and instructors. "Instructors and Staff" is the third domain of focus from the assessment framework that we used to conduct our analysis for this chapter. Given TAF's organization, staff are integrally involved in what and how teaching and learning occurs. Some staff are integral to teaching and learning and we also supplement their efforts by hiring contract facilitators. We sought to address framework questions about how we focus our hiring on maintaining a diversity of staff and facilitators, the mechanisms we use to support our staff, and how we are improving the institutional climate of our organization.

Hiring and Retention

Given our mission, vision, and foundational values and principles as well as our goals to support BIPOC students and adult learners, TAF is committed to hiring staff and facilitators who reflect those communities. A strength revealed through findings of this inquiry was our staff are predominately from the same culture and background as the communities we serve; this provides a deeper understanding of needs and what support should look like. TAF strives to maintain at least 70% BIPOC staff across the whole organization, a metric which we are currently meeting and of which we are very proud. Additionally, 60% of our staff are women and TAF's executive team is all BIPOC women. Maintaining these demographic representations is of great importance to the organization.

Our goal of sustaining a diverse workforce requires us to continuously hold a magnifying glass to our hiring processes. Though we want to maintain a diverse staff, we want our staff to have the expertise that relates to the job and, of course, potential to expand their knowledge and push themselves. Beyond knowledge and skills, we also want new and current staff to be passionate about our mission and have the willingness to collaborate and learn from each other. To reach our hiring goals we have adapted previous practices. For example, we have diversified where and how we market our positions. In addition to the traditional mechanisms for recruitment (i.e., Indeed, LinkedIn, etc.), we are beginning to advertise through unconventional methods in churches, community centers, as well as BIPOC news platforms. We have also conducted a job description audit to determine how we are speaking about positions and what we are looking to as indicators of "formal schooling versus experience." The NWEW department within TAF explicitly names the dismantling of white supremacy culture in our practice and in our schools/universities in job postings. For example, a current program manager job description listed an openness to participate in racial equity work to recognize personal bias and improve performance through a racial equity lens as a required qualification. Our job postings call out a commitment to racial justice and equity that is experienced and not just a talking point, but a part of how applicants see themselves and show up in the world.

We understand that every applicant may not have all the desired skills or competencies, but they must have a willingness to develop them as a member of the team. Applicants moving to the interviewing process must provide authentic commitment and willingness to support equity and our work to be an anti-racist, equitable organization. We utilize interview questions that gauge the degree to which applicant's experiences align to our mission and equity framework. Depending on the roles and who we are interviewing, oftentimes, we can see whether the candidates have what we are looking for by how we stage the questions and how the candidate responds. During the interviews, we ask the candidates where they are at in their racial equity journey. We often have them explain what TAF does in their own words, and we listen in their answers for key words such as "BIPOC students and teachers." Of note, we implement a group interview process and all members of the team have equal voice in the hiring process. We credit these shifts in hiring practices to our current success of having a diverse workforce committed to the mission, vision, and ideals of TAF. We recognize that maintaining our workforce requires ongoing support to their continued professional growth and development.

Ongoing professional development is supported by TAF at the organizational and program levels and aims not only to advance knowledge and skills but serves as a conscious attempt to retain staff over time. Each department and staff member uses an equity rubric (see Table 4.3) to reflect, engage in self-assessment, create individual and organizational plans to address our shortcomings, and set annual goals for professional development. Newly hired staff are introduced to the rubric, and they use it to create initial work plans in collaboration with their supervisor. Time is provided in team and staff meetings to reflect, discuss, and evaluate current placement as a team with quarterly updates and a yearly summary reflection on progress toward goals. Of note, this inquiry led us to recognize how our white staff are becoming strong allies and have demonstrated personal growth and experience in confronting their own complicity in maintaining white supremacy.

In addition to a racial equity approach to recruitment, interviewing, and hiring, TAF's education and organizational equity rubric is used by each staff member and department for professional development purposes to apply to their work. Within the organization, each department at TAF works to ensure that there is a clear through line from their individual workplans for a given fiscal year, the organization's strategic plan and racial equity goals. This tool is an important resource to the ongoing professional development of members of the entire TAF team; it was recognized as a strength through our self-study as it helps to align our work to our mission and core values.

TABLE 4.3 TAF's Racial Equity in Education Rubric

Goal 1.1	Emerging	Progressing	Advancing	Transformative
Stated values are seen and incorporated into internal practices, policies, and culture	Clearly construct and articulate a racial equity vision, mission, and values statements that prioritizes its commitment to racial equity, liberation, and eliminating racial disparities	Enact a racial equity vision, mission, and values statements that prioritizes its commitment to racial equity, liberation, and eliminating racial disparities	Enact a racial equity vision, mission, and values statements that prioritizes its commitment to racial equity, liberation, and eliminating racial disparities and is supported in the strategic plan	Constantly articulate and enact a racial equity vision, mission, and values statements that prioritizes its commitment to racial equity, liberation, and eliminating racial disparities in the strategic plan

Leadership and Working at TAF

Within the FATAE questions on models of organizing staff work, supervising and managing staff were explored through our self-study. We realized that prior to this inquiry we had not spent much time considering our leadership structures and culture. Through this process, we learned our organization operates in a manner typical to others. Structurally, the organization is basically hierarchical. Staff are organized into four teams (operations, development, education, and executive), then smaller groups within those buckets. We have a five-year strategic plan for organizational goals, and an annual work plan to further those goals. Every staff member contributes their departmental objectives and tactics to this annual work plan. We also use technology to help with keeping work organized. One of the mechanisms of communication (from the executive team) to the staff is through the directors. Directors meet with their team members during weekly or biweekly one-to-one meetings and regular reports that name how each staff member aligns to the fiscal year goals and strategic goals. In one-to-one meetings, there is opportunity to provide feedback to each other but not necessarily a strict reporting line. Beyond the weekly one-to-one meetings, we have annual reviews on the work plan that both manager and staff member collaborate to complete, discuss, and sign. Additionally, each team meets weekly to collaborate, support and problem solve. Teams operate together instead of as individuals. The NWEW team meets for recruitment, convening planning, team meetings, check ins with the Executive team, and quarterly step backs. In these quarterly meetings the team reflects on completed/ongoing projects, defines areas for growth, looks ahead to the next quarter, and creates individual work plans for the upcoming quarter.

Our self-assessment data indicated our overall leadership is based in equitable practices, collaboration, and helping others thrive; we keep that in mind in the face of hierarchical structures. Managers do not just act as overseers but have their own work to complete. The executive team meets weekly to collaborate, plan strategically, discuss projects, and troubleshoot any challenges we may be facing. The executive team solicits feedback from staff when making decisions and welcomes staff to join meetings when they have something to share or have a challenge. That said, feedback from our inquiry indicated as we grow from a small organization to mid-size, clarifying a joint culture is vital. For example, although it is not codified in our policies and procedures that we explicitly seek out and foster feedback in our current culture, the executive team is working diligently to create space for staff to have more of a voice by soliciting their feedback as we make decisions. Data indicated we've struggled at times in receiving and responding to feedback from staff across the organization. For example, we have been fortunate and blessed to have people come into the organization who have pushed and/or challenged certain norms and expectations. Although challenging the norms and asking questions are good traits to exemplify, there have been times when we have considered a line between feedback that challenges/questions for the common good as opposed to undermining our vision and goals. Strong leadership means considering feedback that pushes and challenges toward where we want to go and that which will get us off track. This is an area in which we need to explore and develop clearer cultural guidelines and norms.

A suggestion rendered through this process was to create a collective option of management and supervision by creating a flat, versus hierarchical decision-making structure – where all decisions are made by committee. A drawback noted about this model is it may not be ideal for supporting productivity. Instead, we aim to keep the organization as flat as possible by keeping decisions closest to the people doing the work. To help this, we need to develop processes to focus on organizing work rather than logistics or how to do the work. For the organization to continue to move forward on decisions, we do need leaders where the buck stops and who can make good decisions based on the good of whole and putting students and adult learners first. Yet and still, we can create a more egalitarian work environment by doing more planning and thinking together and then delegating tasks. We can also provide work time in meetings and leave smaller tasks for outside of meetings. In addition, it was revealed that given our rapid growth, there is a challenge of maintaining a focus on our goals without leading to a doubling of work/expectations in any given year. It was pointed out that rapid growth can make it easier for individuals to become siloed in their role, not taking advantage of cross team collaborations/learning opportunities as those take more time. We are working on sustainable growth.

Related, feedback provided additional suggestions as to how to better support our staff. Comments indicated inconsistency among how managers supported staff. Recommendations specified developing guidelines and protocols for managers to operate at a level of consistency while allowing them to bring their authentic style to their work. In addition, it was suggested managers need development on providing direct and constructive feedback and helping team members set goals aligned to their individual work and to the work of the whole. Further, it was noted that individuals should still have room to name some of their own goals based on personal preference. People need space to lead their own development as well as guidance about the cultural capital needed to be "successful" (while also potentially being critical of that capital.) We teach students cultural responsiveness and staff members deserve that same kind of balance of support and push.

Finally, feedback for leadership emerged based on current and future plans for expansion of TAF's work. Analysis of interview and survey data indicated the tremendous workloads of staff at every level of the organization and associated stress they are experiencing. Looking forward, we were urged as an organization to be cognizant and more purposeful in what is needed to support all staff to endure, thrive, and sustain this work without promoting and perpetuating harm in the overall quality of life of individuals supporting the organization. By solidifying a joint culture that includes policy and practices for staff members to grow within the organization while supporting and promoting a healthy work-life balance, employing a racial equity model for interviews, and expanding our network for partnerships, TAF can continue growing an impactful organization led by BIPOC people doing the work.

Partnership and Public Impact

Our target audience within the Network for EdWork are those in the K-12 education ecosystem who are working in the service of educational justice for BIPOC students. However, TAF's target audience is ultimately the students in our K-12 public schools. We reach them by training teachers and administrators to provide more equitable school environments. We provide professional development, and recruit/develop/retain teachers and education BIPOC leaders. In addition to the work that we are doing with individual teachers and school administration through the Network for EdWork, we are also building out a partnership network of schools/colleges, districts, and funders. In this section we report results of our self-assessment on the fourth domain of the FATAE, Partnerships and Public Impact. We focus on critical questions directed to our external partnerships and our impact on the public.

Partnerships

TAF's commitment to equity, justice, and value for collaboration influences and guides our partnerships and is evident in the impact of our programming. In diving into reflecting on information gathered on our partnerships and public impact, we explored what we do well, what we learned and contemplated what we can do differently. Here we look at the evolution of TAF's partnership with the MFP, partnerships with colleges and universities as well as the challenges that come with expansion.

Feedback from the former Director of the NWEW indicated, The MFP is known for "having a strong track record of developing BIPOC teachers in Washington state." Over the past 13 years university partners have found value in their relationship with the MFP as it supports early career BIPOC teachers through personal and professional seminars and a network of BIPOC early career teachers while the universities help to support the financial needs for BIPOC students. As students completed their term with Martinez Fellows and expressed continued interest in the specific programming provided, the NWEW was birthed and from its inception was "positioned to become a leader across the state" in its support of educators and leaders of color as outlined in TAF's strategic plan. Over the course of the last year partners were increasingly impressed with the programming and several key stakeholders and partners expressed excitement and support about the future and evolution of NWEW.

Part of the power of the NWEW is that it was an outgrowth of the MFP. As BIPOC students began their teaching careers as Martinez Fellows, with over 85% staying in the teaching profession, many ascended into leadership and wanted to continue with the specific learning program they experienced as Fellows. To ensure that this work was not done in isolation, university and community partners were invited to join a coalition of deans of education and school district leaders. These select partners worked to unite the various organizations and programs to function more cohesively across structures, support financial goals of the organization (TAF), and to communicate regularly across universities and support district partners to create a broader level of support across the spectrum of emergent teachers to school and district leadership.

When we considered the types of partnerships to pursue in support of our social justice and equity goals, we focused on districts and universities in which the attraction and enrollment of BIPOC students were prioritized. We partnered with organizations who had programing that continued to evolve to meet the varied needs of students of color as well as foster environments that daylight bias and racism and push white faculty/staff and students to actively face and work to dismantle racism and foster social justice.

Our partners shift depending on the needs of our adult learners. We have had several major external partners with colleges and universities as our primary partners since the foundation of the NWEW evolved from the MFP. These partners provided access to funding, became thought partners, provided training locations, helped to identify potential Fellows, as well as recruited BIPOC teachers to the state. As Fellows prepared to matriculate from the teacher preparation programs, we worked with districts to find placements for Fellows in schools with a commitment to equity and in which there was work to foster a culturally inclusive and supportive environment. Whenever possible, we attempted to leverage partnerships with schools to place more than one Fellow at a site. Finally, we partnered with community members to serve as consultants and guest facilitators because of our commitment to remain connected to the voices and realities of the broader community. Through these multiple types of partnerships, there has been an enhanced sense of belonging allowing us to better serve our participants.

When considering partnerships between NWEW and universities that actualize "cleaning the pond," our inquiry pointed to several benefits for all parties. The NWEW partnerships with universities benefit both parties in the following ways:

- University partners advertise and recruit BIPOC students in teacher preparation programs to apply and participate in the Martinez Fellowship program.

- University partners also agree to provide scholarships or compensation for BIPOC students in the program.
- The NWEW provides personal and professional support to BIPOC students through the Martinez Fellowship programming.
- The NWEW also opens participation to leadership within education preparation programs to Education EnCounter and Ally Engagement.
- The NWEW offers a network of other universities committed to racial equity in education as partners.
- Collaboration leads to thought partners in co-development of affinity spaces for students.

The NWEW partnerships with school districts benefit in the following ways:

- School districts provide access to high school early educator programs to inspire younger students to become teachers.
- School districts can promote hiring opportunities to a network of over 200 BIPOC teachers from the Martinez Fellowship.
- The NWEW can have a direct impact in schools with cohorts of Martinez Fellows situated in specific schools and school leadership participate in Education EnCounter and Ally Engagement to create a school environment with a critical mass of adults cultivating a racially equitable learning environment for all.

All partners receive benefit from NWEW through:

- Structures of transparent and informative communication which provides opportunities for feedback.
- Opportunities to solicit feedback and collaborate on recruitment of BIPOC teachers and Martinez Fellows.
- Participation in the personal and professional programs of the Network for EdWork to enhance mutual benefits.
- Quality professional development for emergent teachers and established educators within a safe space that is responsive to their needs and the current climate.
- Support of teachers and students from a holistic standpoint, as diverse people with varied lived experiences impact how they learn and at times how they are perceived.
- Access to resources, tools, and practices for growth around equity and leadership in education.

While this process indicated our partnerships with universities, districts and evolution of the Martinez Fellowship are examples of where we shine, challenges remain. One continuing challenge is funding for the MFP.

As noted previously, MFP funded by the Martinez Fellowship Foundation offered full financial support to students. When the program shifted to TAF, we did not have the capacity to match that level of funding and meet the expansion goals. To address this challenge, universities partners were tasked to provide funding for students who participate in the MFP. These partners, too, face funding struggles. Future efforts need to expand our collaborations with university partners, other community-based organizations, and potential funding sources (grants, gifts, etc.) to secure the needed financial resources to support our Fellows and expand the number of BIPOC teachers we mentor into the teaching profession.

An additional challenge noted was changing perceptions about teaching and needing to get involved in advocacy to improve conditions for teachers, specifically BIPOC teachers, who are leaving the teaching profession and public school districts at high rates. Some district and university leaders feel they need to do something new/more. For example, providing support and acknowledging the lived experiences of BIPOC teachers and the impact of daily micro aggressions in addition to the shared stressors of teaching in public schools. Many of our partners are on board in word around the innovative programs of the NWEW but do not consistently follow through on communication and requested tasks necessary to do the work. Recruiting leaders from our partner schools to participate in our Education EnCounter and Ally Engagement programming themselves and sharing up to date data on retention and completion of program of their BIPOC students remains a challenge.

As most of the NWEW programming centers on the BIPOC community it is imperative that organizations that we partner with have an internal priority to ensure that these communities are served well and actively supported. One university leader and board member, stated it best, "Our goal is to create an equitable partnership based on mutually agreed upon values and goals, where we recognize the contributions of all members and have attended to relationships/trust so that we can handle equity/power/challenging issues in the moment." Furthermore, we work to decenter whiteness in our programming. We intentionally root our work centering the lived experiences and wisdom from those most marginalized, most oppressed, and less societal power; thus, we work to ensure that diverse organizations and voices are primary. For example, we have learned to consider the language we use to challenge hierarchical and status relationships (e.g., Community Captains, Guest Guide, and Guest Storyteller instead of Speaker). These types of action continue to center our mission and the goals we have outline to direct us toward that vision.

The data we collected to write this chapter also indicated opportunities for us to grow in our partnership activities. Many stakeholders felt we need to do a better job partnering and involving elected officials/state legislators and existing, individual state and local policies which impact our programming. For example, we are often impacted by decisions that come down from the state legislature, but we have no prior knowledge of decisions which may impact our work before legislation is finalized. Developing relationships with elected officials will help us to understand the impact of these policies and what we organizationally can do to counter or utilize to the benefit for our supported populations. There are several nonprofits that have focused on work that supports aims like ours for a long time, so we have an opportunity to partner and capitalize on their expertise and learning over the years. Though university partners are not new, it is new to think concretely about the policies and practices we would like to see emulated by our partners. Subsequently as we determine the new universities and colleges with whom we work, we want to prioritize those who center equity work or are willing to commit to agreed up on goals to ensure the support and care of our BIPOC educators.

We are doing the following to help set clear expectations around with whom TAF partners: (1) TAF is developing a rubric to help assess if we are doing what we say we intend to do in this area and (2) The NWEW is gathering information about graduation and acceptance rates of BIPOC candidates from current and potential partner universities and teacher prep programs (programs/colleges that have at least 30% BIPOC graduates with expectations for that number to grow over time) to determine which partners are most successful. We are also considering if there is a role, we could play in what has traditionally been the responsibility of universities, especially regarding the recruitment of students. The answers may become clearer as we plan to collaborate in recruitment efforts with our university partners.

As we looked at data on our role as a partner, we recognized our partners must receive reciprocal benefits. The impact of the partnership for our partners manifests by helping them develop tools and resources to address racial inequity/bias and social justice in a very personable and actionable way. Additionally, we are carving out more opportunities for support by opening space for white leaders (many of our university partners) with the Ally Engagement program.

Public Impact

At its core and as previously stated, TAF's mission, values, and programmatic foci intend to transform educational systems for BIPOC students and educators to eliminate historical disparities and improve their social, emotional, academic, and career outcomes. Our work stands to have a strong and positive impact at the individual and community levels. As we track progress over the history of the organization, we are heartened by our successes and strive to increase the scope of our work at the local, state, and national levels.

As we asked stakeholders to consider our public impact, it became clear that challenges at the macro and micro levels continue to test and serve as potential barriers to our work. For example, input from board leadership,

NWEW leadership, and the NWEW program manager revealed macro-level crises including national sentiments and the lack of state, and national policies that focus on the importance of diversity, equity, and inclusion. This included recognition and response to historical "isms" that persist today such as racism, capitalism, sexism, and individualism. Additionally, health care and financial crises are threatening the physiological and safety needs of our community members. The COVID-19 pandemic heightened many of these concerns as well. These issues may detract from the more local level needs TAF addresses. As an organization, it would behoove TAF to be better informed and consider how these more state or national issues ultimately impact our work at the community level and strategies to limit their impact on our work.

Similarly, stakeholders recommended TAF should track and have a better sense of broader social, political, and economic issues. They suggested an annual environmental scan to identify internal and external influences on the organization's ability to perform critical tasks and achieve strategic goals and priorities. This would help us align strategic goals and priorities based on what is within our control (micro) and what is not. Our interdependence on external entities (macro and manufactured) would enable employees to better identify and prioritize their work. In terms of whether a crisis is "manufactured," having training and awareness of how the influences of manufactured crises impact our work would be helpful. Understanding from the environmental scan what is within our control will help identify realistic outcome measures of crisis response/communication efforts.

Of course, even with the best preparation and planning, things happen. When crises do occur, stakeholders recommended seeking feedback and creating formative models of assessment that would allow TAF to identify and monitor potential challenges along the way. These models would push us to define how we are checking and assessing our progress. Having a framework/ rubric that is consistently engaged at an organizational level assessing how our responses correlate to those characteristics that continue injustice, would be helpful. Our work on the equity rubric previously mentioned is one attempt to do so. As we gather this information, having plans for our organizational role in addressing concerns as well as a communication plan for sharing this information should be clearly articulated.

Summary

The FATAE was extensive, in-depth, and illuminating. TAF's foundational governing documents guide us forward in serving adult learners equitably and just and our organizational racial equity rubric offers us an ongoing assessment to ensure that our finance and fundraising aligns with our organizational values. We are challenged to increase our partnerships while also screening them to show that they possess strong and articulated beliefs and policies that support racial equity. Conversely, our depth of programs shows the equitable approach in serving a diverse adult student population. Extending our Liberation Pedagogy to apply to the needs of educational leaders and partnering with more teacher preparatory programs are energizing challenges we welcome.

Examining our hiring and retention, and ongoing professional development centered on racial equity is required for all TAF staff and collaboration is encouraged in helping others thrive. We continue to be challenged to balance the necessity of strong leadership and hierarchical decision making with an egalitarian work environment. Assessing this domain reveals the need to standardize support to staff and strengthen guidelines and protocols for managers to operate at a consistent and firm level while encouraging their authentic styles of leadership to be affirmed. Additionally, providing an annual environmental scan to identify the impact of social, political, and economic issues on staff's ability to perform tasks could prove to be an invaluable tool in creating an equitable, just and affirming culture at TAF.

References

Dee, T. (2004). Teachers, race, and student achievement in a randomized experiment. *The Review of Economics and Statistics, 86*, 195–210.

Egalite, A., Kisida, B., & Winters, M. A. (April 2015). Representation in the classroom: The effect of own-race teachers on student achievement. *Economics of Education Review, 45*, 44–52.

Goldhaber, D., Thoebald, R., & Tien, C. (2019, January 21). *Why we need a diverse teacher workforce.* Phi Delta Kappan: Professional Journal for Educators. https://kappanonline.org/why-we-need-a-diverse-teacher-workforce-segregation-goldhaber-theobald-tien/

Klopfenstein, K. (2005). Beyond test scores: The impact of black teacher role models on rigorous math taking. *Contemporary Economic Policy, 23*, 416–428.

Mahatmya, D., Grooms, A. A., Kim, J. Y., McGinnis, D. A., & Johnson, E. (Winter 2022). Burnout and race-related stress among BIPOC women K–12 educators. *Journal of Education Human Resources, 40*(1), 58–89.

Okun, T. (2021). *White supremacy culture – Still here.* https://www.whitesupremacyculture.info

Technology Access Foundation (2020). *Transformation coaching handbook and resource guide.* Unpublished document.

Vetter, A., Hartman, S. V., & Reynolds, J. M. (2016). Confronting unsuccessful practices: Repositioning teacher identities in English education. *Teaching Education, 27*(3), 305–326. https://doi.org/10.1080/10476210.2016.1145203.

Additional Contributor: Trudy Gritsch

5

BUILDING SKILLS PARTNERSHIP

Collaborations for Opportunity and Justice

Laura Medina, Christian Valdez, and Luis Sandoval

History and Context of Organization

Building Skills Partnership (BSP) began as a pilot in 2000 out of the Justice for Janitors movement that helped hundreds of immigrant janitors achieve a more just way of living and working. The pilot began in June of 2000 by the Justice for Janitors union (SEIU Local 1877, now referred to SEIU-United Service Workers West) in partnership with responsible janitorial companies that were subcontracted to clean the worksites of major businesses across Silicon Valley. Since then, BSP has quickly grown into a one-of-a-kind, statewide model to address the needs of working immigrants. Originally founded as the Leadership Training & Education Fund, BSP's originators believed that learning English is key to janitors' advancement while on the job, as well as to the economic stability, health, educational success, and civic participation of their families. The originators agreed that the best place to offer such classes was at the worksite and during paid work time so that janitors would not have to overcome obstacles to attend class. Those potential obstacles included family obligations, transportation issues, second and third jobs, and numerous additional challenges associated with adjusting to a new country and culture. At the time of its founding, 97% of janitors in the state were Latinx immigrants. Today, Latinx immigrants continue to be overrepresented in this sector at similar levels.

In 2004, BSP developed its first flagship program that consisted of a 70-hour ADVANCE Program (Workplace English & Job Skills). BSP's partnership with SEIU-USWW and employers (labor-management) provided an opportunity to develop this contextualized industry-specific vocational English for speakers of other languages (ESOL) curriculum for janitors. The curriculum

DOI: 10.4324/9781003286998-5

of this ongoing course continues to be based on collaboration and feedback from multiple employers, and it now serves as a model of how we develop and scale programming. In 2006, Los Angeles janitorial employers and the Building Owner & Manager's Association of Greater Los Angeles (BOMA-GLA) requested and provided partial funding to expand the VESL (Vocational ESL) ADVANCE Program to Southern California. In 2007, BSP officially incorporated and become a statewide nonprofit with a board of directors to oversee this new statewide organization with the mission to deliver vocational ESL, computer skills training, parent engagement, and other programming.

During the infancy of the organization, there were multiple individuals who contributed to building this statewide organization that has now become a national model for delivering workplace training. It is important for us to acknowledge contributions of passionate and dedicated individuals such as Aida Cardenas, Alison Ascher-Webber, Kelly Greer, Mike Garcia, Chava Bustamante, David Huerta, Andrew Gross-Gaitan, Victor Narro, Janna Shadduck-Hernández, Lilia Garcia-Brower, Marisol Rivera, Alan Levy, Martha Cox-Nitikman, Jim Altieri, Margarita Vega, Barbara Gurr, and Madeleine Case.

BSP's journey and trajectory is rooted in the belief that together we can positively impact the quality of life of immigrant workers. We believe that we are an example of how a vision can ignite individuals to take collective action toward addressing those who are often forgotten. With a bold vision of creating an equitable playing field for California's working families to succeed in their careers and educational endeavors, we experienced tremendous growth since our inception. Since 2007, we have grown in size, scale, and ability to deliver programming. A core BSP value has been hiring leaders with proximity to the communities impacted and served. Today, BSP has expanded to seven major cities across California and broadened its programming to fully address the unique barriers immigrant janitors and their children face in realizing the benefits of social, civic, and economic integration. This type of action-oriented approach to its mission can be witnessed throughout BSP, including the proximity to the community it serves. This approach is embodied in the life of BSP's founding executive director, Aida Cardenas.

Aida Cardenas is a first-generation Mexican American woman who comes from an immigrant, working background. She began her work in social justice and empowerment while attending community college and subsequently at UCLA. While she was a student of the UCLA Labor and Workplace Studies summer internship program, she was placed with the Justice for Janitors Campaign Division within Service Employees International Union (SEIU), Local 1877 that is based in Los Angeles. The Justice for Janitors movement began in the mid-1980s as a response to working conditions and wages for building service workers who were largely immigrants from Mexico and

Central America working in the shadows of the some of the most expensive real estate property in the United States. By 1990, SEIU Local 1877 was actively organizing local groups of workers to bring regional and national attention and advocacy for the systems that created oppressive conditions for workers in commercial buildings. The Justice for Janitors movement raised awareness of the needs of building service workers, and it also mobilized a generation of individuals like Aida Cardenas to work to create changes in the treatment of Latinx immigrant workers.

Aida was eventually hired by SEIU 1877 as an organizer in the Los Angeles area. Subsequently, in 2000, she was part of a team that organized and created member leaders in Orange County, California. She worked with those leaders to win their first contract with higher wages and health insurance coverage. The work and rationale for BSP built on the union's efforts by empowering workers to advocate for job quality through skills training and access to supportive services to increase the quality of life for both workers and their families. As we describe more fully later in this chapter, BSP seeks to provide programs for multi-generational interventions that stem from quality jobs and access to upskilling opportunities, information, and a comprehensive education program that addresses employees' whole needs. In an industry where 97% of janitorial workers are immigrants from Latin America and more than 60% are women, BSP seeks to operate in a way that supports more workers and their children following the path that was similar to that of Aida Cardenas

Aida Cardenas served as Executive Director for BSP from its founding in 2007 until 2019. Her appointment as the leader of BSP was not only as a result of her aptitude and dedication, but to her expertise within the industry. Her appointment was also an explicit recognition of her leadership in a new movement that aimed to invest in worker education and their families through a collaborative effort among all stakeholders. Many of the population served by the fledgling BSP could identify with Aida as a leader, working mother, daughter of immigrants, and someone who is a highly adept negotiator and a committed advocate to social justice. They could envision this work in relation to either themselves as working parents, or their children who could have the opportunity to succeed through education and work. Through Aida's example, they could also see the benefit of advocacy against systemic oppression. The mission of BSP at its inception was to serve property service workers who were part of the SEIU-United Service Workers West (SEIU-USWW) that evolved from the SEIU 1877. To do that, BSP has always been more than a job-training and skills-development program. It seeks to support the holistic needs that property service workers have in their lives as working parents and community members. BSP seeks to be an advocate that helps to change not just working conditions, but also the systems and societal practices that affect those conditions.

To understand how that is unique, it is important to understand a little about labor law. Labor and employer relations are governed federally by the Taft-Hartley Act (also known as the Labor Management Relations Act). Taft-Hartley legislation allows for employers and bargaining groups to establish agreements where employees can receive benefits like education as part of their bargaining agreement with an employer. Typically, Taft-Hartley funds are managed by an organization which has a board of directors that has equal representation from labor and management. The initial Leadership Training and Education Fund (LTEF) was set up as Taft-Hartley agreement solely in Northern California bargaining agreements between SEIU 1877 (as it was known at the time) and signatory employers who found a need and value for employees to be able to communicate in English at their place of work.

This initial work of developing the LTEF, done largely by two current BSP Board Members, Alison Ascher Webber and Andrew Gross Gaitan, was critical to show both labor and employers the value that training offered to both. Employers, employees, and the organizations that represent them saw vocational ESOL courses for workers at their place of work and on paid time as a benefit to all parties involved. Providing classes on paid time at the workplace was key to providing access to workers who may not have had access to traditional educational opportunities because of competing family responsibilities and multiple jobs. The labor union that represented workers viewed this as a valuable, negotiated benefit for the workers it represented. The employers saw the training as a way to increase the customer service skills of their employees through vocational ESOL courses. Finally, the workers who were largely monolingual, Spanish-speaking had an opportunity to increase their English language skills that would benefit their work and private life. The ESOL courses' success set a foundation for what would eventually become BSP.

This collaborative model was embraced, supported and expanded by industry leaders such as the long-serving President of SEIU-USWW, Mike Garcia, and Alan Levy from Building Owners and Managers of Greater Los Angeles, an industry group that represents property owners and their management companies that employ or subcontract service workers. In 2006, this collaboration of partners supported the first vocational ESOL pilot classes in Los Angeles. The success of these classes served as the catalyst to create a non-profit organization that went beyond the typical functions generated by labor and employer agreements. The labor organization, employers, property owners, and employees came together to create a non-profit, collaborative model among all of these groups. While Taft-Hartley training organizations typically engage some of these groups, the new organization sought to include all of them. Of special significance was the participation and active involvement of the larger commercial real estate and property owner and manager community. That community continues to hold a key role in the industry's decision making and power of negotiations with SEIU-USWW. The partnership also included the participation of community stakeholders who were experts in various fields of social justice, education, and the non-union janitorial industry. BSP officially became 501(c)3 in 2007 with the mission statement:

> Building Skills Partnership programs improve the quality of life of property service workers in low-wage industries, as well as their families and communities, by increasing their access to education, leadership, and career advancement.

By striving to achieve impact not only for workers but also "their families and communities," BSP held a unique perspective and role compared to other labor-management collaborations on employee training. It meant that BSP would bring together all partners around a powerful vision for supporting employees' whole needs. That broader scope acknowledged that employee performance was closely tied to the complexity of employees' lives and the communities in which they live. To meet that mission, having ongoing engagement with all stakeholders was paramount. The board of directors needed to include equal representation from three groups: labor (the union/ SEIU Local 1877); management (janitorial employers) and clients (property owners and managers); and the community (immigrant and worker-focused advocates). Beginning with its board and extending to all levels of the organization, BSP convened partners that can often have competing interests. The result has been a benefit for responsible employers who contribute to the Master Contract Agreements with SEIU-USWW and provide significant value for members, their families, and the communities in which they live.

One of BSP's earliest efforts provides an example of how this all has worked. In 2008, BSP and SEIU Local 1877 connected with the UCLA Institute for Research on Labor and Employment which conducted a survey on workers' needs (Terriquez et al., 2009). The survey sought to determine what the workers whom BSP serves would see as their greatest need. The workers identified the education of their children as being their greatest need, and they believed that providing opportunities for their children was the most important benefit that the union could offer. The union bargained funds in its contract to provide classes that BSP called "Parent University," courses in parenting and advocacy that were co-developed by BSP and UCLA IDEA (Institute for Democracy, Education, and Access) and the UCLA Labor Center, spearheaded by eventual BSP Board Chair, Janna Shadduck-Hernandez. These bargained funds eventually paid for BSP to expand into subjects like health and wellness and financial literacy. Workers saw their union membership as impacting their larger lives. As Ron Herrera, President of the Los Angeles County Federation of Labor, explained, "Labor has to expand beyond a narrow vision of bargaining into the community, into social and economic justice" (Murray, 2022). With time, employers saw the impacts of supporting their employees' larger needs.

Bringing together labor, management, and community resources to impact the needs of workers continues to be BSP's model.

Sal Campos who works at ABM, a contractor company that places property service workers, shares his BSP experience: "I started with ABM at Google in November of 2004 as a day porter. I started attending the BSP classes thereafter. I moved to events (continuing my classes), then worked to be a lead. I continued with BSP for bit longer, becoming a supervisor with ABM. After a while as a supervisor, I became an assistant manager, and now full manager with ABM in 2017. I am grateful for the opportunities, such as BSP classes, ABM has provided to me and others to continue to grow." BSP seeks to provide similar experiences for all workers.

Through its 15-year history, BSP has been anchored by its core focus areas including (1) workforce development, (2) immigrant integration, and (3) community advancement. Also, since its inception and current growth, a key attribute of BSP has been that its leadership and management is deeply committed to social justice and largely reflects the communities and individuals it aims to serve. That began with the first executive director, Aida Cardenas; however, that commitment has extended throughout the organization as BSP seeks to hire people who understand, empathize, and have, at times, experiences that match the lives of the people BSP serves. BSP employs a wide diversity of leaders and staff within the organization who come largely from the Latin American immigrant diaspora and who are passionate about the work because of their engagement with the population whom BSP serves. The richness in understanding the needs of the communities served through close proximity have helped create an organization grounded in values of compassion, empathy, social justice and equity that continues today. In other words, BSP is an organization that aims to serve workers with compassion and empathy and is committed to the ideals of social justice and equity. This commitment is present not only in the firm belief that staff can move an entire industry to invest in worker skills, but it also exists in BSP's ability and capacity to question the inner workings of our own organization. As a now well-established organization, BSP seeks to evolve so that its staff continues to be committed to social justice, diversity, and equity, but also reflects its population as it diversifies. We want our staff to have experiences connected to the industries we serve, and we want them to come from cultural and racial backgrounds of the people we serve. BSP seeks to make our advocacy framework into a framework for operations so that our commitment to social justice and equity is not just something done for others but is also a way of operating daily.

The authors of this chapter write it as people who have committed to this work in that way. As you read this chapter, we hope you will see how we grapple with what it means to both do the work and to live it in our daily efforts. We approach this work from our perspectives as people engaged within BSP and who choose to do this work because of our commitment to the work that BSP performs.

Chapter author Laura Medina grew up in Carson, California, a culturally diverse city in south Los Angeles County. She identifies as a first-generation Mexican American woman and draws her commitment to hard work from her immigrant parents who also placed a large emphasis on education. She attended the Los Angeles Unified School District and later Smith College as a recipient of a STRIDE (Student Research in Departments) Scholarship. She majored in political science and French studies and spent her junior year abroad in France. When she graduated from Smith College, she was awarded a Fulbright Fellowship to France where she taught English and served as a cultural ambassador at a high school in *La Courneuve*, a Parisian suburb known for its immigrant and working-class communities. There, she connected with students by comparing her own experience to the immigrant experience in their respective countries. Laura began working at BSP in 2008 as the organization's first AmeriCorps VISTA employee. Her first project was in the parent education program that focused on helping immigrant, working parents to become involved in their children's education. Since then, she has been involved in the creation and implementation of multiple programs and services at BSP and currently serves as the Chief Operating Officer thanks to the upskilling and professional opportunities she has received throughout her tenure at BSP.

Chapter author Christian Valdez identifies as a cis-gender male and is currently the Development Director at BSP. He joined the organization in 2014 when he coordinated and oversaw BSP's northern California direct service programs. Christian was born in Mexico City, immigrated to the Bay Area at the age of five, and grew up in the predominantly Latinx community of North Fair Oaks surrounded by affluent cities. He is a member of an immigrant family who lacked legal status. Christian's worldview was shaped by common immigrant experiences created by those barriers to community integration tied closely to language access: parents who worked low-wage cleaning and restaurant jobs; a lack of his family's experience with the education system to provide fully engaged support; a lack of access to information and technology despite being in one of the world's most technologically advanced regions; and a mistrust and fear of institutions of authority because of his legal status. Christian was a first-generation college student and current DACA recipient who attended an affluent, mostly white, preparatory school in grades 9–12 and is influenced by his lived experience of the intersectionality of race, socio-economic, and immigrant dynamics. BSP is the longest employment Christian has experienced.

Chapter author Luis Sandoval is BSP's current Executive Director. He grew up in both Mexicali, a border town in Mexico, and Salinas, California where he took notice of the barriers that prevented him and other immigrants from accessing career and educational opportunities. He is inspired by his experiences growing up in a family of workers in property and cleaning services, construction, and agriculture jobs who also sought to improve job quality in these sectors. As a son of farmworkers, as a janitor himself, and as a former worker in low-wage industries – which includes working in a squid factory in Salinas Valley, working in a packing shed in Georgia, or working alongside his parents in the farm fields – he developed a personal view of how essential immigrants are and the challenges and opportunities that exist within his community. He has over 20 years of experience in developing, managing, leading initiatives that reach those most vulnerable communities. Over the years, his skills have allowed him to assist several organizations in a variety of capacities. This includes assisting with strategic planning, board facilitation, fundraising, capacity building and programming as a consultant. He has completed courses in a strategic public relations program at George Washington University. In 2017, he was selected to participate in the Aspen Leadership Seminar Program and has participated in Hispanics in Philanthropy fellowship program. Luis holds a bachelor's degree in Social Behavioral Sciences with a concentration in sociology from California State University Monterey Bay. He is co-founder of the California Advocacy Network for Aging Latinos and is also Co-Founder of the AZ-CA Humanitarian Coalition, an interconnected network responding to the migrant humanitarian crisis. Luis spent the early part of his career in higher education as an administrator of federal and state grant programs outreaching to underserved communities.

In conducting our self-assessment to write this chapter, we discovered much about our organization. The *Framework for Assessment and Transformation in Adult Education* (*FATAE*) allowed us to examine our activities and to determine whether we were living into our intentions. Our commitment to justice and equity has been strong since our founding, but the self-assessment that we conducted helped our leadership team examine our actions as an organization. As we were conducting the self-assessment, BSP's leadership team met to discuss what we were finding. Those conversations were helpful in identifying how we are succeeding and falling short of our intent. While we reviewed all four of the domains in the *FATAE*, we decided to focus on two of those domains because we saw them as critical at this point in our organizational growth. We did, however, review the other two domains and have some brief analysis of our findings from our brief review of those other two domains. In the sections of this chapter that follow, we describe what we have learned about ourselves as an organization that has been committed to justice and equity since our founding. In conducting a self-assessment and subsequently writing this chapter, we found some explanations of how we have evolved to become a successful organization. We also discovered areas where we can enact our vision more fully. We are an evolving organization that works to match our vision and ideals daily. The process of analyzing our work in relation to the *FATAE* helped us to see where we are in that evolution.

Governance and Finance

Organizational Structures and Staff

Using the *FATAE* to assess our current status was helpful to us as we looked at the governance structure that BSP evolved since its beginnings. Our review gave us the chance to look comprehensively at how we operate, from our mission statement through our daily work. This introspection is something we had already begun and the *FATAE* gave us a structure and language for our discussions. Initially, we began by looking at the questions that focused on supporting our staff so that we could then consider changes to our organizational structures that would incorporate what was working well and changes needed more formally. As noted above, BSP was founded to be more than many Taft-Hartley training organizations because of its intent to look beyond narrowly defined, on-the-job skills training and address the whole needs of workers and their families. To build its capacity to provide that level of support, we needed to grow our staff and to ensure formal systems were in place for that growth.

For its first three years, a significant portion of BSP's capacity came from AmeriCorps VISTA (Volunteers in Service to America) members who completed one to two-year terms and were tasked with early program design and implementation in different areas that enabled BSP to carry its mission. AmeriCorps VISTA is an anti-poverty program designed to provide needed resources to nonprofit organizations and public agencies to increase their capacity to lift communities out of poverty. AmeriCorps VISTA provides opportunities for individuals to dedicate a year of full-time service with an organization ("sponsor") to create or expand programs designed to empower individuals and communities in overcome poverty. The VISTA members working with BSP were critical to its early efforts and successes. VISTA members could not legally be considered BSP staff. As per program regulations, they were employees of AmeriCorps. As the organization grew its efforts and scope of work, and by its fifth year, it began to develop the resources to hire more staff directly. Many of BSP's earliest employees were originally AmeriCorps VISTA members who transitioned to becoming BSP employees when their AmeriCorps VISTA term completed and as resources allowed.

With time, BSP grew to the point where it could recruit beyond AmeriCorps VISTA members. However, this relationship between BSP and AmeriCorps influenced the earliest organizational structures of BSP. The hiring of more internal staff allowed BSP to have the stability we needed to examine and develop policies and organizational structures it needed to effectively pursue our strategic vision. As BSP grew its number of internal staff, we recognized organizational needs to structure both the staff and the ways in which our organization supports its staff. BSP created more executive and middle-level managers and sought to hire people with more work experience who could oversee the work. It also began conversations about how to upskill employees – both those who came through AmeriCorps VISTA and those who were hired outside of that relationship.

Our organizational chart and latest job descriptions are two of the more recent results of how that move toward formalization of our organization worked. These documents also allowed us to use the questions posed in the *FATAE* to examine how an organizational chart and job descriptions are more than perfunctory organizational products. In looking at who reports to whom and what managers' responsibilities are, we sought to determine whether our current structure helps or hinders our intentions for staff capacity and advancement. The added middle-management positions could help us offer employees career pathways, in addition to having clearer lines of responsibility and accountability. That is especially important for the staff we select. Early on, several of our staff were early career professionals without extensive experience outside of BSP. Other staff have come to BSP with significant non-profit experience. As an organization, BSP has, therefore, had to balance and create systems that value both types of staff experiences and recognize the need to advance individuals from all capacities.

It has been important, then, for us to provide a management structure that allowed those with advanced knowledge to help guide us while offering opportunities and support for career development for all to grow. It would make little sense for us to provide career advancement opportunities and support for the clients we serve and not similarly offer opportunities for the staff who are critical in moving forward the work of the organization. It is also important that we consider staff who come into BSP with extensive experience and/or high-level skills and how they fit within the framework of recognizing those skills that are invaluable in moving the work forward while providing career opportunities for all BSP employees. While we were already on the path to make the internal changes to make that happen, the questions in the *FATAE* helped us to clarify that intent and to have the language to express it. As we develop new policies and systems that are clear, we now find ourselves better able to address the challenges we face. As we write this chapter, for example, we are still in the pandemic and are seeing the same effects of the "great resignation" that all organizations are facing. Our now well-defined job descriptions and defined structure are helping us fill in as needed while we search for new colleagues more intentionally.

In addition to our operational practices, we have been looking closely at our overall governance. The *FATAE* has been helpful because its questions help us to discuss our governance in more detail around issues of equity and justice. Throughout its existence, BSP has interacted with two, distinct but intersecting board governance structures. Both have been critical to our successes in securing additional support from industry labor-management partners for programming and the expansion toward a broader vision that addresses the needs of workers beyond the workplace. To clarify: BSP works closely with two overlapping governing boards. First, BSP is overseen by a board of directors that provides strategic direction, oversees its operations, and has fiduciary responsibility (similar to other nonprofits); however, BSP is also accountable to a board of trustees comprised of labor-management partners who contribute to the Master Contract Agreements as part of a Taft-Hartley training fund overseen by the LTEF. As noted previously, the LTEF is the longest standing governance structure and is the predecessor to BSP. Originally, founded as a Taft-Hartley Training Fund as the LTEF, in 2007 Buildings Skills Partnership expanded its vision to do more than workplace training. The LTEF trustees form a standard governance board, common to Taft-Hartley collective bargaining agreements, that oversees the funds generated by the collective bargaining agreements. LTEF service agreements provide between 30% and 40% of BSP's annual revenue. LTEF trustees have ultimate approval on how that funding is spent, so BSP collaborates with that board to outline training and service objectives for that funding.

In many Taft-Hartley-funded programs around the nation, the funding only provides direct training for work-related skills and knowledge. Through its relationship with the LTEF and by being able to show the impact of its work, BSP has received approval to expand training into areas beyond direct, job-related skills development. For example, BSP was able to show how workshops and classes in financial literacy positively impacted employees' work. If a worker experiences common financial hardships, that employee will continually have challenges that encroach into the workday. With some lessons on how to navigate the U.S. retail financial system and referrals to community service providers, employees can develop a different relationship and agency to the income they earn through work. That relationship to income can have positive outcomes such as employee retention and satisfaction (Hannon et al., 2017). By showing the positive impacts of financial literacy training, BSP was able to show the LTEF the importance of funding it (Figure 5.1). As the LTEF has expanded its definitions of what it will fund, the funds it provides have given BSP an anchor with which to build programs. BSP has leveraged those resources to pursue other funding through private foundations and public agencies to build out a comprehensive model of services beyond the funding provided by LTEF. Over the years, BSP has been able to show the LTEF trustees how their investment benefits employees and employers as every dollar spent by the LTEF is leveraged (through being able to secure additional dollars) into a dollar-and-a-half return in service to employees.

As a 501(c)3, BSP has a board of directors that operates as the oversight body for the organization. This has been critical to our ability to expand our work to workers' whole needs. While the LTEF provides as much as 40% of our resources, that is not enough to develop and maintain all of the programs that have evolved. Those additional funds are raised and managed separately from

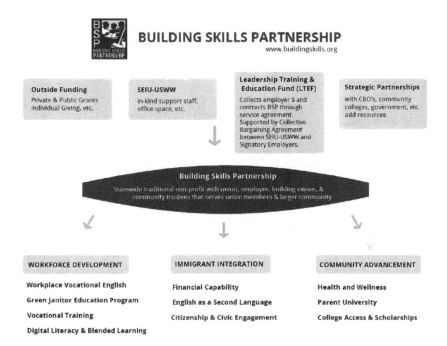

FIGURE 5.1 BSP's Funding Structure to Support Its Multi-Strategy Approach

the funding provided by the LTEF, and being a separate non-profit allows us to do that. As we noted previously, the makeup of BSP's board of directors has been important to us since our founding. The board of directors is always comprised equal representation among labor, industry, and the community. Labor representatives are there to ensure that BSP's service to workers considers the comprehensive needs that workers' lives demand and which are in line with the long-term strategic goals and vision of SEIU-USWW. Industry representatives have included building owners, property managers, commercial real estate representatives or affiliates, and service contractors who are the direct employers of the property service workers. These individuals bring questions of how BSP's work adds value to their needs as for-profit businesses; this is a valued perspective to BSP's industry-led strategies. Community members are as diverse as justice advocates and academics who bring their perspectives in supporting communities to any discussion. The outcome of these three groups' equal representation is that BSP constantly balances its efforts in relation to all three groups. Within the BSP board, there is commitment to the three, previously described core components: immigrant integration; workforce development; community advancement. Those pillars guide us and keep the organization and trustees focused despite what could be disparate aims among the three unique constituencies that the board represents.

Early into BSP's efforts, union members were unclear where BSP's efforts and the union differentiated. They would, at that point, sometimes bring concerns to BSP that were the purview of the union. Over time, as BSP has expanded its services to a larger number of individuals within the membership and developed a larger footprint with an increasingly recognized brand, we have been able to clarify our role as a separate but intermediary of labor and management focused on serving workers; and that type of misunderstanding is less frequent now.

Another early issue arose from the unique, whole-person approach that BSP takes in doing its work. As noted previously, Taft-Hartley funds are typically operated in a transactional manner. Unions traditionally bargain for benefits, wages, and working conditions; and members of management bargain for what will provide employers the greatest return on investment. Moving all of our partners toward understanding and valuing a holistic, worker-centered model took time. BSP has been guided by an action-oriented approach to demonstrate the impact of its programming to all represented at table: workers, employers, union, and the industry. BSP needed to show the efficacy of this approach, and it needed to show that efficacy to both labor and management. Employers needed to see the value in giving employees time during the workday to receive training that would ultimately benefit their bottom lines. Union leaders had to ask for training that did not directly tie to employees' work. Fortunately, BSP entered into this work as other, larger changes supported the efforts.

There is a movement in California for employers to be involved in supporting the well-being of their workers. Certifications like the LEED and WELL standards that apply to the way buildings are built and operated provide a basis for employers to consider the roles of property service workers in the sustainability of their buildings. Furthermore, the State of California has funded projects called High-Road Training Partnerships that focus on sector-based industry partnerships that deliver equity, sustainability, and job quality through projects such as BSP. Also, there is an increasing push to increase definitions of job quality to include worker wellness, digital skills, literacy, financial literacy, and other supportive services. Therefore, being supportive of employees' development in these various areas aligns with leading conversations on job quality and what makes good and innovative business practices.

With the programs that BSP offers, workers can learn basic skills and are also developing those skills that will help create career sustainability. In the past, a large number of property service workers remained in their jobs without opportunities for skill development and had limited career mobility opportunities. Now, employers are seeing the need to attract and retain new employees to the industry with the kinds of programs that BSP offers. As a result, many employers see value in collaborating with BSP to create conditions that attract and retain employees. This evolution beyond the typical training fund's role has advanced the way BSP and the LTEF collaborate and innovate. They have, thus, come to see themselves as partners in the work. We have, as a result, been able to begin to infuse the kinds of fundamental justice and equity principles that are the core of our work into the opportunities where employers and the union collaborate. Rather than seeing skills-based training as the only need, we have been able to find consensus with the LTEF on the importance of supporting the wider needs that any employee brings to work.

An additional group helps us with our mission. The 2016 collective bargaining agreement between SEIU-USWW and employers across Southern California named BSP as the convener of a Labor Management Committee. This Committee was tasked with bringing labor-management and workers to discuss industry and workforce training needs and develop worker-centered training solutions. BSP's Labor Management Committee serves as an advisory group with the goal to create a structure to collaborate and obtain feedback from industry partners, a critical component in developing industry recognized programming. While this group is not part of the daily operational structure, it helps us work with our partners as we review and develop ideas for implementation. The Floor Care Training Program we began in 2019 offers an example of the importance of the Labor Management Committee.

The first impression that people have as they enter a high-rise building comes from the lobby. If the lobby is impeccably maintained, people will develop an immediate and positive impression. The floors of a building are critical to that impression, and building managers and owners hire employees who can maintain the floors to a high standard. As a result, floor care workers are paid more than other property service workers. It is a mistake to see property service work as "unskilled," a term that has been, in the past, applied to it. Floor care is one of the most obvious examples of why. When we first looked at the work being performed by floor care workers, we found that training was typically provided by a vendor who provided the training on the specific machine, but that training typically did not cover overall understanding of the work such as chemical management, safety and safety data sheets, and ergonomics. While this position pays more than other property service work, there had not been a formalized pathway for people to be trained into that position. In the past, after receiving the minimal training from an equipment manufacturer, people with the skills would select the next person they wanted to train into that position. As a result, there was not an open and fair process for everyone to have the opportunity.

Based on its relationship to workers and to management, BSP was able to bring the need for floor care training to both groups and to provide both labor and management an opportunity to discover the potential benefits for each side. The Labor Management Committee consisted of decision makers for both labor and management, so solutions that the group developed were highly likely to be adopted. Over time, BSP staff were able to help both sides see the value, and the Floor Care Training Program emerged. BSP began offering it in 2019. In the time since, this training program has offered a more equitable pathway into the higher-skilled and higher-paying position.

While the Labor Management Committee began in Southern California, it eventually expanded statewide. To ensure that multiple employers and all regions are represented, BSP regional coordinators help identify key leaders from their region to participate. The committee expands or contracts depending on needs, and those needs constantly evolve. For example, the COVID-19 pandemic caused a pause in the Floor Care Training Program because of the shelter in place and social distancing restrictions. However, the pandemic also offered an opportunity. At the beginning of the pandemic, BSP used the Labor Management Committee platform to develop an infectious disease training program with input from all partners that became crucial as property service workers were designated "essential" and needed to work through the pandemic.

As the work of the Labor and Management Committee expanded statewide, we continue to have regional conversations because of the need to be relevant to needs within the multiple regions within the state. The discussions of needs in high-rise buildings in Southern California, for example, are different from the needs in the spread-out mega-campuses in Silicon Valley. Even if two members come from the same company, the conditions may be different in their region, so it has been critical to have as broad of a mixture of members as possible. Participating employers have had to commit to having key executives in various regions participate in the Labor Management Committee since it is important that employers encourage worker participation. Moreover, the union representatives in different regions may see unique needs that exist in their region, so it has been critical to have full regional participation from union leadership.

As the work of the Labor Management Committee continued, the committee was able to support additional programs such as variations of digital skills training that are more highly specialized in the Silicon Valley. Furthermore, BSP developed a Legionella training based on information from a property owner that a trace of Legionella had been found in its unused building as tenants were sheltering in place and working from home. The work that BSP has done as a result of convening the Labor and Management Committee, both on a statewide and regional level, is recognized by the California Workforce Development Board (CWDB) as a model High Road Training Partnerships practice.

BSP also convenes a Worker Advisory Committee which is comprised of workers who have participated in BSP programs across various regions. Participants give workers' perspective to BSP's programming priorities, planning, and quality of services. BSP provides training to committee members on how to work in a committee structure and develop leadership skills such as public speaking. BSP coordinators prioritize recruiting workers across its service regions. That wide recruitment is crucial because just having a voice from industry or just one region is not enough. The Advisory Committee offers many perspectives even if employees come from within one organization that has multiple locations statewide.

Internal Operations

As we noted previously, the evolution to having more full-time staff and away from significant reliance on AmeriCorps Vista members helped us formalize our organizational structure. As we continued to grow and develop those structures, the evolution of BSP has continued over the last three years. We developed an executive management team and now have regional directors that allow us to effectively oversee a statewide effort. As we grew, it became increasingly important to have a model that allowed for information to flow among regions and within our executive team. It also was important for BSP's management team to remain connected to the ideas developed by staff.

Writing this chapter has been helpful as we employed the *FATAE*'s questions to examine who we are and how we came to be who we are as we evolved. The most impactful work that resulted from writing this chapter came as we looked at how our evolving governance structure supports BSP employees. The *FATAE* questions caused us to stop and consider how our past and existing structure supports employees in the same way that we seek to support the people we serve. We have grown to over 30 full-time employees, two part-time employees, and about 15 part-time instructors who deliver our courses and workshops. As we stopped having AmeriCorps VISTA members in 2018, and as we hired more BSP staff, it was important for us to build the capacity of our staff. We began exploring the question of staff support and began to look at staffing levels. The questions in the *FATAE* allowed us to consider the opportunities we were developing for our staff as we hire more people.

We are now having discussions among the executive team and directors to see how our position descriptions allow for flexible hiring that will encourage internal, vertical career development, as well as align with the current strategic priorities of the organization. We are also identifying what those career advancements can be. We expanded to offer more professional development opportunities for staff to gain skills and new knowledge that will prepare them for future leadership opportunities and expertise in their work. We take these steps anticipating that we will see more of our staff (which is reflective of the populations we serve) have the same kinds of growth opportunities we work to provide the people we serve. We expect to evaluate these actions yearly to determine whether these actions will meet our aims of providing career latticing opportunities for staff.

While the *FATAE* allowed us to have focused questions that helped with discussions, internal staff development has been a critical feature since our founding. As structure has evolved and grown, BSP has been able to grow staff into leadership roles. The three authors of this chapter are examples. Laura was the first AmeriCorps Vista member to work with BSP and since her hiring has worked in a variety of roles until becoming the Chief Operating Officer. Christian began in one of the regional centers as a Program and Development Assistant and is now the Development Director. Luis, our current Executive Director, was previously BSP's Chief Development Officer. As a result of the upward mobility and opportunities we have offered, we retained workers and have relatively less turnover compared to other non-profit organizations. In creating job descriptions and new positions, it has been important that we have worked hard to move away from deficit-based framing and into asset-based models. This has allowed us, for example, to look at what qualifications someone might have beyond education and years of experience that qualify for a position. We have also sought to hire children of property service workers to be trainers and staff because we see their life experiences as significant assets to our work.

At the time that we are writing this chapter, we are also undergoing a review of our strategic plan which was upended by the global pandemic. Similarly, changes and growth of BSP's leadership presents an opportunity to embark on a new strategic planning process under the new context of a COVID-19 recovery. This all comes as we are expanding our work significantly and being asked to provide services and support to others who seek to replicate our model in the state and nationally. Additionally, we are encountering the same pressures that all organizations are addressing during the pandemic and the "great resignation" that has come with it. By looking at who we are and the kind of organization we seek to be through the experiences of these pressures and the lens of the *FATAE*, we are discovering that we can define our current circumstances and our future direction more clearly. The external changes force us to think creatively, and the *FATAE* continues to give us some guidelines to help us plan and conduct our work through justice and equity.

It is important for us to have a sense of direction as an organization. We started the process to write a five-year strategic plan in 2018. It was intended to replace BSP's first five-year plan that we wrote in 2014. In 2019, BSP's Board of Directors and Executive Director at the time followed a process that included staff and constituents to have meetings and discussions that informed the creation of a new five-year plan. The document was mostly finished in 2019 when there was a transition in executive leadership. Because BSP has been, from its founding, an organization that engages multiple stakeholders and seeks to practice inclusive governance, that strategic planning process was put on hold until the next executive director was chosen. Soon after, the pandemic struck and Luis Sandoval who was an interim role, led the organization through its key response efforts to the economic and health impacts of COVID-19. In late 2020, Luis was officially named BSP's second Executive Director. With the onset of the pandemic, the challenges of shifting operations and addressing new needs meant that long-term strategic planning was, again, put on hold. However, there was work completed that allowed affirmation of BSP's mission and direction.

In 2021, Luis and the leadership team held a series of meetings that allowed us to discuss and identify strategic priorities in a document describing those priorities. The resulting document was updated again in 2022. We have discovered that in this unique moment as we are managing the complexities of organizational life during a global pandemic and as we are undergoing internal growth, it makes sense to look at one-year periods. This shorter-term process helped each of our directors work with their staff to identify critical questions in their area and determine how they will address the strategic priorities in their area. We are now developing accountability measures, assessments, and definitions of success for this work. Because much of our work is completed virtually, we hold video conferencing sessions where groups can break into teams and have discussions that they can report back to the whole organization. Most significantly, through its self-examination, from developing strategic priorities and in the writing of this chapter, BSP has affirmed its commitment to the mission statement noted previously. We have found that statement still to be representative of who we are and whom we seek to be.

To meet that mission, having ongoing engagement with all stakeholders has been paramount. The board of directors' equal representation from labor (workers); employers (janitorial contractors) and clients (property owners and managers); and the community (immigrant and worker-focused advocates) is crucial to our success in meeting our mission. Bringing together those partners to support workers' needs is what makes BSP successful. Beginning with its board and extending to all additional levels of the organization, BSP is constantly convening partners that can often be at odds. The result has been a benefit for responsible employers who contribute to the Master Contract Agreements with SEIU-USWW and significant value for members and their families. This is work in progress as BSP evolves from informal structures under which it operated at its founding to more formal ones that are required by growth and the need for stability. Having the *FATAE* is helpful as we create those formal structures since it allows us to investigate our actions in relation to the framework and allows us to determine how our actions match our intent.

The year-to-year strategic priorities that we have developed were developed internally among BSP staff and management. As we are evolving as an organization, we seek to have additional stakeholders involved as we live into the plan. In future strategic plans, we will engage the full range of stakeholders;

however, for now, it was important for us to have internal discussions that helped our internal team focus on who we are and what we want to accomplish. With time, and as we evolve our formal organizational structure, we will engage more voices in the process.

It is important to us that our strategic plan is more than a document that we write and revisit. We want our daily actions to match what our mission and values claim. Again, the *FATAE* has been helpful to us as it offers guiding questions that have helped us move from strategic planning to action as we center our efforts on equity and justice. It has provided us with concepts and language that we can look at throughout the organization and determine our effectiveness. Because of the sometimes-competing interests of the stakeholders that BSP serves, we have found that being centered on equity and justice gives us a common point for our discussions with our constituencies.

BSP is unapologetic about its vision of working toward an equitable future for California's property service workers, but we are also acutely aware about the broad support needed from competing partners to address the barriers immigrant workers and their children face. At the heart of this is the need to move toward justice and equity by seeing the whole needs of both the employee and the employer and their relationship to their union. We seek for employees to be more than a resource to employers. We want employers to view that employees are key partners in the workplace and people who fit within the larger contextual needs of a community. Furthermore, we want to lift up how labor can be of additional value to its members, like SEIU-USWW's example, by offering services and benefits to its membership beyond the bread-and-butter issues that can restrict unions solely to focusing on work-related issues. Additionally, we seek to help employers be contributors to the communities in which they operate. We want to help them see that a return on investment can include the larger impacts that the employer has within communities – and how those impacts benefit the employer's ability to conduct business.

This all can leave BSP in an ambiguous position. We are constantly trying to navigate the need for training while recognizing the need for justice and equity through the larger impacts we seek to have beyond job-related skills training. Economic justice, we believe, requires multigenerational approaches that cannot often be quickly measured. At the same time, we must address the needs of our LTEF funding (which demands more immediate metrics which show impact). As we examine our organization and as we operate daily, we are living in the middle of those complexities as we provide services for immediate impact and for longer term supports to our clients. We do this while also being aware of and engaged in the complexities of systems change to help the organization with which we interact see their potential to better serve the people with whom they interact.

Partnerships and Public Impact

Questions in the *FATAE* allowed us to have a critical moment of reflection about a process that is deeply embedded in our year-to-year and day-to-day operations as a non-profit organization: fundraising. The questions helped us to take a step back and look at the process of fundraising itself, what our BSP strategies have been, and the systemic issues by which we as a non-profit, as well as other non-profit organizations, compete for resources. Since we pride ourselves as an organization driven by justice and equity, it is not enough to think solely about our services but to also explore how we as an organization are living out justice and equity in a system that can promote values or longstanding ideologies that promote existing inequitable practices and power dynamics.

As noted previously, the goals of a labor-management partnership around training typically focus on the relationship between workers and employers. As a labor-management convener, BSP fulfills that role in a unique way that not only centers partnership between labor and employers but requires us to think of broader intentional partnerships to create and support a holistic model of supportive services to workers. The need for and impact of partnerships begins with our funding. We previously described how the LTEF is a fundamental and anchoring partnership mechanism that drives programming and services, providing as much as 40% of BSP's operating budget. However, to support working families through a holistic multi-generational, multi-intervention model, we need to create and sustain partnerships beyond the LTEF whose primary focus has been advancing industry-led training solutions for the workforce. With a history of success and strong collaboration with the LTEF to expand its role beyond that of a traditional training fund, we have been able to leverage LTEF resources to pursue and sustain additional funding sources to develop and maintain our comprehensive, model initiatives.

Traditional funding models that many non-profits use do not work for us because of our unique set of circumstances and diverse stakeholders. Since the LTEF does not cover as much as 60% of our budget, we develop and maintain partnerships with private foundations as well as public agencies who understand and support our work and have a complementary mission and funding-initiative portfolio. We have, for example, a relationship with the James Irvine Foundation, whose goal is to have, "A California where all low-income workers have the power to advance economically." They are, because of that goal, developing a strategy for improving job quality and opportunities for workers in traditionally low-wage industries. They started by consulting with experts and field practitioners to inform where investments are needed and the mechanics of how funds can be best leveraged and deployed. BSP was excited and grateful to be part of the research process to provide our unique perspective.

The emerging partnership with the James Irvine Foundation is an example of a symbiotic partnership that supports both our aims and their aims. Similarly, BSP holds longstanding relationships with foundations such as the Silicon Valley Community Foundation, Sobrato Family Foundation, San Francisco Foundation, Siemer Institute, United Way of Greater Los Angeles and Bay Area, as well as UnidosUS. Also BSP holds strong relationships with public agencies such as the CWDB through their High Road Training Partnership, Employment Training Panel and Workforce Accelerator initiatives, and the Labor Workforce Development Agency (LWDA) to support key worker outreach. As an organization, we rely less on individual donors and corporate sponsors than many non-profits. Historically, our partnership with foundations has reflected a collaboration to innovate around BSP's unique set of stakeholders and truly build a comprehensive model of services to impact working families. Similarly, our work with these foundations often helps us develop a community of similar organizations through their connections. These connections allow us to build partnerships that amplify impact on BSP's target population.

While BSP does not fundraise from individual donors as much as traditional nonprofit organizations, what really sparked further conversations within our organization through the *FATAE* was the question of how we might be, "… perpetuating deficit-based ideologies of the people we serve and/or a purely economic framings of the problem." We have had significant initial discussions on this topic. Members of our leadership team have gone as far as to research the historical context for the term "workforce development" and its roots in deficit-based framing. Furthermore, the question has challenged us to think critically about how we can live out our justice and equity goals through our fundraising practices, specifically how we talk and market our programs and the people we serve, both internally and to external audiences. i.e., How do we drive narratives of opportunity, power, and allyship, as well as intentional asset-based language for our target population to disrupt traditional hegemonic narratives of "low-wage/low-income" workers and communities of color which we serve?

As we examined the questions asked by the *FATAE* around these kinds of funding partnerships, we were challenged to think critically about the relationship we hold with philanthropic partners and the philanthropic sector as a whole, as well as how that impacts the process of fundraising not only for us but in direct connection with other nonprofit organizations who share aligned missions to impact the target population we serve. Through this exercise, we acknowledged inherent issues that exist with the traditional funding model for non-profits that serve marginalized populations. As Hispanics in Philanthropy suggests, Latinx-led organizations receive less than 1% of all philanthropic giving in the U.S. (McAllister et al., 2011) Accessing even that limited, existing funding is both time and resource intensive. Funding sources also often demand aggressive competition that fosters what Vu Le, a leader in philanthropy and non-profit structures, calls a "Hunger Games" mentality among non-profits (Le, 2020). This current model of funding by the philanthropic sector inherently discourages increased collaboration among service providers. The model creates challenges for non-profits to amplify the impact of their work through partnership given the critical need for resources on a year-to-year basis. While those pressures to compete for limited resources continue to impact our work, we work toward a model that is collaborative. Our history of partnerships with foundations and collaboration with other service providers help us reflect about the relationship to funders as partners in our work while looking ahead at opportunities to further adopt community-centric, collaborative fundraising principles in our strategy and development practices.

As we went through this exercise and evaluated ourselves against the *FATAE*, what really stood out from the questions that examined "The Hidden Curriculum of Fundraising" was how those questions encouraged us to act more critically and intentionally about partnerships as a core component of our fundraising strategy and activities. We examined not only our role, but we were also able to reflect on the systemic issues that exist with traditional fundraising and how we could leverage our privilege as a healthy organization with diverse funding streams to further partnership and collaboration and move away from stark competition that prevents partnership-based fund raising. We started looking at the community-centric fundraising model which will be something we intentionally evaluate and include in our upcoming fundraising model.

Additionally, traditional funding sources foster a practice where grant applicants establish ambitious project goals within a limited grant term in order to compose the most competitive grant proposal and provide the most substantial return on investment for funders. This dynamic often leads to unrealistic impact measures for a limited timeframe or conversely simplistic measures that can be achieved and tracked within a grant term such as the number of participants served or the number of people who experience a wage increase, which is a traditional impact measure in workforce development. While these simple quantifications can be important and meaningful to evaluate service impact at face value, tackling deep-rooted, systemic issues while prioritizing a worker-centered, multigenerational impact model requires a nuanced approach to evaluation that centers equity and clients' multifaceted experiences. The long-term impacts that BSP programs and services seek to make in workers' lives through our holistic model include not just their own opportunities but also for their families and children – measures that take years to determine.

Similarly, systems-change work described above that BSP continues to conduct is both dynamic and fundamentally relies on partnerships with external agencies that often start with differing understandings, taking time to find alignment through ongoing communication, negotiation, and concession. Evaluating the short-term and long-term impact of this dynamic and time intensive work is both critical and the heart of the justice and equity focus of our work. However, it can be difficult to market nuanced and multiyear work to funders under the traditional funding practices; so we work strategically to have components of our work funded while looking toward how those components contribute to the whole. It is why we appreciate and value creating partnerships with our funders, like the James Irvine Foundation, which seek to create opportunities for non-profits to partner and work collaboratively over time. Because these funders are conducting their own explorations of what is required, they understand a more long-term approach, and they have been supportive of the work we conduct over time. Therefore, seeing funders as partners has been important to the growth and development of our central mission to serve workers holistically.

The *FATAE*'s questions about "Prospects and Partners" allowed our key BSP staff involved in fundraising to reflect on an aspect of fundraising that is not frequently discussed. BSP was happy to identify its unique fundraising model that is anchored by collective bargaining investment. Collective bargaining is a process that happens between SEIU-USWW, driven by elected worker representatives, as well as management representatives. Engaging those key stakeholders as we continuously evaluate priorities and as they continue to invest further into BSP, furthers BSP's mission and justice and equity goals as we have been able to work in partnership with these key stakeholders to do the work that benefits workers.

Also, how we tell our story has been important in our ability to develop partnerships while holding ourselves accountable to our mission and the working families it strives to impact. We continually ask ourselves to identify messages that best support our equity and justice goals internally and externally. Since improving the quality of life of property service workers in low-wage industries requires a multi-generational and systems change approach, we work to refine both the language we use and how we deliver our messages. Our biggest challenge is to shift from deficit to asset-based framing. We seek to intentionally and explicitly name the systemic barriers that contribute to the need for our work while elevating the strengths and opportunities our clients have through our collaborative engagement. As a starting place, property service work and the population that hold those jobs are often thought of as low-wage and low-skilled. Property service work exists across many places that we all inhabit, and it is often low paid. However, BSP operates under the fundamental premise that property service work is dignified work and both the workers and the work are not low-skilled.

As we went through the "Messaging" questions in the *FATAE*, we reflected on our key partnerships with funders and partners. What made those partners such strong partners and how have they played a key role in BSP's growth and successes furthering its mission and impact? It also surfaced the value we place on justice and equity specifically in those partnerships with specific funders and their notable support/alignment with our justice and equity goals to drive our work. Given the existing power dynamics that exist and the need to examine them constantly, these exercise will carry forward, challenging us to think critically about our funder partners and to strengthen our position of advocacy to the philanthropic sector to further our values of justice and equity, ideally incorporating more worker voice in that advocacy to that sector.

The gap between the perceptions of this work as low skilled and the resulting, historically low wages requires us to develop messages that communicate on many levels: How do we change a system that has created this perception? How do we bring together workers and employers to create that change? How can we work within existing systems to generate change? How can we bring together workers and management to think differently? On the labor side: How do you expand the role of labor beyond workplace to create opportunities for workers and their families to address their whole need? We increasingly see our role being to develop partnerships that extend beyond training and into advocacy for systemic change. The organization WorkRise, through its funding and partnerships, promotes the concept of 360° Social Determinants of Work (Workrise, 2021) – which include factors such as financial health, physical wellness, education, access to childcare, and more. WorkRise explores through research potential models and rationale to pursue a more holistic view of work and job quality. By growing partnerships, by working with field practitioners who align under such models while deepening investment, and by having partnerships with funders like the James Irvine Foundation, we are able to advocate for major changes as employers see how they can think differently about their employees.

The resulting outcomes of these funder and research organization partnerships continues to have ongoing impacts in our approach to convene and foster collaboration between labor and industry. We see increasing buy-in from employers and the industry as they actively move away from dated practices where employees are perceived and treated as interchangeable components of business. Instead, employers see a value in addressing employees' job quality, career growth, and broader economic and health security needs. Conversely, employees see their employer supporting and investing in them in a drastically different way. Both labor and management are learning to see their relationship as one of collaboration rather than of employer and asset.

BSP engaged with the *FATAE* as we are developing our own policy advocacy framework (Figure 5.2). Our review of the section of the *FATAE* that asked about "Reframing the Debate" allowed us to think further on our initial policy advocacy goals – not as an independent section of our work but embedded and in direct relationship to other facets of the organization explored through the *FATAE* and centered on its justice and equity values. BSP is

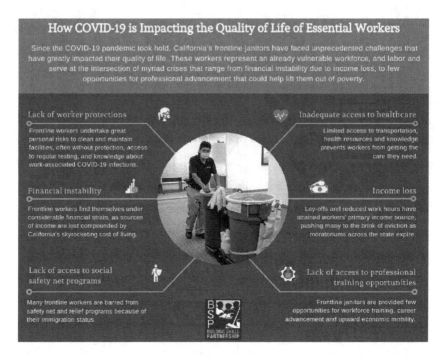

FIGURE 5.2 BSP's Just and Equitable Recovery Framework

setting out a bold and ambitious vision for its policy advocacy work. We do this while remaining aware of how to stay away from deficit-based framing. We also want to be sure our language accurately identifies the locus of the problem, so our solutions are aimed at root causes and don't inadvertently reinforce racist/sexist/etc. notions of individual deficiencies.

As BSP begins work in policy advocacy through questions that focus on "Strategies" in the *FATAE*, we have been able to reflect and identify audiences, existing partnerships, and networks that we will develop to move forward our policy advocacy work. Given BSP's strong partnerships, it is helpful for us to evaluate those partnerships and opportunities to leverage alignment to further our justice and equity aims as central to this work. Similarly, our work provides us an opportunity to identify where there is further engagement, education, and discussions with certain partners to both share and learn to find explicit alignment between our actions and our intentions.

BSP has traditionally prided itself on its unique partnership model as a core driver of its mission and impact. The questions in the *FATAE* that asked us to examine our "Reputation and Models" allowed us to reflect and think critically about those partnerships, anchored by our labor-management partnership through collective bargaining agreements, and expanded to a variety of community partnerships that contribute to BSP's ability to offer a comprehensive and holistic model of services to working families in California. While partnerships are a foundational to BSP as an organization, these questions also surfaced opportunities for BSP to consider how to create a more expansive strategic vision for partnerships.

As labor-management convener, BSP has been able to move perceptions as we have built trust by showing positive outcomes. In traditional practices, the property service industry has often been a race to the bottom where buildings and property-management companies conduct a contract proposal process for services that results in an underbidding race by janitorial contractors to make the lowest bid and win the contract. Those historic practices led employees to be exploited as employers sought to maximize profits on the thin margins that a low bid can sometimes bring. Now, in a competitive job market, employers need to show themselves as more attractive to potential employees. Having BSP programs is now a part of the pitch for some contractors as they bid for property service contracts. This can provide a counterforce to the race to the bottom and show value that investing in a trained workforce can have on the quality of services. Our partnerships with funders and research organizations allow us to create novel programs that are based in solid research. We can then show the efficacy of those programs to both labor and management to create long-term solutions that impact workers' lives.

Because BSP expanded to operate in both northern and southern California, we learned to be sensitive and adaptive to regional differences. As noted above, that helped us to formulate regional approaches that provide services to the widespread, high-tech campuses of Silicon Valley and also the high-rise buildings in Los Angeles, Orange and San Diego Counties, the East Bay, and Sacramento. In addition to the courses, workshops, and other trainings we offer, our flexibility has helped us allow for the kinds of partnerships and funding we develop within regions. For our Green Janitor Education Program and Infectious Disease Certification initiatives, for example, our funding allowed us to train instructors to teach the courses and for staff to provide some light case management so they could point workers to additional opportunities for further development.

In designing some of our workplace courses, we partnered with subject matter experts such as the UCLA Labor Occupational Safety and Health Program (LOSH), the UC Berkeley Labor Occupational Health Program (LOHP), the United States Green Building Council, Los Angeles, The Ashkin Group, and UX/UI design experts. These entities participated in program design consultation and provided notable third-party recognition to the resulting trainings and, thus, provided value recognized by the industry. For citizenship preparation classes, we work with local nonprofit legal service providers to provide support for students, including one-on-one consultations and application preparation services at little to no cost depending on funding availability. We also partnered with the U.S. Citizenship and Immigration Services to provide de-stress tours to help citizenship students reduce the stress of the interview by providing on-site tours to the USCIS offices to walk through what the process will look like during the day of the interview. For our Parent University initiative, which helps parents learn the skills they need to support their children in their education, the UCLA Labor Center and the work spearheaded by BSP Board Chair Janna Shadduck-Hernandez continues to bring their knowledge of schooling and parenting to help design and deliver the courses. We see these partnerships as critical to provide BSP with the authentication we need to do our work, but these partnerships are more than that. They allow us to leverage the knowledge and resources of partners who strengthen our efforts through their assistance and participation.

Our ability to adapt has brought us a new opportunity and significant expansion beyond working with property service workers. In 2015, we began working in a new sector as we expanded to serving workers at Los Angeles International Airport (LAX). The roughly 5,000 workers that are represented at LAX are different than the property service workers we have traditionally served. In addition to having different skills, the workers themselves are a different demographic but nonetheless have similar lived experiences with systemic challenges as BSP's traditional demographic. Whereas the majority of property service workers in California are immigrants from various Latin Spanish-speaking countries, LAX airport workers come from a rich blend of countries and continents. Additionally, the work they perform includes property maintenance, but it also includes other areas such as ticket checking, baggage handling, ramp services, and wheelchair attendants. We maintain our mission, but the mission expands to this new group and requires us to develop new partnerships that will help us address opportunities to serve a more linguistically diverse workforce, workers who perform more varied tasks, and the families of those workers.

As we conduct our work, there are areas where we see opportunities for further growth and development as an organization. We understand that the training and classes we offer have limitations. We want workers to use the training and skills that we provide as a starting point in their career development. We understand the concept of career latticing for adult learners – where adults can use one skill to obtain advancement and wage progression to a new plateau, similar to the Floor Care Certification we provide. That new stabilization can provide employees the opportunity to gain the next skill or certification. In California, certifications beyond what we offer are typically offered in adult schools, technical programs (like apprenticeships), and community colleges. We are now working on how to connect to the workforce programs in those systems so that someone completing the training and workshops that BSP offers will be able to use those as springboards for further opportunities as they stabilize at one level and seek the next level.

We began this chapter by describing BSP's history. Part of the history not fully described in the introduction is directly tied to the partnerships that BSP has had since its founding. It is worth explaining how critical our early partnerships were in establishing who we are and how we operate. Importantly, our evolution to become a holistic statewide organization that impacted workers and their families began from a survey of property service workers conducted by UCLA's Institute for Democracy, Education and Access. The resulting data from that survey emphasized the direction that BSP would make central to its work. The results showed that workers' most identified need was their children's education. This finding was critical because of the source: the workers themselves. Workers said that they wanted a focus on their children. While workers had only seen unions work on salary and benefits, their identified need was more comprehensive. They were asking for a step beyond the traditional labor union's role – a step that eventually led to training like BSP's Parent University and additional services. Thus, this early partnership continues to impact what we do and how we do it.

Because the survey was distributed widely, and because its findings were supported through a partnership of the union, employers, and a major research university, it has had an impact on how BSP shaped its programming. The emphasis on the family from that survey is the genesis of BSP's work as it has expanded statewide. Those efforts have also taken BSP into serving an aging population since property service workers often work well past what is considered retirement age in many jobs. That work, as an extension, led to a focus on health and wellness as we served people in their 50s and 60s. As we expanded our programs and grew statewide, we found a need to expand the partnerships that allow us to meet our mission of being a justice- and equity-based organization. BSP serves as an example of how labor, particularly SEIU-USWW and the Justice for Janitor movement, has been able to have an impact beyond social and economic justice. In our experiences, partnerships help us to make that case with both labor and with employers.

As BSP increased its footprint statewide early on, we needed to identify a unique message that would readily identify our unique mission to partners and potential partners. As we noted previously, in the beginning, workers often confused our work with that of the union early on because of the close relationship we have had with SEIU-USWW. That confusion often extended to funders and other partners and potential partners. With time, we have been able to refine our messaging to clarify our role between labor and employers. We also have worked extensively in the state in partnership with other organizations who now see what we do. At this point, our existing funders and project partners experience us as an organization that leverages its relationship to both labor and employers to achieve economic and social justice. They see that we offer multiple interventions that touch on social determinants of health for workers and families. Achieving that perception has taken time as we have built partnerships in industry, education, government, and labor. The most important trait we have learned to exhibit is a willingness to be equal partners in the work. We look for partners who share our intended mission, and we work alongside them. In brief, we always show up, and we always are willing to work.

As we are expanding beyond property service workers, our mission expands beyond predominantly Spanish-speaking immigrant workers to the airport workers at LAX. We now serve a larger range of communities. Workers from East African, African American, Filipino, and other communities have unique needs; and along with the increase in communities served, we see a need to evolve our programming to meet those needs. It is within partnerships that we can make this adjustment, so we are reaching out to the many organizations and agencies that already provide complementary support to these workers and their families. Moreover, our training efforts can help in workers' career latticing process if the people we serve can articulate the training they receive from us with training available through workforce development. Connecting the workers we serve to increased training opportunities is critical to these workers' career and wage advancement. Through partnerships like these, BSP works to elevate low-wage industries while we also offer workforce partners access to the people they seek to serve.

As we expand as an organization and as we seek out new partnerships, having a clear sense of our direction and mission has been critical. While partners now understand our unique role, organizations and people outside of these partnerships sometimes do not. It has been challenging for people outside of our work to see our separation from the union. At times, people outside of the union process have reached out requesting services. When we reply that we only work within bargaining agreements, we often hear that, "We thought your mission was to help janitorial workers. Why not reach out to non–union workers who have less? Why are you only focusing on commercial building employers?" The simple answer is the funding provided by the LTEF which is foundational to our start and our current work. However, the more complete answer is that our connection to bargained workers and employers is closely tied to our mission for justice and equity. The union exists because of past practices and exploitation. Our close ties and emphasis on bargained employees and employers contribute to breaking those historically exploitative, past practices. The union and the employers who have signed an agreement with the union have come to see our work as more than a provided service. They are engaged in a reimagining of the industry in a way that allows BSP to support the equitable and just needs of the communities it serves.

The connection to bargained employees and employers also can create geographic boundaries. In Los Angeles, for example, the Pico Union area and along the 110 Corridor have long held large populations of union property service workers living there. While these families work in wealthier areas, they live in these lower-income sections of greater Los Angeles. That geographic intensity of workers was a deciding factor on where SEIU-USWW would have its office in the Los Angeles region, and, as a result, where BSP would operate in order to offer services near a large number of workers' homes. It is important to note that having our classes in communities closer to where workers live means that BSP impacts those specific communities. At times, though, it is impossible to exclude community members who are not union members. For example, we offered ESL classes in partnership with a local community college, at the BSP office in Los Angeles, a location where workers could attend easily during the day. However, word spread about the classes and people walked in and asked to participate in the classes. Being in a community meant that we could not turn people away. Rather than excluding nearby community residents, we decided to open some of our classes, depending on our funding restrictions and the type of service, to the surrounding communities. More recently, as we developed virtual classes because of the pandemic, that has created a new question that we are resolving as we now operate in a borderless medium.

It is also challenging when existing key partners want to expand beyond our target group. As suggested above, we have four levels of partnerships: unions, employers, external agencies, and community-based organizations. Because of their broader missions, external agencies sometimes want to extend our shared work into other target groups beyond our core population. We often have to patiently explain to external agencies why we choose to remain focused, and most understand. In contrast, our work with community groups is typically more clearly defined without any pressures to expand. Our work with community-based organizations generates shared projects where we either co-create the project or divide the work between our agencies. A good example is our partnership with the Coalition for Humane Immigrant Rights (CHIRLA) where we partner in offering citizenship and naturalization services to our membership base. BSP offers classes and preparation for the naturalization test, and CHIRLA staff use their legal expertise to provide participants help with the lengthy and complicated naturalization application. The result of these partnership is a valuable advantage for working families who are union members.

It has been important for us to seek and develop partnerships that help us emphasize our core mission as we serve union members and employers/building managers. That gives BSP a clear focus that allows us to succeed at what we intend. The positive outcome of that has been a strong set of funders and project partners who are willing to invest because they understand our purpose and can work alongside us as we meet that mission. The downside is that some funders or agencies with whom we partner can want an expansion that is not consistent with our core mission. However, keeping our focus has been important as we have developed customized and tailored programs that are succeeding at meeting the needs of the workers we serve.

References

Hannon, G., Covington, M., Despard, M., Frank-Miller, E., & Grinstein-Weiss, M. (2017). *Employee Financial Wellness Programs: A review of the literature and directions for future research*. Retrieved from: https://openscholarship.wustl.edu/cgi/viewcontent. cgi?article=1595&context=csd_research

Le, V. (2020). Vu Le on Ending the Nonprofit Hunger Games. *Skoll Foundation*. Retrieved from: https://skoll.org/2020/01/09/vu-le-on-ending-the-nonprofit-hunger-games/

McAllister, G., Mukai, R., & Shah, S. (2011). *Foundation Funding for Hispanics/Latinos in the United States and for Latin America* Retrieved from: https://candid.issuelab. org/resource/foundation-funding-for-hispanics-latinos-in-the-united-states-and-for-latin-america.html

Murray, B. (2022). L.A.'s Labor Movement Goes Back to the Future with Ambitious 'People's Project'. *Capital & Main*. Retrieved from: https://capitalandmain.com/ l-a-s-labor-movement-goes-back-to-the-future-with-ambitious-peoples-project

Terriquez, V., Rogers, J., Blasi, G., Hernandez, J. S., & Appelbaum, L. D. (2009). *Unions and Education Justice: The Case of SEIU Local 1877 Janitors and the "Parent University"*. Retrieved from: https://irle.ucla.edu/wp-content/uploads/2016/03/ ResearchBrief3.pdf

WorkRise (2021). *Bold Ideas for Transforming the Labor Market: Request for Proposal*. Retrieved from: https://www.workrisenetwork.org/bold-ideas-transforming-labor-market-workrise-2021-request-proposals

6

SAINT MARY'S COLLEGE BALOS/GLD

The Water in Which We Swim

Stacey Robbins and Marguerite Welch

Introduction

The authors of this chapter direct two degree-granting programs serving mid-career adult learners in a private Catholic liberal arts institution of higher education. The programs are a Bachelor of Arts (BA) in Leadership and Organizational Studies (BALOS), an undergraduate degree completion program, and a Masters (MA) in Leadership (commonly referred to as GLD for Graduate Leadership). The BALOS program often serves as a pathway for its graduates to then complete the GLD program. For this reason, we approached this project with the intent of examining both. These programs are well aligned with the mission of Saint Mary's College of California (SMC), "that education is a vehicle for transformative leadership and social justice" (https://www.stmarys-ca.edu/academics).

As authors of this chapter and primary program faculty, we begin by acknowledging our privilege and positionality as it may have played out in the gathering and presentation of information on strengths, challenges, and opportunities of how the principles of equity, access, justice, and inclusion are reflected in the BALOS and GLD programs. At the heart of our work are the learners we serve, adult learners with significant work experience. They are often juggling multiple commitments between their families, jobs, and school. Returning to school represents a deep commitment to learning and personal growth and is not undertaken lightly.

While we come to this work with similar commitments to adult learning and the transformative potential of higher education, we arrived at this work at different points in our respective careers. New to SMC in 2020, Stacey brings a focus on adult learning and leadership to her role as director of the

DOI: 10.4324/9781003286998-6

BA completion program. As a pre-tenure ranked faculty member, she notes her relative privilege with the system. As a White woman, she notes the challenge of serving diverse learners while engaging in her own antiracist development. Marguerite joined the faculty of the MA in Leadership program in 2003 and has held administrative responsibilities since 2008. She is a salaried adjunct faculty member, a role that is outside the rank and tenure, faculty structure. A White woman also, Marguerite embraces critical humility (ECCW, 2010), a practice that "embodies a delicate and demanding balance of speaking out for social justice while at the same time remaining aware that our knowledge is partial and evolving" (p. 147).

We note the inequity in the rank of faculty in higher education, a hierarchical system that privileges ranked faculty (those on the "tenure track") over salaried adjunct faculty and per-course adjunct instructors. Based on this hierarchy and length of tenure for ranked faculty, faculty workloads, service responsibilities, job security, and benefits are determined. As program directors, we are guided by our service to our learners and to the faculty in our programs. However, university systems are rigid, hierarchical, and designed to serve traditional undergraduates (typically 18–22 years old, full-time students); as a result, there are limits to how well we can serve our diverse adult learners and the faculty who instruct them.

We chose to undertake this self-study to better understand how well the existing programs are serving the needs of our diverse adult learners. We sought a deeper understanding of the strengths of the programs and awareness of the areas in which the programs needed to continue to evolve to meet our learners' changing needs and build leadership capacity for our increasingly global and interdependent society. We endeavored to better understand the areas that we, as program directors, have the most control over - teaching and learning, and faculty and staff - while also paying attention to the ways in which hierarchy, budgets, systems and processes, and resistance to change impact our ability to serve our diverse adult learners well.

As we work to best serve our learners, we recognize that educational systems are structured for people like us – White middle-class, educated. We note our understanding of how educational systems work given our experiences as undergraduate and graduate learners and our roles within higher education for a combined 30 years. We endeavor to continually question how these systems impact learners in our programs while also using our positions and identities within the system to advocate effectively for our programs and our learners. This tension invites us to use what we know to navigate the system to challenge it, as well as help our learners navigate the system in its current form. One aspect of the system that contributes to challenges for our learners, and us, is the "default" in campus-wide functions to the traditional, undergraduate. Registrar, Financial Aid, and Business offices are not open on the weekends or evenings when our learners are on campus, requiring them to take time from their work to attend to routine tasks. The various forms to complete some of these tasks are also designed with traditional undergraduates in mind. A few years ago, the Graduate and Professional Student Handbook was eliminated and the policies pertaining to graduate and professional students were tacked on to the end of the SMC Student Handbook, which requires graduate and professional students to sort through pages of policies that do not pertain to them.

We experience tension as we push for necessary change, learn what challenges the system will bear, and protect our individual interests. As we do so, we are guided by our values of holding discomfort between our espoused theories and our theories in action, acting with critical humility and an ethic of care. A shared value is supporting adult learners in ways that are meaningful for them, which is operationalized by offering predictability for students so that they can plan around their multiple responsibilities. Aligned with our ethic of care, we strive to meet learners where they are and provide flexibility when necessary. In striving to provide predictability and flexibility, we meet resistance to extending term dates to include weekends, when adult learners are able to come to campus. Building and maintaining positive working relationships among faculty is particularly important to pre-tenured faculty needing colleagues' support for tenure and promotion. This illustrates the tension between advocating for adult learners and protecting one's job security; we have limited social capital and thus need to use it judiciously.

We focused our self-study primarily on two areas of the *Framework for Assessment and Transformation in Adult Education* that as Program Directors, are within our domain of influence: Teaching and Learning, and Instructors and Staff. The individuals we serve – learners and faculty – are our north stars; their needs drive our decisions. As we finished the self-study, we returned to the first section of the framework: Governance and Finance to help us understand how broader institutional factors impact our learners and faculty. As is the case for many institutions of higher education, these are challenging times. Enrollments are declining at the traditional undergraduate level due to demographic shifts. While in the past economic uncertainty has resulted in increases in graduate and professional enrollment, this has not been the case as the COVID pandemic continues to unfold. Institutional stakeholders in higher education face many competing priorities for resources, and SMC is experiencing the same pressures. Toward the end of the chapter, we explore the need for influence at the institutional level to ensure the sustainability of our programs.

Serving Adult Learners in Higher Education

Our programs have a strong foundation for serving adult learners; we understand how their needs are different from those of traditional undergraduate learners. According to the American Council on Education, "Post-traditional learners are students who frequently must balance life, work, and their education.

These students are typically ages 25 and older, care for dependents, and work full time while enrolled" (Soares et al., 2017, p. 1). As working adults with multiple responsibilities, post-traditional learners need flexibility, access, and community. Adult learners benefit from funding for college programs, dedicated campus departments to serve adult learners (with focus on scholarships, child-care services, and academic and career advising), credit for prior learning experiences, and flexible scheduling (Bresnick, 2021; MacDonald, 2018). Our programs improve access and flexibility by utilizing a blended learning format with in-person classes on weekends and asynchronous online discussions and activities between the in-person weekends. To build community to support learners through challenging times and to further develop their leadership and collaborative skills, they move through the program as a cohort, developing deep bonds with their peers.

According to the National Center for Education Statistics (NCES), in 2019 nearly 33.3% of learners enrolled in postsecondary institutions were adults over the age of 25. Projections have the over-25 population increasing to 34.9% by 2030. Given changing demographics and hand wringing about the so-called "enrollment cliff" in which a decline in the U.S. birth rate will lead to a smaller pool of college-aged learners that will reach its peak sometime around 2025 or 2026 (Kline, 2019), it is time for higher education professionals to acknowledge that adult learners will make up a greater percentage of learners in the years to come. It is time to stop referring to adult learners as "non-traditional" and acknowledge the importance of adult serving programs on our campuses. Adult learners in higher education are also becoming more diverse, reflecting the gaps in bachelor's degree achievement by race/ethnicity. While nearly 60% of Asians and 42% of Whites have completed a bachelor's degree or higher, as compared to 27% of Blacks and 19% of Hispanics and Native Americans (Brock & Slater, 2021). Clearly there are populations that higher education could serve that it has not yet succeeded in serving, and a diverse adult learning population is one of those groups. Designing and implementing adult programs that serve diverse learners in equitable and just ways is of increasing importance.

The adult-serving programs we direct are deeply aligned with the College's social justice mission to serve "learners, faculty, administrators and staff from different social, economic and cultural backgrounds" (https://www.stmarys-ca.edu/about-smc/our-mission). However, as an institution, SMC was designed to serve "traditional" undergraduates – learners attending full time, typically aged 18–22 years. As faculty and staff promoting and supporting the BALOS and GLD programs, we find ourselves in conflict with the systems and processes designed to serve "traditional" undergraduate learners in ways that do not accommodate our audience of adult learners. Calendars for traditional students will often include a summer break, while adult learners benefit from year-around courses to keep momentum and allow them to attain their educational goals as efficiently as possible. College-wide communications sent to all learners assume they are "traditional" undergraduates. As a result, these messages often contain inaccurate and confusing information for adult learners. Campus offices are closed after 5 PM and on weekends, and campus services are unavailable or limited on evenings and weekends. The lack of access to these student services degrade adult learners' sense of being a valued part of the campus community.

The Water in Which We Swim

Vision and Goals

Established in 1863, SMC is grounded in the life and work of Saint John Baptist de La Salle, the 17th Century founder of the Christian Brothers. It is one of six Lasallian colleges in the United States. The institution moved to its present location in Moraga, California in 1928. SMC has a long history of service to adult learners. The College created the School for Extended Education (SEED) in 1975. For many years SEED operated satellite campuses around the San Francisco Bay Area to bring classes closer to learners, offering four B.A. completion programs and starting in 2002, the hybrid M.A. in Leadership program. The SEED programs closely aligned with the College's mission:

> [Saint Mary's] College seeks learners, faculty, administrators, and staff from different social, economic, and cultural backgrounds who come together to grow in knowledge, wisdom and love … A distinctive mark of a Lasallian school is its awareness of the consequences of economic and social injustice and its commitment to the poor. (https://www.stmarys-ca.edu/about-smc/our-mission)

The early 2000s were a tumultuous time for SEED. There was a rapid expansion in terms of students, staffing, programs, and outreach. This expansion included the addition of new locations closer to the learners. While aligned with the Lasallian core principles, the expansion and increased visibility faced resistance from traditional undergraduate programs, challenging the rigor of degree completion programs for adult learners and expressing concern that the degree completion programs devalued the traditional undergraduate degree. Finally, the expansion was deemed financially unsustainable and in 2005, SMC made the difficult decision to close SEED. While some programs moved to "teach-out" status, the M.A. in Leadership and the degree completion program for professional dancers were moved to the School of Liberal Arts (SOLA). Building on the BA in Management degree completion program that ended with the closure of SEED, the BALOS program started in 2009 as a hybrid program.

During this time, program directors had significant autonomy in how to run the programs in ways that were innovative and nimble. This autonomy included budgetary responsibility, decisions about how to market the programs and recruit students, deeply collaborative engagement between faculty and staff, and a collaborative teaching model. We established internal systems for supporting our learners, necessary to interact effectively with the college-wide systems; some examples are clear instructions to learners about timing and processes to register for courses and ensuring appropriate classroom assignments.

Since 2015 the GLD and BALOS programs have been housed in the Leadership Department of the Kalmanovitz School of Education (KSOE). This move was precipitated by a SMC initiative to better align like programs, and we joined three existing leadership programs. This integrated the BALOS and GLD programs into a larger system, and program directors had less control and influence over the budget, recruitment, marketing, and program administration of the programs.

While the programs' goals and mission did not change, the additional layers of administrative approvals and corresponding lack of influence left program directors and faculty feeling like a square peg being pounded into a round hole. While the programs shared a focus on leadership through the lens of equity and justice, the college level recruitment processes did not always meet the unique enrollment challenges and opportunities for programs without a "typical" student profile, as learners come from different professional sectors. With smaller cohorts of learners, programs have had fewer resources available to serve learners and carry out the program's mission.

Additional administrative layers also meant that decisions were made further away from the people and programs that were impacted by the decisions. A recent example is the decision by college level administrators to eliminate the trimester calendar that our programs were using, which required us to transition to a new calendar in less than a year and with approvals at the department, school, college, provost, and accreditation body levels.

While the administrative challenges we face are daunting, it is important to highlight the alignment between the mission and vision for our programs and the mission, vision, and goals of the College, as noted above, and the KSOE.

KSOE Vision

KSOE is committed to fostering an accessible, student-centered learning community that co-creates a transformative education, welcoming learners of all backgrounds. Our graduates will become visionary leaders in their respective fields, guided by our shared Lasallian values of social justice, respect for all persons, and quality education to create a more just and equitable world.

KSOE Goals

- Academic and education excellence through transformative learning.
- Diversity equity inclusion and belonging (DEIB), advancing racial justice equity.
- Leadership as Lasallian educators.

The KSOE vision and goals inform the equity and justice focus of school-wide retreats. Additionally, faculty have participated in internal training on trauma informed pedagogy and anti-racist pedagogy by faculty experts as well as external training with Kevin Kumashiro's Leading for Justice program.

The Leadership Department is one of three departments within the KSOE, which is one of four schools within SMC. There are other SMC systems that set and administer policies that impact learners and faculty, including the registrar, financial aid, human resources, and academic affairs, along with a wide variety of faculty committees and task forces.

We are faculty with the additional responsibility of program administration. This encompasses oversight of the academics of the program, other faculty, health of the program, student experience, and administrative processes to ensure smooth functioning. We collaborate with other faculty on changes to curriculum and shepherd curricular revisions through the KSOE and College approval processes. We ensure that all courses are appropriately staffed, and that faculty are supported in their teaching. We are the primary point of contact for learners from enrollment through to graduation.

As the primary contact for learners, we work with them to address challenges of being an adult learner (balancing school with other responsibilities, re-entry into academia). The Enrollment and Student Services department within the KSOE was established in 2020 to centralize the activities related to supporting learners in navigating the SMC systems related to being a student, from signing up for email to registering for classes to applying for commencement. They have approached this work with an orientation toward self-sufficiency, creating a guide and forms for learners to take care of these tasks independently. This works well for many learners for routine tasks; however, it does not work as well for learners who have non-routine needs, such as changing to a new cohort or returning to complete their capstone leadership project. The Marketing and Admissions department promotes the KSOE programs to the public through a variety of activities to generate interest in the programs. We participate in information sessions, make one-on-one calls with prospects, attend recruiting events, and interview prospective learners. We interface with the Associate Dean's office for issues related to faculty, from hiring to workloads to retirements. With a large number of part-time faculty, there are often courses that need to be posted during the year; this involves writing the posting description, reviewing applicants, and making the hiring recommendation.

The various streams within which we swim have varying flow rates, lots of eddies, and often standing waves – sometimes it feels like we are in class IV waters! Some of the turbulence SMC is currently experiencing is related to the national trend of declining enrollments, which the College is experiencing across both undergraduate and graduate programs, exacerbated by the COVID-19 pandemic. With a new president (July 2021) and a new provost (February 2022), along with other changes in leadership positions, the College is working to better align programs with needs of the learners we serve. We are encouraged by our new provost's belief that innovative organizations understand that it is essential to maintain a strong focus on diversity and inclusion, and his recognition that it takes time and intentionality to develop diverse, inclusive teams.

Leadership Education

Our programs are well-aligned with the KSOE vision and the goals. The common elements of the missions of the programs are to provide a quality state-of-the-art transformative education in leadership to enhance the capacity of people to address the challenges and opportunities of today's global and interdependent world more effectively. Given that our world is characterized by high degrees of complexity, uncertainty, and turbulent change, we focus on developing a full spectrum of competencies and intelligences required for facilitating meaningful change in work and lives of our learners.

Because leadership works through relationships, inclusiveness is vital in effective leadership – not just because the dignity of all individuals deserve respect, but because diverse perspectives are essential in addressing today's complex problems, which, as the saying often attributed to Albert Einstein notes, cannot be solved with the kind of thinking that created them. Consequently, we seek diverse perspectives from learners, staff, and faculty to inform both the curriculum and administration of our programs. Yorks and Kasl (2002) "use the concept of learning-within-relationship to describe the importance of … theorizing [about phenomenological understanding of experience] for practice, especially for learning events where groups of learners bring highly diverse (and potentially divisive) lived experience to the learning setting" (p. 177). Furthermore, the critical reflection prompted by engaging diverse perspectives fosters transformative learning.

We establish a focus on the value of diverse perspectives early in students' experiences in our programs through practicing discussion as dialogue that seeks to understand other perspectives, in a respectful environment, rather than defending one's own perspective while attacking others.' This is done in a number of ways throughout the programs. As the cohorts are forming in the first course, they create a set of community agreements, which are revisited and revised throughout the programs. The activities in the first course include theoretical grounding and practice with critical thinking. We ask the learners to use a critical thinking model to reflect on their decision to return to school. In the cross-cultural capacity course, which is mid-way through the program, learners write their "cultural bio" – a document that asks learners reflect on and write about:

- How did the time (era/decade) and your social environment (family, community, education, class, religion, politics, language, geography, etc.) affect your patterns of thinking, behaviors, values, assumptions, and beliefs?
- What were the meaningful events or transformative experiences that changed your sense of self in relation to others, and/or your view of the world?
- What has most contributed to shaping the lenses through which you see reality?

The cultural bios are posted and others in the cohort read and respond to them. This is an assignment that learners are still talking about at the end of the program, noting how the bios deepened their connections to one another. While these are examples of assignments that encourage learners to engage diverse perspectives, the faculty facilitation, thought modeling and evocative questioning, is critical to the success of these activities. Valuing diverse perspectives is an essential element of adaptive leadership and effective organizational practice, which are at the heart of our curriculum.

Our Learners

Learners who come to our programs are diverse in many ways, including their professions, ethnicity, race, gender, gender expression, sexual orientation, and religion. They work in a wide variety of professions with about 20% in the field of public safety (law enforcement, fire service), and others from non-profits organizations, health care, education, and private sector organizations. Their average age is late-30s to mid-40s, with some in their 20s and others in their 60s. Many are from historically marginalized groups; our cohorts are typically 70–80% BIPOC and 20–30% white. Many have partners or children at home and/or are caregiving for elders.

Learners in our program arrive with a pre-existing desire to further their education, many in the hopes of advancing in their careers or embarking on a new career, and most of all to enhance their capacity to make the world better. Because of their historic mission and reputation, SMC and these programs attract learners who are committed to justice and equity. Learners graduate with a clearer sense of who they are and how they want to live their lives. Through coursework and program experiences, they have questioned and reflected on their lived experience in the context of leadership theories and research synthesis and application. They have identified their personal values and developed plans for their personal development.

Whole Person Learning

Leadership education emphasizes understanding the whole person. The cohort model creates a collaborative, learner-centered educational community whose members support one another with mutual understanding and respect. This starts in the first course of the programs where the learners establish their community agreements. These agreements are reviewed and revised regularly throughout the program and serve as a touchpoint when conflict arises.

The emphasis on the whole person is integral to the Lasallian core principles that guide our institution. These principles require that we attend to the intersecting spheres and dimensions of all persons' (learners, staff, and faculty) identities and lives. This is done through building communities that defend the goodness, dignity, and freedom of each person, and fosters sensitivity to social and ethical concerns (https://www.stmarys-ca.edu/about-smc/our-mission).

Our capacity for learner-centered educational communities was evident in our smooth transition to remote learning during the COVID-19 pandemic. We sought input from learners as we created adaptive models for remote and hybrid classes. In addition to the system support, the work we had done with our cohorts to create strong communities was evident during the pandemic and beyond. At the conclusion of a course we recently taught together, learners commented about support and mutual respect:

> There were times I assumed we were running out of time and feared we wouldn't get everything done in time. My assumption was incorrect because we all supported each other by offering assistance to other groups which allowed us to complete the project on time.

> With everyone stepping up, getting involved, and checking in with each other to see where help was needed. I continue to be grateful for how supportive and respectful our cohort has been during this program, cheering each other on throughout.

Both programs are structured as hybrid programs, with weekend in-person meetings (three per term) and weekly asynchronous online work between the weekend meetings. This gives learners the flexibility they need to pursue their education while working. A degree in leadership has broad applicability regardless of their career path. Although they have less-expensive choices, they choose to come to SMC because of its reputation and because the College's programs for working adults are recommended to them by bosses and co-workers, friends, and relatives (60% of learners are alumni referrals).

Integrated into our curriculum are pedagogical approaches that ground learners' learning in their lived experiences and expand their capacity for transformative change. The program rests on a foundation of on-going inquiry of students' assumptions and values, and on engaging a diversity of perspectives and values of others. This inquiry takes place in response to various readings and learning activities, and by interacting with other cohort members both online and during in-person meetings. We purposely attend to and develop effective communication and relational skills that increase learners' capacities for engaging others in authentic and respectful ways. Furthermore, we seek to involve the whole person through employing multiple ways of knowing. We look for a synthesis through recognition of deep personal introspection, an improved knowledge of self, and the enhanced ability to understand others in daily behaviors in the world.

Throughout the program, learners are questioning their own value systems and those of the organizations with which they are associated. They are encouraged to express themselves precisely, eloquently, and intellectually about values, truth, reality, leadership, etc., as these are made manifest in their lives. Furthermore, learners identify, define, and understand a framework of values, and the associated skills and behaviors that serve to support choices as they embrace their practice of Leadership practices. Toward the end of the program, we often hear comments such as "you have no idea how much this program has changed my life" (Student, Cohort 5).

Self-Study Methodology

The two degree programs at Saint Mary's College School of Education – the B.A. in Leadership and Organizational Studies (BALOS) and the MA in Leadership (GLD) – conducted a comprehensive study of their systems and practices based on the *Framework for Assessment and Transformation in Adult Education (FATAE)* for the purpose of noting the strengths of our programs in serving diverse adult learners and acknowledging areas for continued growth and improvement.

According to the Center for Equity in Learning, "Opportunities and obstacles for working learners are gaining increasing attention in conversations around education and equity" (Kyte, 2017, p. 10). While accessibility has improved, barriers still exist for some populations; many educational organizations that serve adults are challenged to be successful in serving all populations. The Organisation for Economic Co-operation and Development (OECD) reports that "Education plays a key role in providing individuals with the knowledge, skills, and competences needed to participate effectively in society and in the economy. In addition, education may improve people's lives in such areas as health, civic participation, political interest, and happiness" (OECD, n.d.). We need models to learn how to equitably support and include all learners. We explored whether and how the BALOS and GLD programs provide support and systems that ensure access, inclusion, and progress that serve the needs of diverse adult learners.

The questions that guided our inquiry are the following:

1. To what extent do the programs incorporate a justice and equity framework in the curriculum and administration of the program?
2. How well do our programs serve diverse populations of adult learners?

This analysis was undertaken using the *FATAE*. This framework's original purpose – to support leaders of colleges of education in centering justice and equity in their leadership decision making – makes it highly applicable to our adult serving higher education programs. The *FATAE* has four key areas: Governance and Finance, Teaching and Learning, Instructors and Staff, and Partnerships and Public Impact.

Given our domains of influence as program directors and faculty, we focused our analysis on (1) Teaching and Learning and (2) Instructors and Staff. However, decisions in all four areas strongly impact on the success of adult serving programs and our ability to meet our highest aspirations to serve diverse learners while building thriving and sustainable programs. In the next sections, we will focus on the areas within our domain of influence. We will return to the remaining frames — Governance and Finance, and Partnership and Public Impact — and consider how decisions made in these domains impact our ability to center justice and equity and meet the needs of our diverse learners.

To help us avoid bias when studying programs for which we are responsible, we partnered with learners in a doctoral level research course to assist in the collection and analysis of data. First, in partnership with the doctoral students, we highlighted the most salient areas of the framework for our inquiry – teaching and learning, and instructors and staff. Next, within those areas we focused on two priority areas in Teaching and Learning (i.e., "Strengthening our Programs and Curriculum" and "Supporting Our Students) and two areas in Instructors and Staff (i.e., "Increasing the Racial Diversity of Our Instructors" and "Supporting Our Instructors"). These were chosen because of the direct alignment to the responsibilities of Program Directors. Finally, we used the "Questions for Assessing and Action Planning" to develop survey and interview/focus group questions appropriate to the experience of our audiences of alumni and faculty.

For example, the "Strengthening Our Programs and Curriculum" priority area encouraged us to explore how our instructors could "more substantively explore and draw on the scholarship and models developed by colleagues across the country and world about how to center justice and equity in our programs and curriculum." Survey questions assessing these areas asked how well "The program curriculum offered a multicultural approach to leadership, offered opportunities to examine my own biases, prepared me to lead diverse communities, explored a variety of leadership theories that represented many cultures and perspectives, employed resources (e.g., texts, videos, etc.) from a diverse set of authors, and has social justice woven throughout each class." Surveys were developed from these prompts and distributed to our graduates to understand how they experienced the instructors, curriculum, student services, and accessibility of the programs. Surveys were distributed electronically to graduates of the programs within the last ten years.

Similarly, we used the questions in the framework from the Instructors and Staff domain to develop interview and focus group questions for program faculty. Examples of questions included: In what ways does the program incorporate justice and equity into the curriculum? In what ways does the program align with the Lasallian principles? Which one of these principles does your pedagogy align with? Why? Social justice was at the forefront for many students; to what extent did you discuss these social justice issues – especially around justice and equity – with students in your classes? Part-time and full-time program faculty were invited to participate in interviews and focus groups to better understand faculty experience. Faculty interviews provided insight into how faculty of various rankings and positionalities experienced working in these programs. We note here that our full-time faculty are not representative of the racial and ethnic diversity of our learners. Part-time faculty are more representative of our learners with respect to race.

Teaching and Learning

To better understand how well our programs center learning and teaching for justice and equity, we focused on two, main priority areas within the *FATAE*: (1) curriculum and (2) student support. We selected these two areas because they are both our responsibilities as programs directors and domains in which we have some capacity to influence outcomes. To better understand how well our curriculum serves diverse adult learners, we explored how well our work was situated in broader movements for justice and equity, collaborative, and collective processes for learning and teaching, use of existing justice and equity models, and availability and utilization of resources. In our analysis of student support, we considered who our learners are, how the diversity of our student population is related to our mission and strategic plans, pathways through our program, and financial burdens and supports.

To gain insight into these areas, alumni of the programs participated in a survey with both closed- and open-ended questions, and instructors in the programs participated in interviews and focus groups conducted by the doctoral students not connected to the two programs. Survey data were analyzed using descriptive statistics and interview and focus groups were recorded, transcribed, and analyzed for themes. Overall, we examined the data to better understand strengths and opportunities for improvement.

Our Learners

The percentage of adults aged 25 and older nationally who completed some college but had not earned a degree in 2016 was highest for American Indian/ Alaska Native adults (26%) followed by 25% each for adults of two or more races, Pacific Islander adults, and Black adults. Among the other racial/ethnic groups, 21% of White adults, 18% of Hispanic adults, and 12% of Asian adults had completed some college but had not earned a degree (2016 https:// nces.ed.gov/). The need for degree completion programs is significant but these programs vary in how successful they are in supporting students to achieve their goal of graduation. Private 4-year institutions, such as ours, are more successful with rates of completion around 60% (2016 https://nces. ed.gov/). The B.A. completion program at our institution boasts an even higher completion rate of 90%. Our data indicated this rate was achieved in part due to the ability of our learners to transfer previous experiences and academic credits courses from other work/educational institutions. This offers a faster and cheaper route to degree completion and acknowledges the educational value of these experiences. Student data indicated that in both programs instructors engage with learners flexibly, acknowledging the unique needs of adult learners with multiple responsibilities; this allows learners to continue their studies through challenging times both individually and collectively, such as the coronavirus pandemic.

Program Strengths

Data indicated strengths of the program included our cohort and community-based approaches to learning, acknowledgment of prior learning toward degree completion, and access to diverse perspectives. Each of these is addressed in more detail below.

Cohort and Community-Based Learning

Learners and faculty noted the richness of the cohort-based learning experience. Not only are learners able to build meaningful, supportive relationships with peers but they are also able to build on their collaborative, leadership, and teaming skills in real time. In this way, the classroom becomes a laboratory to apply the theories, skills, and tools to their experience working on collaborative team projects and consulting to a community-based organization on real organizational challenges.

Acknowledgment of Prior Learning toward Degree Completion

Learners noted the importance of acknowledgement of prior learning toward degree completion. Learners bring to the programs a variety of lived experiences in the academic and professional realms that are relevant to higher education. Honoring those experiences is multifaceted. In the degree completion program, learners submit transcripts from previously attended higher education institutions, certificated professional development courses, and prior learning essays to demonstrate competency in college courses and earn upper division units. These options provide students credit for learning both in and beyond college courses. Learners also bring personal and professional experiences that deepen the cohort's learning; faculty recognize and validate the knowledge, skills, and experience that learners bring to the classroom.

Access to Diverse Perspectives

Student feedback highlighted how our instructors held space for learners who were diverse with respect to race, ethnicity, age, profession, and socioeconomic status to share their experiences on various classroom topics, which resulted in rich discussion; however, these discussions were not necessarily enriched by course materials or course instructors (an opportunity to address in the future!). But, rather, the unique experiences of the learners guided the social justice and equity threads in class discussion. Faculty noted that learners in the program had become increasingly more diverse over the past 20 years.

Opportunities for Improvement

While learners and faculty noted several program strengths including the community of learners created in the programs, the opportunity to meaningfully engage across differences, and acknowledgement of the needs and experience of adult learners, they also offered insight into how the program could better serve diverse adult learners. Their recommendations are grouped into four areas: student centered leadership model, curricular materials, faculty and training, and financial support to improve access and retention.

Student Centered Leadership Model

Learners perceived diversity to be a program value that is shared by the program director, instructors, and learners and embodied by the focus on collaborative learning and projects with community partners. To further center justice and equity, they suggested the program should embrace a dynamic, student-centered leadership model by using a diverse leadership team of instructors, community members, and learners to develop a stronger curriculum with equity, diversity, and justice at its core.

Curricular Materials

Learners and instructors noted that course texts needed to be updated to reflect the student body as well as leadership frameworks centering justice, equity, and inclusion. While some instructors made explicit connections to current events, including the global coronavirus pandemic, protests about racial injustice and police brutality, and climate change, and connected these to leadership challenges facing justice-focused leaders, many failed to connect theory and leadership frameworks to current events.

Faculty and Training

Our self-study revealed differences in the faculty and training for each of the programs. In one program, faculty have remained less diverse than learners and are overrepresented by White women. Adjunct faculty members are hired based on a collective bargaining agreement, which privileges years of teaching and experience with the specific course over representativeness of diverse racial or ethnic backgrounds. However, the other program's per-course adjunct instructors who co-teach with full time program faculty are more representative of the learners. We attribute this to the particular focus on diversity and representativeness in recruiting and hiring per-course faculty.

We also note differences in faculty preparedness and training across the programs. While some faculty noted a lack of training in working with diverse student groups, others noted the importance of the co-learning they did as faculty to support their development of antiracist pedagogy. Others noted that they would benefit from training on culturally responsive pedagogy and antiracism. Faculty and students alike advocated for requiring qualifications for adjunct instructors should include experience working with diverse adult learners, proven ability to establish an inclusive classroom culture, and skills in confronting bias and microaggressions and facilitating cross-cultural communication.

Financial Support to Improve Access and Retention

While there is significant demographic diversity among learners in the program, learners noted that the cost of the program (at a private institution of higher education) was challenging and limited participation across socioeconomic groups. Learners also noted challenges with receiving financial aid in a timely manner and limits of scholarship and grant availability.

Instructors and Staff

The section addressing faculty and staff of the *Framework for Assessment and Transformation in Adult Education* encourages organization personnel to look at how faculty and staff are selected/hired, integrated into the organization, and what is offered in terms of professional development. In particular, the framework draws attention to how justice and equity are attended to in these processes. First, we will first focus on the areas of strength as described by program alumni and faculty in surveys, and focus groups and interviews, respectively. Areas of strength include improving the racial diversity of faculty, collaborative teaching, and professional development. Next, we will explore opportunities for improvement for instructors and staff.

Strengths

Based on our self-study we determined three areas of strength for our programs: improving the racial diversity of faculty, collaborative teaching, and professional development. Each theme will be explored primarily using data from the faculty focus groups and interviews; themes were triangulated with student survey data to verify the strength.

Increasing the Racial Diversity of Our Faculty

While the framework speaks more to full-time, ranked faculty and our faculty is primarily per-course adjuncts, this issue has been a topic of discussion within both programs over the last few years. It is particularly pertinent for the GLD program, as all three of our full-time, salaried, adjunct faculty are in their early-to-mid 60s and are interested in transitioning from full-time to part-time teaching. Additionally, many of our per-course adjuncts (in both programs) are also in their 60s or 70s and have been teaching in the programs for over ten years. While we bring much wisdom to our teaching, we are at an inflection point and recognize that the time is coming for others to build on the foundation we have created. SMC has done well at diversifying the ranked faculty and should additional tenure track lines be added, we believe the hiring process will bring diverse faculty for the programs. We have noticed that learners are more engaged when they have faculty that look like them. This is also supported by the literature. The per-course hiring process involves posting the courses and considering applications. While this falls in the domain of program director responsibilities, the full-time faculty have discussed candidates and sought faculty who are racially diverse, facilitative in their style, experienced in working with learning communities, and are social justice advocates. We know that with this diversity will come the kinds of diverse interests and focus areas that will expand our programs to be more responsive to more students' diverse needs.

Collaborative Teaching

In the overview section we mentioned that many of our courses are co-taught and that this has been a signature feature of our programs, particularly the GLD program. We expand on that concept here as we believe it is critical for programs embracing a justice and equity framework. We have of late been referring to co-teaching as collaborative teaching as it is more description of how we do this. Typically, co-teaching means that two or more faculty are each responsible for specific sections or learning units of a course. Collaborative Teaching is "the way two or more teachers teach the same group of students together" (BIT.AI Editorial Board, 2021). The emphasis on "together" speaks to how we do our collaborative teaching. "In our practice, two (or more) faculty share the entire teaching experiences as a team, including design, curriculum development, course delivery and assessment" (Paxton, 2022). We pair adult educators with leadership practitioners with attention to creating cross-racial and cross-gender teaching teams. This practice provides multiple perspectives which enhance the learning experience and provides greater possibilities for connections between learners and faculty. The adult educators (our full-time faculty) typically handle most of the administrative responsibilities associated with teaching a course (setting up the course in the learning management system, permissions for readings, etc.). Our per-course faculty have expressed a desire to do more collaborative teaching.

It is unfortunate that with the transition of the BALOS and GLD programs to the KSOE in 2015 and the implementation of a collective bargaining agreement in 2016, our ability to engage in collaborative teaching has diminished. We had been compensating faculty at 0.667 FTE for co-teaching and we were asked to bring the compensation in line with other programs at 0.5 for co-teaching, which was perceived as a pay cut by many faculty. The collective bargaining agreement now requires that courses be staffed based on seniority, which does not allow for rotating assignments among teaching teams of three or more faculty. We share this information here because we believe collaborative teaching is essential in creating learning environments where justice and equity are foregrounded.

Professional Development

The data revealed several aspects of professional development that are a strength. In addition to the collaborative teaching, our faculty (within our programs and both programs together) have gathered several times a year to share activities we use in our courses, discuss assessment practices, reflect on the development of our cohorts, consider new texts, etc. We think of ourselves as an additional program cohort. This process has substantially enriched the learner experience and contributed to the joy of teaching for faculty.

We have met less frequently over the past few years due to budget constraints, as there were no funds to compensate faculty or provide food (the meetings were often about six hours). Through this process, our per-course faculty identified these meetings as a strength and requested we return to increased faculty meetings. This remarkable commitment indicates that serving as faculty in the program is more than just a job for many of our per course faculty.

Another noted strength of supporting faculty were financial resources to support their ongoing learning. The college provides faculty development funding to full-time faculty and per course adjuncts who teach more than five courses. The amount varies based on rank and time of service; more funding is provided for early career ranked faculty.

A final strength called out by the data in professional development is our work with colleagues within SMC and from other institutions. Stacey and Marguerite are founding members of the SMC Standing Up for Racial Justice (SURJ) group. Another faculty member has led racial justice events for the campus community. One of our salaried adjuncts has been part of a group of White people inquiring into whiteness for over 20 years. Several of our faculty (both full-time and part-time) have presented and attended at the White Privilege Conference, International Leadership Association Global Conference, and the International Transformative Learning Conference. Stacey is part of a multicultural research team examining whiteness in Diversity, Equity, and Inclusion (DEI) work. These activities provide opportunities for conversation about bringing a focus on equity and justice into our work.

Opportunities for Improvement

Several opportunities for improvement emerged from data regarding faculty and staff support. These include addressing faculty concerns primarily around the status and integration of adjunct faculty, staffing, and governance. Each of these are elaborated next.

Faculty Concerns

As we look to create pipelines and pathways for additional faculty we must advocate for more resources for involvement of per-course adjuncts. While many of our per-course adjuncts who are later in their careers have expressed willingness to contribute labor to the programs, this is not a sustainable practice as we nurture new faculty in our system. Our discussions about nurturing new faculty have centered around creating partnerships with full-time faculty who are stepping down from full-time roles with new faculty from all ranks. This might include doing some of the administrative work of setting up the online course; many of our per course adjuncts either have full-time jobs or are teaching at multiple institutions. Both scenarios provide limited time for updating course content. For many years, we held faculty meetings with both full-time and adjunct faculty several times each year. The faculty thought of themselves as another "cohort of learners" and at the meetings we would share activities led in courses, discuss how to best give feedback on written work, how to support learners who were struggling, and other such topics. These meetings created a sense of community among all faculty teaching in the programs. The introduction of the collective bargaining agreement meant that we could not hold these meetings without paying faculty. Additional funding to resume faculty meetings would ensure a continued, shared understanding of the programs as a whole, which enables faculty to scaffold content more effectively. Finally, another opportunity for improvement is to allocate more funds for marketing the programs. As the programs are a fit for people from a wide range of backgrounds, organizations, and level of responsibility, thus there is no specific niche for prospects. We have relied heavily on alumni referrals, which requires a replenishment of the pool of alumni! We have done some social media marketing in fits and starts, more consistency in this area is another opportunity.

As directors of programs embedded in an institution of higher education, we are acutely aware of the inequities around job security, autonomy, and benefits. We have discussed the rank and tenure issues above, and there are significant differences in benefits eligibility between full-time and per course faculty. Benefits eligibility for per course faculty comes with teaching five courses, which rarely happens in our programs – mostly because of limited course availability and due to part-time faculty engaged in work in the world; very few, if any, have spent their entire career in academia. We have stretched the boundaries of curriculum revising in our faculty meetings and we do so, knowing the courses and program as a whole, benefits from the input of per course adjuncts.

Staff

Many of the administrative functions that support our programs are done by staff members in other departments, where we have minimal influence. There is one staff person, the Senior Admin Assistant (SAA), assigned to the leadership department who reports to the department chair. A staff reorganization in July 2020 shifted the administrative functions to a centralized process for all of the KSOE. The SAA plays a critical role as the link between programs and the administrative functions. We consider her a full member of the program director team and she participates in the program director monthly meetings. While students appreciate all the support of our Senior Administrative Assistant, they noted several challenges which have emerged in their interactions with staff in administrative functions in other departments. These challenges include issues with financial aid packages, unclear and inaccurate information regarding graduation, and untimely processing of units for prior learning credit.

Governance

Like many institutions of higher education, at the highest level SMC is governed by a Board of Trustees, to whom the President of the College reports. The President has direct responsibility for the administration of the College in areas outside of academics. The provost, who reports to the President, has direct responsibility for academic affairs (faculty and curriculum). The College follows a shared governance structure between faculty and administrators, which is comprised of a multitude of committees that advise, review, and/or approve policies. The committees are responsible to the Academic Senate; membership to the Senate and committees is through elections. The committees focus on new academic programs, regular review of academic programs, faculty development, faculty promotion (rank and tenure), faculty welfare (compensation and benefits), and educational technology, to name a few, as well as an abundance of ad hoc task forces. There is also faculty representation on the Board of Trustees through the Senate Chair and Past Chair. Our opportunities for influence depend on which committees we are elected to join and our relationship with our colleagues. As the reader might gather from this description, governance in higher education is often a hierarchical, cumbersome, and time consuming activity. Faculty recognize this and are currently starting discussions in the Academic Senate to design a new, more nimble structure that is better adapted to the pace of change happening in higher education today.

During this past academic year, the Provost's Office started a "Graduate Council," made up of the deans, associate deans, program director, and chairs to talk about issues related to the governance and directing of graduate programs. We are excited about this new group as it provides an opportunity to collaborate across the campus with other graduate and adult serving programs, with which we have more affinity than the undergraduate programs. The first few meetings were an opportunity to get to know one another and the programs and toward the end of the last academic year the group had a fruitful discussion about recruiting and admissions.

Conclusion

As program directors and primary program faculty, we have agency to embark upon many of the recommendations that emerged from this self-study. Inspired by adrienne marie brown's (2017) work on emergent strategy for just social change, we are committed to "create a world [within higher education] that works for more people, more of the time" (p. 156). To bring this vision to fruition for diverse adult learners in higher education, "we have to collaborate on the process of dreaming and visioning and implementing that world" (p. 156). We need institutional support for collaborative design efforts that involve students and a diverse group of faculty, staff, administrators, and community members. We acknowledge the challenge of doing this work at a time of resource scarcity; however, to maintain our commitment to equity, we must compensate students, adjunct faculty, and community members for their time and efforts and acknowledge the labor of full-time faculty.

Guided by brown's (2017) framing of social change as fractal in nature, such that "what we do at small scale reverberates to the largest scale" (p. 52), we focused our analysis on the areas where we have control as program directors – Teaching and Learning, and Instructors and Staff. However, system wide decisions and processes constrain or support our ability to serve the diverse adult learners in our program. Notwithstanding the social justice grounding of the university's mission "to make lasting change in the world" (https://www.stmarys-ca.edu/about-smc/our-mission), the way the organization is structured and the way that works get done here "reflect the status quo" (p. 52).

When organizations with social justice missions are structured to reflect the status quo, our creativity and liberation are limited (brown, 2017). In higher education for a combined 30 years, we note the following examples of status quo: hierarchy, bullying, top-down structures, money driven programs, ineffective processes for handing conflict, and unsustainable overwork culture. While not surprising, this is "the water in which we swim" (brown, 2017, p. 53), the structures and culture limit our ability to meet our social justice mission. What we do on a small scale – in our departments, committees, faculty and staff meetings, and classrooms – sends ripples through the college, the community, and the world.

We are committed to navigating these challenging waters to create ripples to change, to "empower students to lead change according to the principles of social justice and the common good" (https://www.stmarys-ca.edu/kalmano-vitz-school-of-education). We are called to dismantle oppressive systems and change the harmful aspects of our work culture to rebuild with courageous collaboration and to create space for the practice of the inclusive, adaptive, and community-engaged leadership frameworks we teach to our learners.

To make meaningful change we must name and address the turbulence in our waters and take collaborative action and build capacity for adaptation. These adult-serving leadership programs manifest the university's mission in unique and important ways and have rippling effects on the communities our learners service. In serving adult learners focusing on leadership through the lens of equity and justice, these programs expand the equity proposition of the university. The Lasallian values of the institution indicate a commitment to justice and to care.

Undertaking this self-study through the lens of equity and justice offered great insight into both the needs of our diverse learners and to how we would like to influence the system to help us do this important work. As part of the ongoing work of the university we stand read to engage its mission and focus on justice and equity more deeply. We invite our colleagues, administrators, and past, current, and future learners to partner with us in evolving and strengthening our adult serving leadership programs.

References

BIT.AI Editorial Board. (2021). *Collaborative teaching: What is it & how to do it the right way?* https://blog.bit.ai/collaborative-teaching/

Bresnick, P. (May, 2021). *4 ways colleges and universities can support adult learners.* https://www.fierceeducation.com/best-practices/4-ways-colleges-and-universities-can-support-adult-learners

Brock, T., & Slater, D. (2021). *Strategies for improving postsecondary credential attainment among Black, Hispanic, and native American adults.* https://ccrc.tc.columbia.edu/publications/credential-attainment-black-hispanic-native-american-adults.html

brown, a. m. (2017). *Emergent strategy: Shaping change, changing worlds.* AK Press.

European-American Collaborative Challenging Whiteness (2010). White on white: Developing capacity to communicate about race with critical humility. In V. Sheared, S. Brookfield, S. Colin, J. Johnson-Bailey, & E. Peterson (Eds.), *Handbook on race: A dialogue between adult and higher education scholars* (pp. 145–157). Jossey-Bass.

Kline, M. (2019). *The looming higher ed enrollment cliff.* Higher Ed HR Magazine. https://www.cupahr.org/issue/feature/higher-ed-enrollment-cliff/

Kyte, S. B. (2017). Who does work work for? Understanding equity in working learner college and career success. *ACT Center for Equity in Learning.* http://equityinlearning.act.org/research-doc/who-does-work-work-for

MacDonald, K. (2018). A review of the literature: The needs of nontraditional students in post-secondary education. *Strategic Enrollment Quarterly, 5*(4), 159–164. https://doi.org/10.1002/sem3.20115.

Organisation for Economic Co-operation and Development (n.d.). *OECD Better Life Index.* https://www.oecdbetterlifeindex.org/topics/education

Paxton (2022). *Collaborative teaching: Five benefits and one crucial reason for adaptive innovation.* https://www.linkedin.com/pulse/collaborative-teaching-five-benefits-one-crucial-reason-doug-paxton/?trackingId=TtQ7RtLIQOGNJ2wzowohtQ%3D%3D

Soares, L., Gagliardi, J. S., & Nellum, C. J. (2017). *The post-traditional learners manifesto revisited: Aligning postsecondary education with real life for adult student success. American Council on Education.* http://hdl.voced.edu.au/10707/445646

Yorks, L., & Kasl, E. (2002). Toward a theory and practice for whole-person learning: Reconceptualizing experience and the role of affect. *Adult Education Quarterly, 52*(3), 176–192.

7

FINDINGS

Reflections That Lead to Action and Change

Bob Hughes, Deanna Iceman Sands, and Ted Kalmus

Common Characteristics in the Four Cases

Commitment to Justice and Equity

The commitment all four organizations made to equity and justice is not a commitment to a specific model or a specific set of practices. They all have unique approaches, models, and practices. However, they all possess a central commitment to justice and equity. They strive to improve how they meet this commitment. Their intent is to center justice and equity in everything they do. Establishment of a unifying goal is important throughout the literature on effective organizations (e.g., Elmore, 1996; Hall & Hord, 2014; Hands et al., 2015). For each of the four organizations in this book, justice and equity is that focus. They begin that focus as they hire people who exhibit a longstanding commitment to serving the communities that the organization serves. These employees then challenge the organization to live to its ideals through regular self-analyses, internal dialogue, and external review. For example, BSP committed to matching the makeup its communities in the hire of their first executive director and then through the current position descriptions. In this first act of commitment, these organizations seek to act beyond hiring for diversity. They seek to build organizations that act daily in commitment to equity and justice. To do that, they need people who add to the work they perform from their own commitment to equity and justice.

Commitment to Self-Exploration

As Schein (2010) suggests, organizations evolve through stages of organizational culture to achieve the complexity they need to accomplish their work. Being an organization that centers equity and justice in its work means that

DOI: 10.4324/9781003286998-7

these organizations' self-analyses are ongoing and consistent. As explained further in Chapter 8, the reflections they completed for this project complemented other work they had underway. In addition to those formal evaluations, however, as the chapters attest, these organizations have ongoing informal evaluations where they challenge themselves to live into their ideals. BSP describes biweekly meetings among the management group where they can discuss not only ongoing operations, but also see how the issues they are facing can be aligned with their mission. TAF brings together staff, board, and the community to examine how its efforts align with its intent. BeLit met the challenge of merger by bringing together multiple stakeholder and internal groups in conversations that continued well after the official date of merger. St. Mary's BALOS/GLD faculty meet regularly and with colleagues outside of the programs to have check-ins about their work and how to situate it within the larger institution. The result is that each organization constantly examines its daily work while allowing for multiple voices to inform, support, and challenge that work.

Multiple members of each organization's community became engaged in this project by being interviewed, completing questionnaires, providing materials and background, and helping to edit their final chapter. This all happened in the life of each of these organizations when they were pushed for time, resources, energy, and focus. The effects of the pandemic, especially, demanded attention from each organization. Their willingness to undertake and successfully complete their chapter attests to and represents their commitment to the larger work of justice and equity. Indeed, during our meetings with project coordinators, the coordinators indicated this process inspired and energized their staff to move forward from conditions created by the pandemic. Rather than seeing this project as an adjunct task, they expanded their work to include this project.

In a Continual State of Evolution

The descriptions above might suggest that these organizations live in a constant state of flux. That would not be entirely accurate. A better perspective is that the organizations are in a constant state of evolution, as Schein's (2010) work proposes. The changes they undergo are perpetual; however, they are not aimless. Each organization exists in a sector of adult learning that demands constant adaptation. Project coordinators from each organization indicated that a benefit of navigating change was the catalyst it created to question how current services align with the needs of individuals/groups and/or whether services provided are offered in a manner that aligns to the cultural, cognitive, or affective needs of individuals/groups. For example, BSP began serving property service workers and then expanded into opportunities to support other types of service workers at one of the world's busiest airports.

At the same time, they needed to help their traditional constituents adapt to changes in the property service industry. Concurrently, they are growing into new regions of the state while being asked to help other organizations in other states which seek to replicate their work. To meet the demands of all these changes, BSP evolves as an organization. All three of the organizations describe similar pressures.

The informal and formal self-evaluation and reflection in this project and other analyses these organizations conduct assist the organizations to examine their work formatively. However, just studying their issues would not have been adequate to support the needed evolution. To meet these pressures strategically and intentionally, each organization has needed to develop the operational structures and systems they identify in their chapters. Those structures allow the organizations to engage actively in establishing intentional directions for their evolution. The four organizations are unique in how they evolve, but the common feature is their evolution. Like BSP, TAF, for example, has undergone a significant evolution since its founding. As they worked with children, they found they needed to support the educators who served those children. As they evolved to include adult learning into their structure, they had to ensure that this new work did not get shuffled off as an adjunct to their core mission of serving children. Instead, TAF expanded its work to adult learners while maintaining fidelity to its core mission.

Commitment to Clients and Employees

The four organizations each have longstanding commitments to the people they serve. It is the level of commitment that Caffarella noted as common among adult learning organizations in her 1996 opinion essay in *Adult Learning* (Caffarella, 1996). In that essay, she warns of commitment easily leading to overextension. As we note in Chapter 2, we cast a wide net to find organizations that are successfully serving diverse groups of adult learners. In making our final selections, we were not surprised to find that all of the organizations exhibited commitments to their served populations. The hypothesis that adult learning often attracts altruistic and dedicated workers is easily provable in any of the organizations we interviewed for this project. Therefore, we were also not surprised to see that strong dedication reflected in how the selected four conduct their work, how they revere their clients, or how they make decisions. As we completed the project with each organization, we came to admire their connection to their communities. This is less "work" than "mission" to the organizations and their staff.

What we were surprised by, however, was the concurrent commitment that the organizations also make to the people who work there. While the leaders in the four organizations have most likely not read Caffarella's 1996 warning, they express awareness of the need to support their staff. More than once in our meetings with the organizations, someone told us something similar to, "We decided that if we're going to provide opportunity for our clients, we would be hypocritical not to offer similar opportunities for the people who do the work."

The one organization where employee growth and development were not explicitly tied to goals of equity and justice is St. Mary's BALOS/GLD programs. Because these two programs are housed with a school of education which is housed within a larger college, systems of development and growth for employees are managed at the larger institutional level. However, the dean of the school of education clearly saw this project as an opportunity for growth for the two chapter authors. Within the larger systems of St. Mary's College, that dean has been able to support growth for her staff by seeking opportunities for their growth and by assisting them in those opportunities. In this project, the dean was able to bring together an experienced faculty member and a relatively new faculty member. The project allowed them to use their separate lenses to their self-examination. Equally important, though, this was an excellent professional development opportunity for those two faculty members to expand their skills and knowledge through co-constructing the knowledge represented in the chapter. In many ways, the dean established an ideal learning opportunity through this project.

Willingness to Try New Ideas

All four of these organizations are learning organizations. Garvin (1993), Hunter-Johnson and Closson (2012), and Odor (2018) all emphasize the importance of willingness to innovate as a hallmark of any organization that sees itself as a "learning organization." Despite the many challenges and pressures that they describe in their chapters, each organization shows not only willingness, but, at times, eagerness to explore new ideas. The pressure to evolve continually has not created, as it at times can, a retreat to the safety of what is known. Instead, these organizations seek solutions and are open to multiple sources of knowledge information that they had not considered.

For example, TAF brings together groups of stakeholders to engage them in problem solving. BSP has wide partnerships that allow them to draw from industry partners, unions, state agencies, research centers, foundations, and more. The program directors of BALOS/GLD are developing strategic partnerships across the wider campus to help inform and shape the programs' future. BeLit, as now the largest and longest-serving adult literacy provider in its region, maintains an extensive network of partners from which to learn, and develop new ideas. These organizations are not trapped in following past practices, nor are they trapped by change for change's sake. They have strategic and clear processes for examining the value of new ideas; and they also have similar processes for examining the efficacy of those ideas once they are implemented.

By Unique Domains Explored

It was important to us as editors and guides to this work that each organization used the *FATAE* in ways that supported their aims as an organization. We did not want to create an academic exercise where organizations followed guidelines and developed an abstract relationship to those guidelines. As explained in more detail in Chapter 8, we used a participatory action research model that intended to provide a useful process well beyond the publication of this book. Therefore, we asked them, instead of attempting to evaluate themselves on all four domains, to identify two domains that they could comfortably complete within the six months (eventually extended to nine months) we provided for the self-analysis. We also asked them to consider which of the domains might be helpful to them to consider as an organization; and which of the domains would be most helpful in explicating the story of how their organization came to be successful at equitably serving their communities. It would be fine, we explained to the project leaders, if they looked beyond the two domains they selected, but we wanted their chapter to have a focus within the two domains they selected.

We found, as organizations completed their evaluations, that organizations used the framework in a more nuanced way than we had anticipated. While one organization limited itself to two of the domains, the others found that it was more useful to identify questions in multiple domains. They found critical questions of the framework were valuable without limiting themselves to only two domains. As we worked with the organizations, we found that both approaches (limiting to two domains or selecting questions from multiple domains) had value to the organizations. While such an approach may seem random or intended to highlight only positive aspects, neither happened. Coordinators from the four organizations selected areas of the framework that aligned with their current work as well as questions that would reveal strengths and opportunities for growth. As we note in Chapter 8, our flexibility in supporting each organization allowed us to adapt to these changes and for each organization to find value in the process. The resulting chapters written by each organization offer an opportunity to look at commonalities in their responses to the domains.

The domains within the FATAE from which organizations selected questions to explore are:

- TAF: Governance and Finance; Teaching and Learning; Instructors and Staff; Partnerships and Public Impact
- BSP: Governance and Finance; Partnerships and Public Impact
- BeLit: Governance and Finance; Teaching and Learning; Partnerships and Public Impact
- St. Mary's BALOS/GLD programs: Governance and Finance; Teaching and Learning; Instructors and Staff

As the faculty at St. Mary's note in their chapter, their look at the Governance and Finance domain came after they looked exhaustively at the other two domains they selected. They chose to examine Governance and Finance after completing their analyses of the other two selected domains to ground their understanding within the larger institutional context in which they operate. Their focus on those other two domains makes sense since as faculty, even faculty charged with directing programs, they have little control over the governance of the institution. Yet, as they acknowledge, that structure impacts how they operate and needed to be evaluated, even if briefly.

The first observation we made is the effect of having one of the organizations, St. Mary's BALOS/GLD programs, subsumed within the larger system of a school of education, which is, itself, part of the larger college. As their chapter notes, the resulting experiences of St. Mary's leadership programs are often shaped by those larger systems. The other three organizations are more autonomous entities. Even the TAF adult learning programs, which are housed within the larger TAF organization, have more institutional autonomy than St. Mary's leadership programs. The analysis that follows includes observations of the impacts of that lack of direct autonomy.

In the comparisons and contrasts that follow, our observations follow the *FATAE's* sections and structure. Those sections of the *FATAE* where we do not offer analysis are because we did not have enough data from the case studies to make a comparison or contrast. The process which we followed in conducting our analyses is explained in Chapter 2.

Governance and Finance

BSP, TAF, and BeLit have substantial number of leaders and employees who come from historically excluded backgrounds, and these people help to ensure that equity and justice remain at the center of the organization's efforts. St. Mary's adult learning leadership programs are directed by White women, who retain their commitment by, as the authors note, "...acknowledging our privilege and positionality as it may have played out in the gathering and presentation of information on strengths, challenges, and opportunities of how the principles of equity, access, justice, and inclusion are reflected in the BALOS and GLD programs." In all four organizations, a focus on creating a more equitable and just world through their mission is at the center of their daily efforts. All of these organizations believe that the adult education they offer is critical to reducing barriers and gaps for historically marginalized communities.

At the time of this project, BeLit was in the early stages of re-examining of the mission and vision statements from the two merged organizations, negotiating and integrating their mission and vision statements into new foundational statements. They used their self-analysis and reflections during this project to reaffirm their mission and to hone their vision to anchor the development of their strategic plan while aligning operational processes with that emerging vision. The other three organizations have evolved robust missions and visions since their founding. These three organizations all rely on these statements to keep focused on their work. Also, these statements have not radically changed since their founding. Each of the three organizations that have had their mission, vision, and values statements for years has not altered either direction or vision. Instead, they have used these documents to remain true to their founding while expanding their operations.

Using the *FATAE* was helpful for each of the four organizations to measure their strategic planning processes against the concepts of equity and justice addressed in the framework. TAF staff worked to develop a strategic plan in 2021 over a six-month period as they were concurrently completing this project. Their plan includes both internal and external goals that impact operations and the organization's ability to expand its voice regionally and nationally. As a result, TAF staff spent a significant amount of time in the year using the *FATAE* analyzing how their intentions match their actions. Similarly, BeLit, as they were completing their merger and analyzing their work in relation to the *FATAE*, found that completing an analysis of their work helped them to interrogate how their beliefs matched their actions. For the faculty in the leadership programs at St. Mary's College, the project helped them to look closely at the strategic plan of the school of education where they are housed to see how and where their efforts matched the intent of that plan. Their analysis was useful at a time when they need to advocate for support for their programs. As they note in their chapter, BSP's strategic planning is on hold, but their time with the *FATAE* will be helpful since it provides them a tool for analysis as they analyze their annual plans and progress toward a future strategic plan.

As staff work through how their organizations are led, each has unique needs. BSP is growing in size and scope, and it is transitioning from a very flat organization that was useful when it was smaller. BSP leadership seeks to empower its levels of leadership while allowing those with expertise to step forward and be recognized. BeLit is, in its initial steps after the merger, structuring roles and responsibilities to ensure continuity and success as it brings more of its staff into leadership roles. St. Mary's will be recruiting someone to replace one of the chapter authors who is the longer-serving leader of the GLD program. TAF describes its leadership as stable with well-defined roles. All four organizations, regardless of the circumstances, need leaders with demonstrated experience and skills as leaders, along with a deep and longstanding commitment to justice and equity.

As the editors of this book, we began this project with the hopes that we would attract organizations to participate that would represent a broad swath of adult education. We believe we succeeded since the four organizations are each performing different work with unique populations of adults. However, one aspect of organizational trait we observed as we worked with the four organizations helped us to understand an important issue about leaders and leadership specifically. BSP, TAF, and BeLit all employ a very common leadership structure as autonomous from a larger entity in which they could be housed. These organizations are wholly or in part managed and led by leaders of color who have been intentionally sought for their ability to represent, understand, and serve their communities.

In contrast, St. Mary's College and its associated schools, departments, and programs has a different leadership. The two White women who lead the BALOS/GLD programs seek to diversify the faculty who teach their courses, and they understand their positions of privilege that are different than most of the students they serve. The college and school of education have a mission that is complementary to the BALOS/GLD programs' justice and equity aims, but that larger institution is operated very much in the hierarchical model of academia. That means that there are multiple layers of systems and authority that the two directors must navigate when leading their programs. Their experiences highlight the challenges faced by adult educators who operate their programs within larger structures where they do not have direct control over factors such as working conditions, hiring standards, or salaries. Because they exist within that larger system, their efforts can be limited by the constraints established by that larger system which can see adult learning program as secondary to the larger organizational aims.

Those challenges which the leadership programs faculty experience at St. Mary's due to their subsumed positions also extend to how democratic they can operate within a larger and more hierarchical system. As the authors explain within their chapter, "Additional administrative layers also meant that decisions were made further away from the people and programs that were impacted by the decisions." For BSP, BeLit, and TAF, their size creates fewer layers. However, more importantly, their organizational focus on serving a targeted, adult population narrows their overall mission. That, in turn, allows them to keep decisions at the lowest levels. While they each are refining their efforts to be more inclusive in their decision-making, and leadership, the three autonomous programs can have discussions in small teams that keep many people in their organization engaged in those discussions. Thus, they can operate more democratically.

At the action level, all four organizations strive toward collective, as opposed to autocratic, action as much as possible. BSP emphasizes the importance of communication and openness, and the importance at all levels of understanding their three core focus areas – for both internal staff and external partners. TAF describes how much they rely on adherence to their mission and vision, and everyone's commitment to those. BeLit is working on building formal systems, but they see openness and communication as keys to their current and future ability to do so. The faculty who direct the BALOS/GLD programs seek to work as collectively as they can, within the constraints of the system in which they operate. However, often decisions are top-down, starting at college then school then department levels; and this leads to their inability to influence some policies and decisions to serve students better.

While faculty who write about St. Mary's describe the resistance they experience within their systems, the other three organizations do not. This is important to note since there are critical factors that contribute to the lack of internal resistance. Certainly, as noted in the chapters, the lack of resistance does not come from a lack of changes that the three autonomous organizations experienced. Each of those three organizations underwent significant changes at the time of their participation in the project – the pandemic being one of many external pressures. They, however, identify causes that contribute to their lack of resistance. First, the mission-focused approach of each organization allows them to hire people who are committed to their mission and model of operation. Second, these organizations have all committed to open and consistent communication to ensure that everyone understands what is changing and why. Finally, they have each normalized change. Change is not something that occurred at a specific moment for these organizations. It is what they experience routinely and have come to expect. As a result, people within the organization are not surprised by changes.

At the same time, even for these organizations, moments of significant change such a major shift in governance, a merger, or a significant influx or drop in funding presented significant challenges to stability. A disposition toward iterative change equipped the autonomous organizations to manage larger, singular challenges. Both TAF and BeLit took advantage of major shifts to invite a more deliberate period of reflection and reorganization. In both cases, affirming organizational values and clarifying priorities led to some turnover of staff and mid-level leadership. Rather than creating a destabilizing event, that turnover was viewed as opportunity to hire and promote with a greater sense of purpose and mission alignment. BSP's change in executive directors follows that same pattern. Adherence to founding principles keeps these organizations grounded and focused, even as they experience personnel changes.

Also, the autonomous programs make decisions at levels much closer to the people impacted. For the BALOS/GLD program directors, decision-making at the larger institutional levels still privilege the "traditional student" (e.g., the elimination of graduate student handbook). Closing the college's school of extended education (which served adult learners) and forcing integration within the system set for "traditional learners" created an institutional resistance to change. Because the program directors work within a larger system that is often unaware of their students' needs, the program directors experience resistance to efforts to meet adult learners' needs. The resulting issues impact much of the college experience for the adult learners that the programs serve.

All four of the organizations share a common commitment to working with as diverse group of people as they can – both the people they serve and the people who work within the organization. TAF seeks to impact diverse educators and has worked hard to ensure that the people within the organization reflect the populations they seek to impact. That includes staff, management, and board members. While BeLit understands and is working on its need for having a more diverse governing board, it has intentionally structured its hiring practices to ensure that its staff and managers reflect the diversity of the communities BeLit serves. From its founding, BSP has reflected the communities it serves to create programs. St. Mary's faculty are working within the larger institution's hiring practices to bring more diversity to its adjunct teaching corps, a group they recognize has not historically represented the diversity of their students and the communities they aim to serve.

The ways in which the three autonomous organizations manage their funds reflect their commitment to justice and equity. For TAF, budgeting is a collaborative effort that involves staff and management. Each budget begins with proposed program-level action items and then the management team prioritizes and allocates resources for those identified needs. To maintain this bottom-up approach, TAF engaged with an external researcher to develop a rubric that allows them to determine the equity of decisions like resource allocations. Budgeting, therefore, becomes a process of continual questioning to determine if resources match their equity and justice goals. The 30–40% of BSP's budget that comes from the Leadership Training Education Fund grounds their organizational expenditures to focus on workers' needs and keeps resources allocated toward core services. The base funding also allows them to seek partnerships that build on that base and allows them to look for funding partnerships that complement the organization's mission. As BeLit began allocating its resources as a newly merged organization, it discovered inequities in workload and salaries, so it reallocated funding to create equitable systems for BeLit employees. It has been important for all three organizations to use their resources in alignment with their commitment to equity and justice.

That alignment between action and commitment was clear in the actions of all four organizations. Their use of the *FATAE* was useful to their continued explorations of how they matched their intentions to their beliefs; however, that work did not begin with this project. All four organizations have been self-examining their intentions and actions from their founding. Their chapters each identify that clear commitment to living into their beliefs consistently. This project was another step in that exploration for them.

As it operates daily, BSP is still trying to find the best ways to manage operational decision-making as it grows and develops systems that support more inclusive decision-making while giving authority where it is needed. TAF has more clearly established procedures, but they similarly seek to put decisions at the lowest levels. As the newly merged BeLit develops its organizational culture and systems, they also seek to find more inclusive management practices. While St. Mary's College is bound by institutional systems and culture, the two program directors have found ways to collaborate and manage their programs together within the larger system. That collaboration is no small feat in any higher education institution.

The three autonomous organizations all express a clear understanding of the internal and external funding world in which they must be engaged. That world is most clearly described by BSP in their chapter, where they explain the often competitive and quick-result-driven nature of seeking external funding, particularly linked to grants and contracts. TAF partnered to develop an equity rubric they plan to increasingly employ in making and evaluating the impact of their decisions of external funding streams to seek as well as potential partners they may engage in that process. BeLit seeks to be more engaged with its state systems so that it can advocate for the funding that they and similar organizations need. These three organizations seek to remain current in their understanding and capacity to address funding.

BSP's description of their approach to funding beyond the LTEF is one that applies to all three of the autonomous organizations. They seek those partners whose work is complementary to their efforts while also helping to expand their thinking about the work. They seek funding sources that have similar goals and then develop more than a funding relationship that extends into operations, evaluation, and development of a community of partners. That desire and perspective is common among the three autonomous organizations as they wish to avoid chasing funding that would take them away from their core work.

Of the four organizations, TAF and BSP have explored the hidden curriculum of funders most thoroughly. BSP commits to finding partnerships, not just funders. They are constantly examining the larger implications of relationships with external funders beyond just receiving funding. TAF's six, central values help keep them focused and, as a result, somewhat sheltered from pressures to chase funding while maintaining relationships with those funders that have similar values. These two organizations have had time to be able to evolve to these positions. BeLit is early in its development as a merged organization to have had these discussions; or if they have, they did not include those discussions in their explanations. As is often the case in higher education, BALOS/GLD faculty in the school of education do not routinely or autonomously seek funding outside of their college budget.

The four organizations all explain the importance of how they tell their story as an organization and how they tell the stories of the people they serve. BeLit's example of how they advocated for elimination of the term "formerly incarcerated" shows a desire to self-examine how their messaging reflects and evolves with their awareness and values – and how they sought to impact the larger conversations as a result. BSP is careful not to equate "low wage" with "low skill" in describing the work that their learners perform. St. Mary's faculty seek to move the college away from using terms like "traditional student" to highlight that the students they serve do not fit that profile, and that the profile is outdated. For these organizations, it is important to have a message that explains not only the work they do, but their perspectives on that work. They intend, through their messages, to impact larger conversations about the people they serve.

Teaching and Learning

Only the BALOS/GLD programs at St. Mary's focused specifically on the Teaching and Learning section of the *FATAE*. However, there are statements embedded in the chapters that give some picture of how these organizations manage teaching and learning. We hope that, at some future time, someone uses this framework to look across multiple organizations at the teaching and learning that is at the core of adult learning. Perhaps, we hope, someone will follow this study with one, using this model of inquiry, that solely focuses on the teaching and learning components of the framework.

One of those areas where three of the four organizations gave evidence of their teaching and learning practices is on the topic of educating for democracy. St. Mary's BALOS/GLD programs' detailed description of how they operate their cohort and courses provides a clear example of what educating for democracy looks like in higher education. They focus on relationships, inclusivity, respect, diverse perspectives, and critical reflection; they seek to make their learning environment learner centered. Another model example was BSP's work in training workers based on participatory models so that they can fully participate on committees and community action. TAF encourages their participants to utilize democratic processes in their own educational work as the program models this for them by the way they structure sessions and cohort activities.

Having a process that is collaborative in designing and delivering curricula to students is critical to St. Mary's BALOS/GLD directors. In their teaching, they seek perspectives from learners, staff, and faculty to inform curriculum and administration of programs. In analyzing their efforts, the St. Mary's program directors discovered an opportunity for growth, i.e., creating student/community leadership team to develop stronger curricular focus on equity, diversity, and justice. Also, they see a value in co-teaching. Even though co-teaching has been restricted by collective bargaining and financial implications, the directors are seeking to reinstate it. TAF also develops and designs curricula through a shared process that brings instructors together for design and implementation.

The organizations base their beliefs in collaboration and democratically based learning within strongly held philosophies. St. Mary's BALOS/GLD directors ground their work through the Lasallian core principles that also guide the larger institution of which they are a part. They also align their work to whole-person approaches that they cite from the literature, as well as often citing the importance of education as a transformative learning experience. TAF's reliance on liberation pedagogy undergirds its emphasis on education for growth and change. TAF's foundational thinking draws from Paulo Freire, bell hooks, and others; it also is rooted in literature of anti-oppressive, asset-based, community engaged, critical, culturally affirming, responsive, inclusive, intersectional perspectives. They use a metaphor of "cleaning the pond" to describe how they are transforming school environments where BIPOC students, teachers, and leaders can thrive and lead. While the other two organizations do not provide as detailed explanation of the theoretical foundations that underpin their actions, the ideas, and actions they describe in their chapters readily complement the descriptions of philosophical foundations provided by St. Mary's and TAF.

The chapters show that each of these organizations see people as their greatest instructional resource. BSP writes about the people who helped found and continue to provide ideas and support to their efforts to design and deliver support to low-wage workers. TAF touts the importance of the community expertise from which it draws. BeLit describes how the people with whom it has connected through partnerships help it to develop and expand programming. The St. Mary's program directors explain the importance of the assets that adult learners with significant work experience, multiple commitments, families, etc. bring to their program. All these programs show that the diversity of their communities, and of the resulting learners they attract, help create vibrant learning experiences for learners.

All four organizations recognize that the populations they serve are often excluded or marginalized. As a result, the instructional practices they identify intentionally counter that. It is important to BSP, for example, to hire only instructors who have direct personal experience or have a family experience with the served population. TAF realizes that their population needs a community of practice to engage in countering the larger forces that seek to marginalize them or minimize their voices. St. Mary's and BeLit understand that creating pathways to economic mobility is critical to their students, so making those pathways accessible and manageable are important.

To those ends, all four organizations seek to have instructors who represent the communities of their students. While BSP, TAF, and BeLit have been successful, St. Mary's directors struggle to find ways to attract and hire a more diverse teaching corps of adjunct instructors who teach most of the courses in the two programs – something they attribute to institutional constraints. For all four programs, however, having a diverse instructor cadre can provide role models and can advocate for learners' needs from a personal perspective.

These programs use a "career lattice" approach as they serve learners. All four programs respond to learners' needs for non-linear career progression. Learners in their programs can complete one level, use that level to gain the stability they need, and then move to another level as their lives allow. BSP's Floor Care Training program is an example of a pathway where property service workers can obtain additional skills and higher wages to reach a new plateau in their career lattice. For BeLit, the progression leads to workforce development programs that allow for skills development and wage progression. St. Mary's, offers flexible bachelor's or master's degrees that open opportunities. Although TAF does not explicitly describe career progression pathways, the experiences that their learners have can open both informal and formal leadership opportunities for educators who understand and can better serve students of color.

All four organizations intentionally address the potential financial and/or attendance needs of their learners. TAF offers direct scholarships for people entering teaching, and it works with colleges of education to support additional funding. They also explore alternative supports (e.g., childcare, alternative meeting times, dates, length of sessions) to encourage participation in their seminars and workshops that are provided at no cost. BSP provides its training at no cost at work sites or near to where workers live. They also provide alternative supports like childcare to assist families. BeLit provides its services at no cost while offering an increasing number of workforce-focused courses that lead to employment. While the BALOS/GLD programs cannot adjust their pricing, faculty modifies program structures to use blended learning and a cohort model to make their courses more accessible and supportive of their adult learners.

The four organizations provide examples of the support they offer students to assist in their success. BSP and BeLit hire instructors and navigators who understand learners' experiences because of their own personal experiences. TAF intentionally designed its Fellows program to ensure that participants have an established learning community that extends into their careers. St. Mary's employs a cohort model for the same reasons, and they intentionally build activities and assignments into learners' experiences where they can build their trust and support for each other. These organizations commit to supporting learners' academic needs well beyond classroom instruction or course materials.

While the other three organizations have assessments of growth and learning, of special note is TAF's work. They partner with university academics to help design assessments that determine their success in supporting learners. They seek to analyze complex goals that include the impacts of their approach to teaching and learning. They provide multiple opportunities for the learners they serve to exhibit understanding and mastery, and they track results to see how they can create more effective practices.

Instructors and Staff

As they work to put their beliefs into actions, each organization finds what their own employees' barriers are. They all work to dismantle those barriers. When the BALOS/GLO directors discovered that ranked faculty were more diverse than adjunct faculty, they sought to understand why and continued to work within the campus structure to address the problem. TAF actively seeks to dismantle systems of oppression for both the learners it serves directly and the larger systems those learners encounter. BSP commits to developing systems and processes that create advancement and opportunities for low-wage workers while being aware of work assignments and salaries of its own staff. BeLit clarifies its staffs' needs as they review work assignments and salaries that make those equitable.

TAF's work with adult learners is about the creation of a pipeline. They are committed to creating a pipeline for people of color to become educators and to become leaders in education who understand the needs of education to adapt to all learners. The other three organizations are looking for ways to develop pipelines of instructors who can teach in their programs. St. Mary's faculty see this need as a reason to be more engaged with advocating for additional resources from their campus. BSP and BeLit rely on people within the communities they serve to be instructors, and they look for ways to offer those instructors career advancement opportunities. The people engaged in all four organizations, thus, become part of a pipeline of people who come to the organization and commit to the core ideals of that organization while participating in equitable and just learning for the served communities. Each of the four organization becomes the center of that pipeline by providing the structure for learning to occur.

To maintain that central role, these organizations question their practices to ensure that their operations match their intent. Both BeLit's and BSP's extensive workload and compensation studies led to adjusted work assignments and compensation to create more equitable responsibilities and salaries. TAF understands that work assignments vary according to the role that an employee has. Workload and compensation, to the three autonomous organizations, is an extension of their equity and justice focus. The authors of St. Mary's chapter see this also, but they explain that they are constrained by the larger systems in which they work.

All four organizations see staff outside of instruction as being critical to their instructional efforts. The directors from St. Mary's noted how critical their assigned staff member has been in helping their students navigate the college's systems. The other three organizations similarly show that their staff is vital to the ability of instructors and learners to focus on their work. Both TAF and BeLit write about their needs to address staff morale. Their chapters explain how that need led to an opportunity for organization-wide reflection and conversations. Those conversations, in turn, led to changes in structure and, in BeLit's case, pay equity. For these four organizations, non-instructional staff are central to their work.

Partnerships and Public Impact

St. Mary's BALOS/GLD faculty did not select the Partnerships and Public Impact area of the *FATAE* for their analysis beyond noting that they, as a program seeking to maintain itself, needed to extend more of a presence across campus and in the surrounding communities. That will allow them to advocate for their students and to seek resources while understanding more of the larger systems in which they operate. However, the other three organizations focus on this area as critical. Though important for recruitment, internship placements, and possibly for potential instructors, partnerships are less vital for how St. Mary's is structured.

The external reputations that the three autonomous organizations have established have been central to their growth and stability. TAF's Martinez Fellows program has established itself in the State of Washington as a critical pipeline for attracting and supporting teachers of color. BSP's reputation with both labor and employers makes it an important resource to both groups. The two predecessor organizations to BeLit each brought unique reputations to the merger, and BeLit is now building on those strong reputations to forge its future.

BSP's expansion of partnerships beyond its initial funding-based relationship with the Leadership Training Education Fund allows it to provide whole-person support to the learners it serves. It also brought community members from academia, government, and advocacy groups together to strengthen that work. Additionally, BSP has expanded its partnerships to foundation and research groups that help it to develop mission-critical assessments and models in ways that align with BSP's core mission. Now, BSP seeks to develop more partnerships that will allow them to create transition pathways into career development for the people they serve. Similarly, as BeLit expanded its work to look at career opportunities and the ways in they can support career development, they have found new ways to engage both government and industry into their work. TAF began its partnerships within its K-12 work and sought school districts and universities that aligned with its core mission. With time, they have expanded to look at funding relationships that complement their mission. For these organizations, partnerships have been, are, and will be central to the work they do. They are each planning expansions into additional partnerships that extend their work.

Both BSP and BeLit identify the competitive culture of philanthropic funding as a barrier. Developing and sustaining partnerships with external funders is important to both organizations as a counterbalance to those competitive pressures. TAF, because the overall organization's focus in K–12 education, seeks to develop key partnerships in government to reduce barriers they experience in conducting their work – as well as the barriers created by systems that hinder the educators they train and support.

The three organizations which address their partnerships and public impact within their chapters all maintain curricula in their programs that are embedded within the needs of the communities they serve. Partnerships have been critical to maintaining that embedded curricula. BSP describes how they adapt to offer workshops and courses that address both the current and anticipated needs of the workers they serve. BeLit expanded into workforce development as they saw a need for their learners to have opportunities beyond the courses they offered at the time. TAF works closely with the educators they serve to custom-fit the courses and workshops they offer. It is important to all three to have partnerships that help challenge them to do more. As a result, they are able to maintain nimble educational programming that adjusts to learners' needs as those needs evolve.

To maintain that nimbleness, these three organizations continually assess both their programs and the impact of their programs on learners. BSP has relied on foundation and academic partners to assess and evaluate their programs. It has been important for BeLit to use state and federal metrics to be able to show their impact on learners to funders and policy makers. TAF explains that assessment and evaluation are built into all activities. They conduct constant and consistent self-assessment at the individual, unit, organizational, and partnership levels. Assessment of learners and evaluation of their programs are critical operational habits for all three organizations.

Each of the three organizations understands that they must have a larger voice beyond the management of their programs. In their chapters, they describe how they are gaining that voice and having an impact that expands beyond just their internal operations. In their use of the *FATAE*, TAF discovered a need to conduct annual environmental scans after external stakeholders recommended that they should have "a better sense of broader social, political, and economic issues." These scans will help them understand the macro-level issues and challenges in which they operate. BSP remains active in supporting community-level issues. For example, during the pandemic, they created programming specifically to address a community need for vaccinations. BeLit finds opportunities to be engaged with state-level policy issues, and they are inserting their voice as policies and regulations are generated.

All three of the autonomous organizations do not face institutional constraints that limit their ability to seek and develop partnerships that enhance their work. Such partnerships are encouraged by their mission, their governance boards, and by their management teams. In this, St. Mary's leadership programs are disadvantaged by being housed in a much larger system where partner-making happens at the higher levels of the organization.

Lessons for Leadership Development

Need for Clear Pathways of Staff Development toward Leadership

The four project participants offer lessons about leadership development, and one common lesson that all of them can offer is on the topic of leadership development. That applies to formal roles as managers, as well as the informal leadership that emerges as staff takes on roles to help the organization meet its aims (Hughes, 2017). The organizations' processes and procedures for informal and formal leadership all uniquely complement the organization and the work it performs. However, within those differences, common themes emerge.

First, the four organizations all see a need to allow internal leadership to emerge through intentional nurturing and practical experiences (Cranston & Kusanovich, 2014; Lauer et al., 2014). As we noted previously, the dean of the school of education at St. Mary's College was very intentional in how she engaged the two faculty within this project. In her discussions with us as we were selecting participating organizations, she explained that this would provide an important professional development opportunity for the faculty members. Similarly, BSP and BeLit explain in their chapters that they look for opportunities to stretch staff's understanding of larger roles within the organization and, thereby, the organization itself. TAF, as a growing organization, offers continual opportunities for its staff to expand their responsibilities and knowledge of its work. These organizations understand that their staff is their strongest asset and that they need to provide them with opportunities for growth and development.

As a result, the three autonomous organizations have been looked internally to fill key roles. The clearest example of this is BSP, where three, top executive leaders all began in other positions and grew into their roles. As BSP explicitly notes in its chapter, and as is the case for three of the four organizations, this commitment to the development and growth of their employees allows the organizations to be reflective of the communities they serve. St. Mary's BALOS/GLD is an exception to this. The two programs only have two full-time faculty, and the adjunct (part-time) faculty who teach additional courses are not engaged in governance of the programs or the college. However, all four organizations are practicing what Edwards Groves and Rönnerman (2013) identify as "ecologies of practice" where members of an organization extend and expand their knowledge while providing leadership to the knowledge and direction of the overall organization.

Secondly, as Takayama et al. (2017) suggest it must be, especially for organizations that seek to be inclusive and diverse, leadership development is a component of each organization's strategic direction. As they grow and evolve as organizations, each of these organizations have people who can bridge from the past to the future. That has been especially critical for BeLit as two organizations merged to form the new one. Helping people within the organization understand the larger directions of the newly merged organization was critical to being able to live into the changes that a merger required. Developing both informal and formal leadership opportunities for the staff ensured a cleaner transition from two organizations to the newly merged BeLit. While the other organizations did not experience such a dramatic organizational change as a merger, the nature of their constant evolution requires them to support existing staff to become that critical bridge. As St. Mary's BALOS/GLD programs, for example, continue to exist within layers of college structures, it is vital for them to have faculty who understand the larger systems in which they operate and can navigate that structure for their needs.

Specific Funds Built into Budgets That Allow for Leadership Development

Another leadership development lesson from the organizations is that supporting staff for growth into leadership takes an organizational commitment; however, that commitment needs to be a pragmatic commitment by each of the four organizations. For each of them, that meant creation of funding that supported individuals' development. BSP has established and expanded professional development funds that employees can use for training and skills development. As the new organization emerged from its merger, the BeLit board of directors made a significant investment in professional development funds. Each of the organizations saw and reacted to their present and future needs by making an investment into their own staff.

A Relational Approach

Fenwick (2004) argues for human resource development that emphasizes relationships over utility. Looking at private industry, she offers the perspective that profit and shareholder value are less valuable than a focus on justice and equity for employees. While none of these organizations are in the for-profit economy, Fenwick's admonition still applies, and these four organizations show why. Each of the organizations writes about requiring or needing colleagues who reflect the diversity of their communities; and that is critical to their ability to serve those communities in ways that they explain within their chapters. However, another benefit accrues to that diversity that became clear as we looked across the four cases. As each organization has grown, each has fostered a culture based on internal relationships. Because the work is more mission than job to the people currently employed in each of these organizations, they look for new colleagues who can further the relations they want with the multiple communities they serve – and also the relations that existing colleagues have with each other. In their chapter, TAF eloquently sums what each of these organizations seeks, as the writers note that:

> Every applicant may not have all the desired skills or competencies, but they must have a willingness to develop them as a member of the team. We also look at their relationship to equity and our work to be an anti-racist, equitable organization; these align strongly to our mission and values.

A Commitment to Each Staff Member May Result in Losing Staff – and Being Okay with That

Finally, each of these organizations understands that as they help support the development of their employees into leadership, those employees may, at times, outgrow the positions available within the organization and move on to other opportunities. The leaders of these organizations see that as a benefit to their profession since these employees will take the positive culture they learned and spread the lessons of that culture to other organizations. The commitment and relationships that develop from supporting employees to become leaders expands each of these organizations' network within their sector as former employees become connected colleagues.

Lessons for Organizational Development

Belief in the Evolving Nature of the Organization

As explained earlier in this chapter, these organizations are in a constant state of evolution. Each organization believes that to be normal and they plan and operate accordingly. They live into what Hall and Hord (2014) identify as the "stages of concern" where organizations begin with an informational level of understanding of issues and progress to collaboration and refocusing of the organization.

St. Mary's BALOS/GLD faculty work in a very different higher education environment than a decade ago. Their participation in this project was important to their ability to evolve into those changes. BSP and TAF have both experienced rapidly growth and have had to remain a step ahead of that growth through planning, conversations, and developing strategic partners. BeLit is the most obvious example of evolution as circumstances shifted and caused two organizations to merge. Most importantly, as BeLit describes the processes for the merger and their self-analysis using the *FATAE*, it is clear to see that they have set the foundation for future evolution by establishing systems, open lines of communication, and opportunities for internal staff development. All four organizations prepare for an evolving future.

Comfort in Discomfort

The literature on organizational change (e.g., Berthoud & Ray, 2010; Hall & Hord, 2014) suggests that cycles of change can cause discomfort. BeLit, for example, realized that their focus on compensation equity created some uneasiness among staff because they conducted their analysis of salaries before looking closely at work assignment equity. BSP found that staff were worried when the organization started formalizing job descriptions – until the administrative team was able to provide a transparent process that communicated changes and engaged staff in helping define those changes. Participant feedback on TAF's initial formulation of the Network for EdWork, which was inclusive of all leaders (BIPOC and White) revealed it was flailing because it integrated multiple groups. Participants requested affinity-like groups. As a result, TAF leaders decided to divide the programming in two, thereby creating Education Encounter (targeted to BIPOC participants) and Ally Engagement (White participants).

Despite these very real and potential challenges from change, the organizations developed cultures where they support staff's understanding of that change. Even as part of a larger campus, St. Mary's BALOS/GLD faculty found that as they understood more about the larger campus systems, they could adapt to those systems. The most recent example came as they altered their curricula to adapt to a college-wide change to trimesters. The process of consolidating curriculum taught historically across four quarters to a three-semester system is laborious, time consuming, and requires multiple levels of review across departments, schools, and the college. Despite those challenges, the faculty looked to this as an opportunity to employ emerging teaching and learning strategies that focused more squarely on equity and justice and aligned to contemporary theories of adult learning. These organizations are finding comfort in the potentially discomfort of change.

Proof of each organization's comfort came in 2020. Despite the multiple other issues they were experiencing, each had to adapt to the pressures created by the pandemic. Because they are adaptive organizations, they adjusted and thrived as they completely renovated their instructional practices, adjusted to remote working, and still found time for the self-analyses that helped them improve present practices while planning the future.

Having the Right People in the Right Places

In all four of their chapters, each organization explores the importance of having the right people leading and working in the organization. In their histories, we learn how important it was in their past to have key leaders at key moments. Their present and future require the organizations to look for the people whom future histories will also see as key to progress and success.

Each organization has intentionally created a learning organization by carefully using strategies that build a strong staff. Both BSP and BeLit explain how their recent management hires have come from internal promotions. TAF built a team that came both internal and external to the organization as it sought out people who have complementary visions to theirs. St. Mary's school of education hired Stacey Robinson as a new faculty member to complement experienced professor Marguerite Welch; in creating that team and recommending this project to them, their dean helped to bridge past and future with two strong educators.

These four organizations are poised to address the kinds of institutional barriers that Evans and Chun (2007) warn against to hiring a diverse, vibrant, and engaged workforce. These authors suggest that the institutional culture of higher education, especially, limits the kinds of employees that organizations attract and retain. The four organizations' commitment to justice and equity lead them to practices that help avoid those potential traps as they create organizations that avoid issues of dominance and power that can exclude some potential applicants. As Guskey (2003) shows, there is not a uniformly available formula for building staff's leadership abilities; however, the actions and strategies that each organization is using are clearly intended to support to leadership.

Importance of Communication – Especially in Times of Stress and Change

Each chapter describes how the organizations seek to make both internal and external communications that are clear and aligned with their core mission. To these organizations, language matters. For example, BeLit describes how it became more aware of using the term "returning citizen" to describe one segment of their community. BSP explains how their interactions with the Framework allowed them to have language they can use in describing their equity and justice focus.

Beyond their intentional use of language, though, each organization describes how they also want to provide transparent communications that engage both their staff and stakeholders. TAF explains that they have developed systems that keep internal and external constituencies informed while giving opportunity for feedback. St. Mary's BALOS/GLD describes how they practice open communications with their students, while modeling and teaching students to do the same within their professional lives – even though the larger college systems do not sometimes offer similar modeling.

Importance of a Shared Vision

The final lesson on organizational development that these organizations share in their chapters may be the most important. These are all mission- and vision-driven organizations, and the centrality of their mission and vision to their operation cannot be understated. For each organization, these are more than words in a document or something they bring out for donors or annual reports. In reading these chapters, the commitment to living into their intentions is a thread that appears throughout each chapter. BeLit's exercise at the start of the merger where they brought together the new board of directors and 53 staff is an example of how critical mission and vision are to all of the organizations. Through the conversations BeLit had and the inclusion they all experienced, the organization began its work in ensuring that each board and staff member saw their role as contributing to the mission and vision. As all the chapters show, each organization renewed and revisited their commitment with similar transparency and organization-wide engagement. The other organizations did not begin their efforts at developing and living into mission and vision *de novo*, but, as they all note, they have come back to their vision and mission to have discussions about their fidelity to those foundational statements. All four organizations used the *FATAE* as one more tool to look at their mission, vision, and actions through a lens of equity and justice.

Lessons for the Organizational Application of Justice and Equity

An Ongoing Dialogue and a Continual Revisiting of Ideals

The four case studies provide examples of how justice and equity need to be embedded into the work of an organization. In selecting participating organizations, we wanted those which had history of self-examining issues like power, privilege, race, and gender. As we selected the final organizations, within each of the selected four organizations' past experiences and practices, we could see that. Even within BeLit, the newest organization, the brief history they describe in the chapter shows how each of the two merged organizations had, in each organization's past, committed to exploring and responding to needs for justice and equity in their separate, past work. The *FATAE*, as all four have written, helped them to focus carefully on elements of equity and justice and examine their practices. However, this project is not the first, nor will it be the last, time these organizations will self-examine their practices. As they each note, this project represents a further step in their organizational extant application of justice and equity. The four organizations have been, and will continue to be, exemplars of what Fenwick (2004) argues must be an ongoing critical examination of organizations that seek to be just and equitable organizations, not just in their mission but also in the ways in which they operate.

There is, also, a tension that all of these organizations experienced in conducting the self-evaluation that the *FATAE* demanded. That tension became most evident as the organizations moved from the analysis to the writing phase of the project. As they began to write, they realized that not everything they discovered was ideal and that their discoveries identified challenges either within their organization or the larger contexts in which they exist. As editors, we encouraged them to tell that part of their story as honestly as they could, understanding that their work needs to carry forward within the relationships that will long outlast this book. Within the chapters, each organization found ways to explain those challenges honestly while showing the potential for growth and change beyond the challenges. As their chapters suggest, focusing on justice demands that honesty, as well as an ability to provide solutions that address issues.

Engaging Outside Voices – i.e., Partnering with Others Who Are Doing Similar Work

Knox (2003) emphasizes the need for adult education organizations to develop partnerships in conducting their work. He explains that adult education providers are in a unique position to bring together multiple partnerships within any community. Describing a case study of health education, Ramanadhan et al. (2020) show how complex that can be while describing the positive impacts that cross-organizational partnerships can have. In the four organizations, a resulting characteristic of their commitment to self-evaluation around justice and equity is their willingness to engage with multiple partners that help them with that work. As we explain in more detail in Chapter 8, we intended to be a partner in this project, and we did not want to assume a more common consultative role as experts who provide answers. In our screening of organizations, we found that each of the four organizations has some history of developing similar relationships with outside partners. St. Mary's BALOS/GLD faculty create their partnerships through the professional connections of the faculty, and they are learning to create partners on campus to give them connections within the structure of their college. BSP is, by design and historically, an organization that exists to connect multiple organizations and resources. TAF found strong relationships with academics, K-12 schools, funders, and private industry. BeLit, as it seeks to leverage the relationships that each of the two, merged organizations brought to the merger, developed critical affiliations in government, within the adult literacy sector, and with industries that, at first glance, may have no connection to their work. These relationships help each organization in its intended mission as they bring multiple stakeholders together to provide diverse perspectives to their work.

Relying on Internal Voices – i.e., Foregrounding Internal Expertise and Knowledge

Sparks (2009) writes about professional development for K-12 teachers; however, his observations on the importance of developing internal expertise within an organization are applicable to any organization that promotes learning and teaching. Sparks sees a need for real-time professional development where all stakeholders and employees in an educational organization should be concurrently developing new skills while strategically responding to the needs of daily operation. Encouraging, supporting, and listening to internal voices within the organization are, therefore, critical to these organizations' intended efforts at justice and equity. In their chapters, both BSP and BeLit explain that building internal capacity is critical to their future. Both of these organizations put a premium value on creating a management team that is promoted from the organization. TAF's growth has meant they needed to hire a lot of external applicants; however, they have emphasized systems that foreground the expertise of all internal voices as they make decisions. The development of staff is a key common thread throughout all four chapters. Equally important is the ability of the organizations to avail themselves of the existing and emerging skills that come from their employees. They offer evidence in each chapter that they create communication structures and systems to hear and learn from all employees.

The ideas of "internal" and "external" are complicated for St. Mary's BALOS/GLD. While the two described programs are internal to St. Mary's College, in many ways that are common in institutions of higher education, they make operational decisions independently of the larger college. The two directors need to negotiate the complexity of being housed within a school of education that is, itself, one branch of the college. Colleges are typically hierarchically managed. At each level of the organization, there are rules that apply to the levels beneath them on the organizational chart. This gets further complicated by the nature of the faculty role. Because of the needs of academic freedom, faculty operate a parallel structure to manage instructional processes. This is typically called a "faculty senate" (or something similar) and works alongside the structure that manages the college's daily operations. In order to manage instructional programs in higher education, St. Mary's BALOS/GLD faculty have to work within all of those structures.

As a result, what is "internal" to the program changes depending on the conversation. In a budget discussion for a program, for example, "internal" typically means within the school or division in which the program is housed because program budgets are managed at that level. In contrast, when a program is discussing changes to its curriculum, "internal" can mean within its school/division, the faculty senate, or within the chief academic officer's office. In seeing the BALOS/GLD faculty describe themselves in their chapter, it was clear that their ability to be more intentional in understanding and managing internal relations in all of these areas was a major discovery for them. That discovery will be critical to both programs' futures. Their dean's intentional development of the two key faculty who wrote the chapter acknowledged and supported those futures. Although Marguerite retired at the end of the academic year in which the chapter was written, the work that she and Stacey completed sets a foundation for Stacey to work with Marguerite's eventual replacement to build their internal relationships within all of the levels required for the programs to thrive.

Doing More Than Talking; Talking That Leads to Doing

This is a point that we make indirectly multiple times above; however, it is worth stating directly. An attribute that is also often common among adult learning providers is how these organizations emphasize action. All four chapters show that they are committed to discussions and explorations. As we worked with them, however, we observed how each of them saw the discussions and explorations they undertook as worthwhile because they helped to define and refine action. As we were selecting the four organizations, we saw evidence of those discussions in their past. As we worked with them, we saw and experienced how they focus their ideas into action. The *FATAE* was new to them; however, their ability and willingness to act based on what they discovered in using a framework was not.

Allowing Voices to Emerge While Being Clear about Direction and Purpose

The last organizational attribute that we saw in all four organizations is their willingness to allow for multiple voices to emerge in their explorations. In conducting its self-analysis, St. Mary's faculty drew on its students' perceptions of the program – as well as having students conduct the survey as the faculty engaged them in the process. TAF hosted multiple discussions with everyone from the board to management, staff, and external partners. Both BeLit and BSP held regular conversations that brought together stakeholders to examine and respond to the questions posed by the *FATAE*. For these organizations, using inclusive practices to foreground multiple voices is a natural outcome of the inclusive organizations they seek to be.

Organizational Challenges to the Process

Engaging the FATAE was a long process for each of the organizations and a variety of obstacles arose. Few adult learning agencies have spare resources of time, staff, or finances. The work of engaging constituencies over six months came at times with a cost, particularly in the context of managing resources during a pandemic. While some of those obstacles, such as the scarcity of time or the challenge of organizing data, are common to all organizations endeavoring a process of strategic review, there were some elements that felt unique or amplified by the nature of the *FATAE* and/or the domain of adult learning.

It was critically important to each organization to implement a process of meaningful review that includes its broad constituencies. Integrating the perspective of staff, trustees, clients, and funders presented logistic hurdles like organizing times to meet via pandemic-mandated videoconferencing. The coordinators also needed to balance those voices so that each felt recognized for the ways they represented the mission and as an agent of improvement and change. The four organizations needed to remain focused on information collection for an extended period to allow information to emerge. It is challenging for any organization that is as results-focused as these four organizations not to jump immediately to solutions to each challenge their analysis uncovered.

Another challenge that emerged towards to latter half of this project was the tenor of the stories initially penned by many of the organizations. As researchers, we had prior experiences with case study inquiries wherein the "results" were written in a more narrative, storytelling manner, one that captured the depth, breadth, and affective tone (e.g., positive, negative) of findings. We wanted the organizations' work similarly to reflect the authenticity of the gathered information. Also, we wanted them to analyze their information in a manner less schematic and constraining of conventional formats for presenting results (Miles et al., 2014). Our organizational authors, on the other hand, were more experienced in other narrative or forms of storytelling. Instead of writing up results from research projects, they generated initial drafts to serve the purposes of branding, public relations, marketing, and funding development. Often the focus of their work was on highlights of the organization's work and outcomes, and often, did not include challenges faced or opportunities for growth.

Not one of our four organizations would have thrived without developing a talent for advocacy. The resources needed to sustain and expand often depend on a cycle of organizational promotion, and the skills to speak clearly and distinctly about the outcomes and impact of programs. Indeed, for many organizations the rationale for self-examination is, in part, promotional. The desire to present their organizations in the best possible light presented a challenge to the work of applying the *FATAE* in an authentic way. There is a vulnerability required to examine organizational practices rigorously in pursuit of self-discovery and iterative improvement. In a funding environment that constantly requires organizations to highlight successes and expand on performance goals, it is natural for organizations to demure about misaligned internal practices.

There are many reasons that the four organizations chose to take on the work of this project. For some, the goals were primarily internal, a chance to evaluate processes with the support of a framework and coach. For others, the initial lure was more external – the opportunity to tell their organization's story in a way that might add value to a case statement or funding proposal.

Integrating these forces in a meaningful way became a central goal for us as editors. Using a case study model required each organization to unpack performance or cultural gaps, and to reveal assumptions that might have affected morale or impact. For some of the organizations, fear about negative exposure initially inhibited the breadth of the story they wanted to tell.

Despite these concerns, an opportunity for powerful growth and advocacy lay in the vulnerability of authentic reflection. Each organization spoke with visible pride about the discovery of their challenges and the galvanizing power of bridging those gaps among staff and constituents. TAF spoke of the impact of building a sense of shared leadership and agency during a period of strategic growth. BSP's evaluation of its funding partnerships invigorated a pride in the integrity and shared values expressed in its origins. Be Lit found itself elevating professional standards across a newly merged organization and able to tell a story that directly resulted in new levels of state funding. St. Mary's BALOS/GLD found new ways it needed to engage with their campus.

Lessons for the Field of Adult Learning

Understanding the Complex Nature of What It Means to Be a Learning Organization

As adult learning looks at these four organizations to see what it can learn from their experiences, seeing both the positive impacts and the challenges they experience are critical. They provide learning to very different groups of adults, yet these are all organizations that are actively learning themselves. The term "learning organization" is one that is often overused to the point of having an unclear meaning. The chapters in this book suggest an affinity with the definition that Barker Scott offers. To Barker Scott, a learning organization is:

> ...a multilevel process whereby members individually and collectively acquire knowledge by acting together and reflecting together. Knowledge is acquired, or created, and applied by individuals. In turn, individual knowledge is shared, combined, expanded, tested, and applied amongst individuals to become group or community knowledge. As that knowledge is captured, spread and embedded in organizational features, such as strategies and protocols, it becomes part of an organizational context, or code, that, in turn, influences what and how groups, communities, and individuals learn. The code continues to evolve as it consumes the learning of individuals and groups.
>
> *Barker Scott, 2011, p. 20*

That description fits what the four organizational chapter authors describe of their organizations, and it also describes our experiences in working with them. Being a learning organization requires a commitment beyond workshops and trainings that are commonly understood as "learning." As these four organizations show, they learn daily by establishing processes and systems that encourage and nurture their ability to grow as an organization. In many ways, these learning organizations are like plants that need the right conditions. Farmers tell us that crops grow in ideal conditions. If the growing season is delayed because of a late spring, there may not be enough warm days to bring crops to fruition. If the conditions are right, crops need to be fed and kept from pests and weeds. It is that same attention to environment and supports that make learning an organizational characteristic rather than an event or activity alone. As we worked with each organization, we saw and heard their commitments to fostering the dialogues that led to their deep explorations of what they do and how they do it.

Their commitment to being learning organizations is a significant factor in their commitment to justice and equity. The ideals of justice and equity that are explicated within the *FATAE* require a commitment to self-examination that is well beyond merely providing assent to ideals. The work that all four organizations conducted for this book is hard work. It demands honest, extensive interactions that Barker Scott's definition of a learning organization suggest.

Providing Support for Individuals and the Whole Organization to Evolve

These are four organizations in evolution. As noted previously, being in a constant state of change is normative for the people and organizations. As other case studies of organizations that seek to be collaborative and supportive suggest (e.g., Berthoud & Ray, 2010; Hands et al., 2015) an organization needs to balance its needs while balancing the needs of the people within the organization to evolve with the changes. Throughout each chapter, the authors offer examples of this. For example, BSP holds biweekly check in meetings with its internal management, while encouraging managers to similarly check in with their staff. BeLit is building similar conversations into its structure as it merges the two cultures and groups. All four organizations seek to be intentional about how they watch for the signs of stress that results from change. All four seek to be responsive to the needs that arise from the resulting tensions of change.

Allowing for the Social Construction of Knowledge

In their seminal work on the social construction of knowledge, *Situated Learning: Legitimate Peripheral Participation* (1991), Lave and Wenger emphasize the need for learning to exist within the contexts of people's lives. They show the importance of understanding that learning happens within conversations as people learn from and adapt to each other's ideas. In these four cases, we see that the organizations establish opportunities for that. Of course, this happens, as it typically does, around the daily work of the organization as people engage around curriculum development or fund raising or personnel management. It is more difficult for organizations to have sustained conversations about who they are and whether they are living into their ideals. In socially constructing their knowledge of who they are, each of the four organizations initiates and maintains the discussions without becoming mired in the ideas. As noted previously, they each already were already conducting other self-analyses, so their work for this book was not novel activity. What is worth noting, however, is their commitment to whole-organization engagement led to meaningful conversations that eventually informed action.

Lessons from the Field of Organizational Design and Leadership

The regular practice of iterative learning and managing change represents critical skills in navigating some of the default patterns and behaviors embedded in an organization's culture. All four of the organizations identified the historical systems in which they were created, and felt, at the onset of this exercise, that they would discover ways in which their practices misaligned with their beliefs about equity.

The *FATAE* supports the idea that agencies are created by and operate within the systems they were often created to change. Organizations, like people, manifest behaviors that reflect the social schema of their environment. Victor Ray explains that, "...schemas can be thought of as a kind of unwritten rulebook explaining how to write rules" (Ray, 2019, p. 31) and that "individual racial attitudes and discriminations are enabled or constrained by organizational routines. More than a mere 'link' between macro- and micro-level processes, organizations are key to stability and change" (Ray, 2019, p. 32).

Organizations, even those designed to promote change, gravitate toward an internal stability that allows them to manage unpredictable external environments. Behaviors or systems put in place to extend that stability sometimes reflect a desire to minimize inertia rather than a desire to align with organization values. Examining those practices can feel both empowering and disorienting. BSP's evaluation of their funding structure, for example, presented a potential set of targeted funding sources while promising to deepen their case statement for future grants. Similarly, despite a history of funding success, BeLit's board membership revealed the opportunity to imagine a governance structure far more reflective of the communities the organization served. For St. Mary's, a schema was perhaps the most intensely visible, manifested in the structures and policies of the broader college's system.

It is in the acknowledgement and exploration of such structures that each of four organizations thrives. Each organization assumes there is room for growth and implements systems for self-reflection and course correction, sometimes in small ways, and other times on the scale of the questions posed by the *FATAE*.

Each prioritizes the agency and well-being of its staff, drawing energy to programs from the shared personal and organizational expression of mission.

These are themes that suggest a picture of organizational well-being, an idea explored in recent years by scholars concerned with the combination of factors that allow organizations to thrive in addressing issues of equity and justice. In a 2020 article for the Stanford Social Innovation Review, Mary-Frances Winter writes,

> To truly address systemic racism; enhance the experience of equity, belonging, and inclusion among all employees; and support individual and organizational well-being, organizations [need to engage] a continuous process of examination and change to organizational culture. It can be useful to think of the process as having three main parts: building internal capacity to develop new skills and competencies, creating an environment where people can productively talk about issues related to race, and developing equitable systems internally and externally.
>
> *Winters, 2020*

Extended further, the application of an equity framework such as the *FATAE* suggests a practical model for organizational development that aligns closely with the elements of the Social Action, Leadership and Transformation (SALT) Model (Museus et al., 2017) which shines a light on the critical actions for leadership focused on building both internal and external systems of equity and social justice: A capacity for empathy, the development of a critical consciousness, a visible commitment to justice goals, equity in purpose, the value of collective action, and the engagement of controversy with courage. The SALT model echoes the need to visualize the organization as a manifestation of collective social body capable of experiencing, healing from and even transcending social schema (Ray, 2019).

Thus, the work of these four organizations is instructive to leadership practices. While many agencies have moved beyond traditional models of organization and planning, several of these organizations experienced notable gains in the level of staff morale, community trust, program quality, and even funding following their extended inquiry into their organizational habits and default behaviors. As such, opportunities abound for organizational leaders who build in iterative, structured systems for the critical investigation of not only strategy but also organization-wide alignment with their expressed equity values.

Lessons for the Field of K-12 and Higher Education

In the thought-provoking, *The Book of Learning and Forgetting*, written in 1998, Frank Smith penned a chapter on "Liberating Schools and Education" (pp. 90–103). His focus was on liberating education from "the official theory of learning," by advocating for the abolition of tests, fragmented instructional materials and procedures, drills, memorization and recapitulation exercises, segregation of ability groups, coercion, and time constraints. He proposed a three-step solution to achieving change. The first step is conscious raising – engaging in collaborative conversations to uncover the consequences of what people do, what is working well, and what is not. Secondly, he proposed increasing focus on what is working well, and decreasing efforts on what is not, expecting this may run counter to established systems, structures, policies, and procedures. Finally, the third step is being honest about what is not working well and the costs and consequences of maintaining those traditional practices as opposed to implementing change toward more humanizing, inclusive, and liberating practices.

In many ways, the original *EDJE Framework* and the adapted *FATAE* provoke inquiry, reflection, and action to liberate educational organizations from historical, structural, systemic, and cultural discrimination based on race, ethnicity, gender, ability, and sexual orientation. The guided self-assessment and reflection processes supported by these frameworks provide the basis by which we can raise our consciousness to what is working well, what is not working well, and opportunities for growth and change. This process allows for purposive planning and change in future endeavors and efforts to advance equity, justice, and inclusion. The work of the four organizations highlighted in this book offers possibilities, challenges, and rewards of liberation based in equity, justice, an inclusion. Their stories provide hope and specific strategies for advancing education.

References

Barker Scott, B. (2011). *Organizational learning: A literature review*. Queen's University Industrial Relations Centre.

Berthoud, H., & Ray, J. (2010). Diversity initiative in a social change organization: A case study. *Tamara Journal of Critical Organisation Inquiry, 8*(3), 62–88.

Caffarella, R. S. (1996). Can I really do it all? *Adult Learning, 8*(1), 8. doi: 10.1177/104515959600800105.

Cranston, J. A., & Kusanovich, K. A. (2014). How shall I act? Nurturing the dramatic and ethical imagination of educational leaders. *International Studies in Educational Administration (Commonwealth Council for Educational Administration & Management (CCEAM)), 42*(2), 45–62.

Edwards Groves, C., & Rönnerman, K. (2013). Generating leading practices through professional learning. *Professional Development in Education, 39*(1), 122–140. doi: 10.1080/19415257.2012.724439.

Elmore, R. F. (1996). Getting to scale with good educational practice. *Harvard Educational Review, 66*(1), 1–26.

Evans, A., & Chun, E. B. (2007). The theoretical framework: Psychosocial oppression and diversity. *ASHE Higher Education Report, 33*(1): 1–26.

Fenwick, T. J. (2004). Toward a critical HRD in theory and practice. *Adult Education Quarterly, 54*(3), 193–209. doi: 10.1177/0741713604263051.

Garvin, D. A. (1993). Building a Learning Organization. *Harvard Business Review.* Retrieved from: https://hbr.org/1993/07/building-a-learning-organization

Guskey, T. R. (2003). Analyzing lists of the characteristics of effective professional development to promote visionary leadership. *NASSP Bulletin, 87*(637), 4.

Hall, G., & Hord, S. (2014). *Implementing change: Patterns, principles, and potholes.* Pearson Allyn & Bacon.

Hands, C., Guzar, K., & Rodrigue, A. (2015). The art and science of leadership in learning environments: Facilitating a professional learning community across districts. *Alberta Journal of Educational Research, 61*(2), 226–242.

Hughes, B. (2017). I've known Rivers. In P. Mitchell (Ed.), *African American males in higher education leadership: Challenges and opportunities.* Peter Lang Publishing.

Hunter-Johnson, Y., & Closson, R. (2012). Adult educators' perceptions of their organization promoting learning practices and culture: A Caribbean law enforcement context. *Adult Learning, 23*(4), 178–187. doi: 10.1177/1045159512457919.

Knox, A. B. (2003). Future directions for collaborative strategies. *Adult Learning, 14*(2), 29–30.

Lauer, P. A., Christopher, D. E., Firpo-Triplett, R., & Buchting, F. (2014). The impact of short-term professional development on participant outcomes: A review of the literature. *Professional Development in Education, 40*(2), 207–227. doi: 10.1080/19415257.2013.776619.

Lave, J., & Wenger, E. (1991). *Situated learning: Legitimate peripheral participation (learning in doing: Social, cognitive and computational perspectives).* Cambridge University Press.

Miles, M. B., Huberman, A. M., & Saldana, J. (2014). *Qualitative data analysis: A methods sourcebook.* SAGE.

Museus, S., Lee, N., Calhoun, K., Sánchez-Parkinson, L., & Ting, M. (2017). *The Social Action, Leadership, and Transformation (SALT) Model.* Retrieved from: https://lsa.umich.edu/content/dam/ncid-assets/ncid-documents/publications/Museus%20et%20al%20(2017)%20SALT%20Model%20Brief.pdf

Odor, H. (2018). A literature review on organizational learning and learning organizations. *International Journal of Economics & Management Sciences, 7*(1). doi: 10.4172/2162-6359.1000494.

Ramanadhan, S., Aronstein, D., Martinez-Dominguez, V., Xuan, Z., & Viswanath, K. (2020). Designing capacity-building supports to promote evidence-based programs in community-based organizations working with underserved populations. *Progress in Community Health Partnerships, 14*(2), 149–160.

Ray, V. (February 2019). A theory of racialized organizations. *American Sociological Review, 84*(1), 26–53.

Schein, E. H. (2010). *Organizational culture and leadership.* Jossey-Bass.

Smith, F. (1998). *The book of learning and forgetting.* Teachers College Press.

Sparks, D. (2009). What I believe about leadership development. *Phi Delta Kappan, 90*(7), 514–517.

Takayama, K., Kaplan, M., & Cook-Sather, A. (2017). Advancing diversity and inclusion through strategic multilevel leadership. *Liberal Education, 103*(3–4), 7.

Winters, M.-F. (2020). Equity and Inclusion: The Roots of Organizational Well-Being. *Stanford Social Innovation Review.* doi: 10.48558/SD1P-J693.

8

OBSERVATIONS

What We Learned in the Process

Deanna Iceman Sands, Bob Hughes, and Ted Kalmus

Introduction

We began this project with the idea that the people best suited to tell a story are the people who are engaged in the story. Oftentimes, academics come into a situation, study that situation with qualitative and quantitative tools, and then tell the story from their external perspective. That etic view is, however, limited. We can observe, we can measure, and we can report, but we cannot experience what the people engaged in the activity experience. We may have a good idea of what happens because of our past experiences, training, and research; but we do not have an intimate, emic understanding that comes from daily living within the studied context. Even if we, as anthropologists and sociologists often do, immerse ourselves in the culture, and context of that experience, we are, at best, close observers. At worst, we are tourists who stop to see the sights and quickly move to the next sight/study.

Our goal for this book was different. While all three of us have been immersed in education for most of our adult lives, and while we have been educational leaders for a good part of that time, we understand that our knowledge is external to each of these organizations. We did not want to rely on our outsiders' knowledge to tell these four stories. Instead, we wanted to find a way that we could help them tell their stories. As noted in the opening chapters, we were careful to select organizations that had existing evidence that they were successful at equitably serving the diverse communities in which they operate. Our task was to help them in a self-exploration that told how and why they came to this success. Adapting the *EDJE Framework* to this project was critical as it provided a common set of standards for each organization to tell their story. But even in that, we wanted each organization to use

DOI: 10.4324/9781003286998-8

the framework consistently with their own aims and needs. That is why we encouraged each organization to select which parts of the *FATAE* were most important to their self-exploration.

All this stems from our belief that our job is to co-construct knowledge rather than to teach or discover it. Within a social construction (Lave & Wenger, 1991) of knowledge, that idea is central to the role of any external participant. We sought to help the four organizations look at themselves and use the *FATAE* and our support to examine critical questions and then see those relate to goals and objectives that they already have. This perspective creates a symbiotic relationship where we became consultants who helped organizations in their explorations in the initial stage of their project. Later, we became editors of their work so that it reflected their intent. The *FATAE* gave us a common language in both of those stages, and it also provided a research-based set of knowledge that grounded all of the work.

This all required us to develop a unique relationship with each organization. Each of us worked with one or two organizations as their primary consultant, and each of us adapted to emerging needs as they occurred. The consultation we provided was unique to the needs of each organization. In working with them, each of the three editors drew on our experiences as educational leaders, and we also used the *FATAE* that was the basis of this work as a guideline for the support and counsel we provided. That meant being available to meet with both the writing team within the organization and, at times, to meet with their supervisors. We sometimes helped the organizations make sense of challenges they were uncovering, and, at other times, helped them to see strengths that they had not identified.

As a result, each organization came away from this project with different lessons to share. While we saw many common traits across these organizations (explored previously in Chapter 7), co-constructing a chapter with each allowed the organizations to make their work individually meaningful to each of them. That is important since each organization has a unique set of challenges and exists in a unique context. For Building Skills Partnership, for example, that meant applying this work into a rapidly expanding, statewide organization that is fitting into its role as a leader in workforce development. The program directors of the BALOS and GLD programs explored how the larger institutional context impacts their ability to meet their aims at serving adult learners.

As consultants or editors, we could not apply a common set of activities and rules in our work. Each writing team encountered different pressures and needs as they prepared their chapters. When one organization became "stuck" in their process, the assigned editor met with the writing team, interviewed them using the questions of the framework, and then used their words from the interview to draft text that they could use as the foundation for their chapter. In another case, the writing team changed over time and needed to have one of us as the bridge between one writing team and the next. In all the organizations, we were able to ask probing questions that helped them to explore their work and to tell their stories as honestly and clearly as possible. We know that self-evaluation exercises can easily become self-promotion exercises, but that did not happen since each writing team had the framework and one of us to critically examine what they do. We also gave organizations recommendations for other voices to include in their analyses so that they were, also, co-constructing their knowledge with their many stakeholders.

The result of the collaboration is that we feel confident that the four cases are reflective of the experiences within these organizations. Their stories include the challenges they continue to face, so they have done more than just tell of their successes. Like all organizations, their successes are mixed with challenges; their triumphs are mixed with setbacks. Co-constructing these chapters allowed those complexities to be told.

Model of Action Research

As we noted in Chapters 1 and 2, we deliberately selected the organizations that are in this book. That intentionality allows the book to tell the stories of four unique organizations that have differing missions and perform within different structures and systems. They were also at different stages in their development. Given the diversity of what is meant by "adult learning," we believe in the importance of capturing part of that diversity. Participatory action research (PAR) is a model of inquiry that allows exploration of the complexity created by such diversity (Fetterman et al., 2014). As you read the four cases, you discovered how the context, mission, and structure of each organization shaped the ways in which they live into their intended goals to focus on equity and justice. Conducting self-studies and then actively creating their own story allowed these organizations to show how they work toward their intended goals. Using a PAR model allowed this project to have themes and trends emerge naturally as each organization conducted its exploration and told its story. Our role as co-constructors of the work was secondary to their explorations.

PAR also allowed us flexibility in how each organization conducted its inquiry. While we provided a template for how to conduct the self-study and to write the chapter, every team either significantly modified what we provided or completely created their own process. As noted in Chapter 7, each organization conducted other self-analyses as they completed their work for this chapter. They used internal systems or, in some cases external consultants, to move forward on the same topics they explored for their chapter. Not duplicating efforts, especially in the pandemic-pressured time in which they were working, was imperative. Using an adaptable PAR process allowed for the adjustments that each organization needed, while the framework and our consultancy kept the work focused on the equity and justice principles at the center of this book. We helped the organizations create complementary processes that met the aims of this book while using their findings to inform the other analyses they conducted simultaneously.

TAF, used this project concurrently with a review of their systems and programming, both of which had grown dramatically as they expanded their support of educators. Faculty at St. Mary's in the BALOS and GLD programs completed their study while conducting a program review required by their college and while they also engaged in major curriculum redesign to respond to the college's shift to a new semester system. BeLit was evaluating the organizational needs stemming from their merger. BSP was in the midst of analyzing both its systems and processes as it experienced exponential growth and increased demands for its services. The PAR model allowed us to fit within the complexities of each of these circumstances while ensuring that the findings reflected the realities of each organization – eventually leading to actionable information that they can use to continue to grow.

Consultative, Not Authoritative

Our role, as suggested above, was to be consultative, rather than authoritative. As noted, each of the three editors has significant experience in education; however, we believe that imposing our knowledge on these organizations would have been mistaken. When we use the word "consult," we may use it differently than it is often used. Metaphorically, we consulted alongside rather than from the front. Being alongside meant listening to what the organizations needed and adjusting to those needs. Being alongside meant using our past knowledge and experiences to suggest ideas that might shape their inquiry or to frame the results of the inquiry. Being alongside meant being aware of the limitations that each organization experienced and then to support them in negotiating those limitations. In some consultation work, the client comes to the consultant and asks for a solution. In contrast, we sought to understand each organization and then help them understand how their efforts aligned with the principles of justice and equity identified in the *FATAE*. As they explored those alignments or misalignments, we helped them discuss what they were learning and what they could do.

In order to understand each organization, we immersed ourselves into what they do and how they do it. In a face-to-face PAR project, we would spend time on site, interviewing, observing, taking field notes, etc. Not only was that impossible because of the pandemic travel limitations, it was impossible because the organizations had limited face-to-face operations as they completed this project. Along with the rest of the world, we adapted. As noted in Chapter 2, we met via videoconference with each organization as individual editors, and we also had ongoing whole-group meetings with the coordinators from each organization throughout the discovery process and as organizations wrote their early drafts. As they moved into fully writing their chapters, all of the organizations agreed that their time would be better spent working on their individual efforts. Depending on the organization, editors supported the process of editing and providing feedback on up to six interim drafts of a chapter. Each editor continued to meet with their individual organizations approximately every two weeks until the organization submitted a final draft.

The result of the whole-group and individual conversations allowed us, as editors and consultants, to learn more about these organizations. We kept extensive field notes on these conversations and, in one case, recorded and summarized discussions that we could use in helping with organizational analyses, as well as the cross-case analysis that is included in Chapter 7. The meetings and discussions allowed us to create a community of practice that allowed all of us (editors and project teams alike) to learn from our conversations in the "situated" processes that Wenger et al. (2002) suggest are critical to organizational learning. Although we could not embed ourselves in the sites and learn from the traditional PAR tools, we found that creating an intentional learning community and being available to provide support as needed allowed us to develop rich understanding of each organization so that we could consult alongside.

The three editors of this book met regularly throughout this process to discuss our experiences and to support one another as we supported the organizations. Those meetings offered invaluable moments to reflect on the process and to reach new understandings of both the organizations and our overall work. We kept notes in these meetings, and the notes allowed us to return to these meetings and see the project and the organizations evolve. For anyone attempting a similar project in the future our most important advice is to have a collaborative, coherent team who develops and implements the project. As in any socially constructed learning, developing our awareness together enriched us and the final book immeasurably.

Scholar Practitioners

PAR requires inquiry as its foundation (Greenwood & Levin, 2006). Unlike hypothesis-driven social science, PAR's inquiry comes as participants in a given community of practice seek to examine questions related to their practices. In light of the participatory action research design and methods applied in this project, we regard our colleagues from the four, organizational communities of practice as scholar practitioners (Distefano et al., 2004). They engaged in this project "informed by experiential knowledge, and motivated by personal values, political commitments, and ethical conduct .... Were committed to the well-being of clients and colleagues, to learning new ways of being effective, and to conceptualizing their work in relation to broader organizational, community, political, and cultural contexts" (p. 393). We have noted a few times in prior chapters how self-analytical these four organizations have been, even without this project. This project helped to complement those explorations while helping to focus on gathering information about the specific questions asked in the framework. Where they gathered their information was as varied as questionnaires, interviews, the use of historical records, and notes from meetings. Each organization drew on multiple existing sources of information while it also generated new information that helped its explorations. In completing this project, each organization examined itself deeply and included multiple stakeholders in that examination. The result is a "thick description" (Geertz, 1973; Ryle, 1971) that examines each organization from multiple perspectives while triangulating their findings through multiple sources.

"Action" is a critical word in the description of PAR. While identifying and measuring outcomes was not a component of this project, it is clear from the chapters that each organization underwent some evolution as a result of their work on this project. We discuss those changes in Chapter 7 in some detail. These organizations are not satisfied to explore. Instead, they are action-oriented organizations that seek positive outcomes from all of their work. Therefore, it makes sense that, as the chapters show, each of them found ways to use this project in their self-improvement. Whether it was changing their human resources policies or working within a larger system or examining the equity impacts of a merger, these organizations discovered new ways to operate that better align with their intentions to be just and equitable in their work. We suspected that might happen because of the nature of the process and the profiles of the organizations. However, when we began this project, we did not make organizational change an intentional outcome of the project. That happened organically as these four organizations learned about themselves and, as they have always done, sought to be better.

Self-Reflections

Our roles as editors took on meaningful consultative elements over the period of engagement with the organizations we were supporting. In the early stages, that often meant working closely among ourselves to develop a process of engagement and inquiry that reflected the needs, style, and life cycle of each organization. The logistical challenges of "finding the time" were substantial, but in some cases secondary to common elements of organizational inertia. We provided models and sample questions, workshopped plans for engagement and helped to problem solve when issues arose. At times, we needed to encourage progress or reinforce deadlines, sometimes reminding organizations why they had started the process in the first place. However, once the flow of data began, we quickly moved to a reflective stance, more often helping to frame observations and questions around the guiding elements of the *FATAE*.

Our extended engagement with these organizations certainly required us to be flexible as changes occurred but it also meant being involved in more than just supporting the writing of a chapter. The desire to catalyze learning into action led to deep conversations with each organization about its strategies, identity, joys, and frustrations. The work we did deepened our appreciation for the dynamic efforts these organizations are making and personally connected us to their impact. We learned that learning beside one another develops lasting and meaningful relationships, whether on a personal or organizational level. As educators and as editors, we reflected on the ways this work impacted us.

Deanna

I served on the board of directors for one of these organizations for a while in a previous, professional role. The organization I worked with also had a partnership with this organization, one that supported their efforts in teacher training. Though I was an active board member and the organization worked to connect its staff and an understanding of their respective programs/work with board members, being in this process helped me understand that I still had much to learn. This project helped me understand at a deeper level the inner workings of the organization and importantly, the challenges faced and the dedication, effort, and time devoted by staff to keep up with ever-changing landscapes, needs, and resources required to support their adult learners. Prior to this process, I held the organization, its staff and work with the highest regard; now, I realize my understanding of and respect for them and their respective work has deepened in unimaginable ways. Working side by side with the staff who led this process was invaluable – our relationship deepened over time and I for one, am grateful for the opportunity.

Ted

Professionally, I have worked with educational nonprofits for decades who struggle with the dissonance of providing powerful programs without the resources or governance to ensure sustainability or to grow the way they believe they should to manifest their vision. The inertia many of the organizations felt around their growth felt familiar to me and, having seen many others falter, I wondered if the idea of formally centering equity would prove to align vision with practice in meaningful ways. The results were more powerful than I expected. We talk often about the ways that managing change requires vulnerability, but I was humbled by the willingness of our agencies to look deeper, receive feedback, and ultimately elevate learning as a core strength of who they are and how they operate.

Bob

In my professional life, I have twice been a community college dean who oversaw basic skills programs that connected with workforce development. As a professor of adult education, I taught many students who worked in workforce development; and I have consulted with many workforce-development programs. I have, as a result, understood and admired the benefits that workforce development programs like BSP provide. I also understand how they often operate at the margins of adult education – despite the central role they play in supporting the occupational and educational growth of the people they serve. Working with BSP, because of the comprehensive nature of their intended mission and the wonderfully committed folks they employ, was a joy. Even though we were working at a distance of hundreds of miles from each other, I quickly came to see how dedicated they are and how much they care about the work they perform. The distance which separated us was a non-issue for us because BSP was so committed to using the project to learn about itself and improve.

Thoughts about the Process

We kept notes throughout the project, and often paused to consider how we might refine the process going forward. We invited organizations to refine or narrow the questions posed in the *FATAE* to generate language that was most useful and accessible to their constituents. Unsurprisingly, given its source, we heard at times that the base language felt overly academic. Opportunities exist for the continued refinement of the *FATAE's* language. Future users of this tool will benefit, as this project did, from not seeing it as a reified instrument to be followed prescriptively, but, rather, as a foundation for dialogue and exploration.

As noted previously, over the course of a year, almost none of our organizations were immune from staffing changes that affected the process, and all of the organizations engaged in meaningful changes, even during the process of inquiry and reflection. With that in mind, we recommend greater scaffolding for anticipating and managing that change. For example, helping to distribute the work of the project more broadly would have benefitted several of our organizations.

Working with the Framework

We engaged in conversations both as editors and with coordinators from each organization to consider the usefulness of the FATAE for the work of this project as well as more broadly, for other organizations to consider as they pursue operating in a manner that lives into and is consistent with principles of equity and justice. As we considered those discussions, we organized them according to both positive aspects as well as challenges/limitations of the framework. We predict these themes apply not only to the adapted version, the *FATAE*, but also to the original *EDJE Framework*.

Positive Responses to the FATAE

The positive responses that organizations offered about the *FATAE* focused on its use for organizing the work of this project as well as for use by organizations more broadly. Importantly, we recognize how, across the various domains, areas of focus, and questions, it provides connectedness to core principles of justice and equity across its four areas. The *FATAE* also provides a common language and set of guidelines for discussing equity and justice that helps make abstractions more comprehensible and applicable to practice and practitioners, as well as among academics and for researchers to conduct inquiry across designs and disciplines in systemic and systematic ways. As organizations use the *FATAE*, it provides an opportunity to engage a range and variety of internal and external stakeholders in the self-examination process. Leadership teams, departments, program-level staff, and governing boards can employ FATAE's questions to center conversations. It reveals strengths, challenges, and opportunities for growth and assists in tracking and planning for subsequent iterations of an organization's development. To this end, the framework helps us to know and understand what factors help to produce equitable and just outcomes from an asset-based, versus a deficit-based, perspective.

Participants' additional comments on the positive nature of the framework focused on how it ties practice to research-based principles that address equity and justice. The content of the framework reflects research-based principles and provokes/inspires practice to align accordingly. Significantly, the framework is not the work of one person and is not reflective of one line of thought; instead, it is based on the scholarship of many who have developed their ideas through examination, inquiry, and application of those ideas.

Challenges and Limits of the FATAE

Through ongoing conversations, the editors and coordinators provided several comments as constructive feedback to the original developers of the *EDJE Framework* as well as to those considering additional adaptations such as the *FATAE*. In addition, they offered process suggestions for organizations to consider in their use of the framework. One of the most significant comments participants in our work suggested about the *FATAE* is the need to develop of a set of instructions or guidelines to aid prospective users to understand the flexibility of and many ways the tool can be used. Currently, the *EDJE Framework* does not have a set of objectives or instructions for its use.

For example, an organization has great latitude in its selections of domains, areas of focus, and questions it may focus on or pursue at any point in time or under certain conditions faced by the organization. This suggestion is particularly pertinent given the length of the tool.

At first glance, without understanding how the tool may be used, the comprehensive nature and length of the tool could be overwhelming and off-putting, discouraging organizations from using it. The coordinators in our project noted the need to carefully plan the time and coordination a self-assessment process will demand of the people responsible for its implementation. They urged careful consideration of and narrowing of what domains, areas of focus and questions any one person, group, or program area may be responsible for managing. They advocated for creating a plan for how to analyze, condense, and communicate findings.

Also, individuals or groups who consider using the *FATAE* and making adaptions for their context, need to be aware there remain remnants of language reminiscent of the culture of academic or higher education organizations in the version used for this project. Finally, feedback indicated a need to reword pertinent questions in the *FATAE* to shift parts of it from a deficit based to and asset based perspective as the current version seems to be based in assumptions that work towards justice, equity and inclusion is not happening. That change will be especially valuable for organizations like the four in this project who have spent significant time and energy working toward justice and equity previously.

Summary

The history and context that we outlined in Chapter 1 show a need for adult learning to evolve in ways that more authentically and overtly respond to the needs of diverse learners and embrace equity, access, inclusion, and justice in doing so. While the U.S. has seen a slow march toward that needed inclusion, access, equity, and justice, that march has not concluded. Barriers still exist for many who still find themselves not served or not served well by what exists. In the four case studies, we found examples of organizations that see the problems and successfully work toward solutions. Whether the issue is the need for support among educators of color in Washington state, adult learners who seek new opportunities in Philadelphia, or career progression for property service workers or for mid-career professionals in California, the four organizations' case studies show how they counter the contexts that can limit significant numbers of adult learners.

For us, as editors of this work, working with these impressive organizations exceeded our expectations. The relationships we established with instructors and staff in our four organizations, our observations of the seriousness by which they took on and were responsible for their self-studies and respective write ups of their stories, the professionalism by which they engaged internally and externally throughout the process were invigorating and inspirational to us. As we reflect on this project, we decided to summarize this book with the following personal statements of our growth from this experience.

Deanna

I served on the original group of deans who designed and developed the EDJE *Framework for Assessment and Transformation*. Subsequently, I had two opportunities to engage the framework within an institution of higher education. As a dean, I led a group of faculty and staff through processes by which they independently and then collectively ranked and selected portions of the framework to advance our work in a college of education. I also advised a group of doctoral students as they used portions of the framework to gather evidence on the marketing, application, and admission processes of a targeted program for evidence of policies and procedures that either served as barriers to or supported equity, access, and inclusion. The opportunity to adapt the original *EDJE Framework* for use external to higher education was exciting. This project helped me learn about a far broader application of the framework than initially intended or expected. In addition, the experience reinforced evidence that structural and systemic oppression, discrimination, exclusion, and unjust practices are inherent to many types of organizations. More importantly, the work of these organizations revealed their ability to dismantle unjust and exclusionary practices with conscious and sustained attention and effort guided by the *FATAE*. I learned much through this project, especially about grounded, authentic, and practical systems, structures, policies, and procedures to mitigate and reverse historical injustices. With continued adaptions, I believe the *EDJE Framework* provides a useful tool for a myriad of organizations.

Ted

In many ways the *FATAE*, along with the original *EDJE Framework*, was designed to provoke engagement with silenced spaces within organizations. On a broad level, we understand that organizations, even those designed to pursue justice, are built of the same materials as those which perpetuate injustice and so carry the DNA to replicate the very systems they are designed to combat. That is insipid and yet, I have been fortunate to work with individuals and organizations who believe in transformational change and who possess the will, resiliency, and love to actively pursue it. Many agencies are inhibited in their efforts but undaunted in their desire. Completing this project reinforced for me the idea that centering equity is a powerful tool for meaningful organizational alignment, and that organizations that are authentically grounded in their purpose and practice are energized, magnetic, and more likely to thrive.

There are no secret intrinsic qualities to the organizations we chose to engage. Rather they are exemplars of distributive learning leadership and represent a powerful and inspiring case for reflective inquiry for organizations with a similar public purpose.

Bob

I hope someone will read this book and see examples of what excellence looks like, in all its complexity and messiness. I hope you'll see the organizations' chapters and our analyses to be a model for how you might conduct your own explorations as adult educators. As a teacher, researcher, consultant, administrator, or professor, I have been fortunate to have seen education in many forms and through many lenses. All of my past experiences had convinced me of the model we used to develop this book. Completing this project affirmed that belief. The four organizations are each comprised of amazing individuals who work very long hours because of their dedication to the adults they seek to serve. As you found in the chapters, these are not perfect organizations that have found a magic formula. They are organizations that have made commitments to striving toward excellence in every act they take. By supporting them to explore and then tell their own story, we have been able to allow others to see what justice and equity look like as they are wrestled into existence in real places. I found that to be humbling. I worry less about the future of a society that has such organizations and people in it.

References

Distefano, A., Rudestam, K. E., & Silverman, R. J. (2004). Scholar practitioner model. In *Encyclopedia of distributed learning* (Vol. 1, pp. 393–396). SAGE Publications, Inc.. https://dx.doi.org/10.4135/9781412950596.n134.

Fetterman, D., Kaftarian, S. J., & Wandersman, A. (2014). *Empowerment evaluation: Knowledge and tools for self-assessment, evaluation capacity building, and accountability.* SAGE Publications, Inc.

Geertz, C. (1973). Thick description: Toward an interpretive theory of culture. In *The interpretation of cultures, selected essays* (pp. 3–30). Basic Books, Inc.

Greenwood, D. J., & Levin, M. (2006). *Introduction to action research: Social research for social change.* SAGE Publications.

Lave, J., & Wenger, E. (1991). *Situated learning: Legitimate peripheral participation (learning in doing: Social, cognitive and computational perspectives).* Cambridge University Press.

Ryle, G. (1971). *Collected papers.* Barnes and Noble.

Wenger, E., McDermott, R., & Snyder, W. M. (2002). *Cultivating communities of practice* (1st ed.). Harvard Business School Press.

APPENDIX

A Framework for Assessment and Transformation in Adult Education*

Priority Areas of Work	Questions for Assessing & Action Planning
1. Centering Justice and Equity in Our Organization's Strategic Planning and Implementation	a. ASSUMPTIONS: What do we typically say is "supposed" to be in our mission statements, and strategic plans? What are the ways that such items, and the processes to develop/implement such items, can impede justice and equity goals? b. OUR GUIDING DOCUMENTS: Do our vision/mission statements, core values, program goals, and other guiding documents explicitly and fully reflect our commitment to justice and equity? Are these conceptualized and worded effectively? To what extent does our organization advance these effectively, and how do we know? c. OUR STRATEGIC PLAN: When strategic plans include justice and equity goals, how and why do organizations like us typically fail to meet such goals? To what extent does our strategic plan center on justice and equity goals, and how could it be revised to better do so? Specifically: does our plan include measurable outcomes, clear activities and timelines, adequate supports and resources, appropriate assessments and opportunities to revise in the interim, and so on (see, for example, the elements of the Action Plan in the section below this chart)? Does our plan account for existing and forthcoming challenges to implementation, including subsequent changes to policies and budgets, competing perspectives of our CEO/president, etc.? Does our plan require that all significant "new" undertakings (writing grant proposals, hiring new instructors, launching new centers, etc.), as well as ongoing work, involve asking complex questions about diversity, equity, and justice? d. RESOURCES: What are the examples of other organizations' strategic plans (and accompanying tools to implement, track, and/or assess the plans) that center justice and equity?

*Adapted from Education Deans for Justice & Equity ("The EDJE Framework")

(Continued)

Priority Areas of Work	Questions for Assessing & Action Planning
2. Democratizing Our Governance and Leadership	a. GOVERNANCE MODELS: What are common models (and less common but more promising models) of governance, and how does each model advance and/or hinder justice and equity goals? Where does our organization fit, how do we describe our governance model, and how often are we assessing and improving our governance structures, policies, and procedures?
	b. DEFINITIONS OF LEADERSHIP: What are common definitions of effective or impactful leaders and leadership, and qualities of desirable emerging leaders? How might these definitions limit the diversity of candidates for leadership positions and/or the capacity of leaders to be transformative? What is our definition of leadership? How might this advance and/or limit the diversity of candidates for leadership positions and/or the capacity of our faculty and staff to be leaders?
	c. WHO IS LEADING: Who is the "we" that is governing and is being governed? How are the voices of our stakeholders included and our governing structures, policies, and procedures? What is the role of partners outside of the organization in governance?
	d. DEMOCRATIC PROCESSES: What does it mean for decision-making processes to be "democratic" and for leading to be a "collective" responsibility, especially in very hierarchical environments? For example, when is majority vote or consensus helpful and not? How transparent do we make our decision-making processes, especially when the process might differ from issue to issue? To what extent are these happening and not happening in our organization, and why?
	e. COLLECTIVITY: What conversations need to happen to build an organization-wide consensus of and commitment to democratic governance and collective leadership? What areas of work would be "low-hanging fruit" to begin to deepen the organization's engagement in such forms of governance and leadership?
	f. RESISTANCE TO CHANGE: What forms of passive inertia or active resistance can we anticipate when leading anti-oppressively, and what are the examples inside and outside of our organization of resistances to democratic governance and to collective leadership? How could the organization raise awareness and anticipation of, and self-reflection about, how leading for social justice can spark resistance both inside and outside of the organization? What are the areas where such resistance is currently strong, and what are the strategies to address this?
	g. DIVERSITY: How diverse (by race, gender, and other dimensions of diversity) is our current and prospective pools of leaders? How can our organization improve and expand its pipelines and pathways for a more diverse, inclusive, and effective pool of emerging leaders?
	h. RESOURCES: What trainings, supports, and resources can the organization provide for the above areas of work to be successful? Where are the examples of how other organizations have done so, and what were the lessons learned?

(Continued)

Priority Areas of Work	Questions for Assessing & Action Planning
3. Aligning Our Budgets and Budgeting	a. MODELS: What are the common models (and less common but more promising models) for budgeting, and how does each model advance and/or hinder justice and equity goals? Which models does our organization use, and how often are we assessing and improving our budgeting structures, policies, and procedures?
	b. MISSION AND STRATEGIC-PLAN ALIGNMENT: To what extent are our decisions about budget allocations guided by our vision, mission, and strategic plan (versus, say, relying on "legacy" budgets, or how we historically have budgeted)? To what extent are our decisions about allocations guided by an action plan to advance diversity, equity, and justice, including plans that support "reparations"? To what extent are our allocations responsive to our accreditation and program-assessment processes? How can our broader goals as an organization, as well as the career goals of our instructors/staff, be advanced through creative re-thinking about budgets?
	c. DECISION MAKING: Who makes decisions about budgets? How are elements of power and privilege reproduced in the budgeting process? How involved are instructors and staff in reviewing and making recommendations? Are the budgeting process and budget statuses shared with instructors and partners in an open and transparent way?
	d. PAY EQUITY: What contributes to pay inequities (by gender, race, etc.) for employees, such as criteria for salary/wage determination and renegotiation, policies for salary increases and compression over time, and so on? How can our organization address these?
4. Increasing Our Fundraising & Development	a. TRENDS: What contributes to the need for organization to fundraise? How do our fundraising strategies reinforce and/or challenge existing ideologies and trends?
	b. CURRENT STRATEGIES: How do organizations like us typically raise funds, and how do our fundraising activities either advance or hinder our justice and equity goals? For example, are wealthy individuals incentivizing certain work over justice-oriented work; are the messages we use perpetuating deficit-based ideologies of the people we serve and/or purely economic framings of the "problem"; are the criteria we use to identify prospects and evaluate offers centered on our justice and equity goals, etc.?
	c. HIDDEN CURRICULUM OF FUNDRAISING: Who has the social capital to raise funding more easily (because of connection or cultural upbringing)? Are we creating systems to teach this hidden curriculum of fundraising? What are the institutional norms we have accepted about individualism and competition that prevent us from sharing relationships and resources, particularly with organizations with less economic, racial, and gender privilege than us? What are the barriers to working together to raise funds for our programs?

(Continued)

Priority Areas of Work	Questions for Assessing & Action Planning
	d. PROSPECTS AND PARTNERS: Why, for whom, and with whom are we raising funds (e.g., are we raising primarily to support our institution, or are we raising in collaboration with partners to support the communities with the least capacity to enroll)? Who are the potential donors and funders that align with our justice and equity goals? Who are the current or potential partners (such as partner organizations, public officials, etc.) that can assist with fundraising? Who is the primary partner with donors?
	e. MESSAGING: What is the messaging that can best animate our justice and equity goals while also speaking to the priorities of our potential funders? How do we want to define the problem/need, and what do we believe is the most impactful use of funding to address these? How do we raise the awareness of our potential fundraising partners of our justice and equity goals? How might regional differences require adapting our fundraising strategies?
	f. RESOURCES: What trainings, supports, and resources can the organization provide for such work to be successful? Where are the examples of justice-oriented fundraising plans and communications at other organizations?
5. **Strengthening Our Programs and Curriculum**	a. EDUCATION FOR DEMOCRACY: What would it mean for our organization to situate its work in larger social movements for justice and equity? How would that require that we do our work differently? Who in our communities would we reach out to and work with? And how should we prepare our students to approach their own work in education differently as well?
	b. TEACHING COLLECTIVELY: To what extent do we approach the design, implementation, and assessment of our programs and curriculum collectively (versus, say, allowing programs to be run primarily by one instructor/staff)? Where, when, and how are instructors talking about the legacies of injustice and the external challenges facing similar organizations, and what these mean for our programs and curriculum? (See also Sections 7 and 10).
	c. DEEPLY ENGAGING IN EXISTING RESEARCH AND THEORY: How can our instructors and staff more substantively explore and draw on the scholarship and models developed by colleagues across the country and world about how to center justice and equity in our programs and curriculum? That is, how can we engage even more deeply in the expansive literatures about and models for education that are anti-oppressive, asset-based, community-engaged, critical, culturally affirming and responsive, feminist, inclusive, indigenous-centered, interdisciplinary, intersectional, multicultural, nonnormative, post-colonial and post-imperial, queer, and so on?

(*Continued*)

Priority Areas of Work	Questions for Assessing & Action Planning
	d. RESOURCES: What resources and supports can our organization offer to support instructors in such learning, reflecting, and implementing? How can we make use of the resources and connections of our networks to facilitate this exchange and engagement across institutions?
6. Supporting Our Students	a. ASSUMPTIONS ABOUT TARGET STUDENT POPULATION: What are the characteristics of the individual student, and of the overall student population, that we strive to serve in our organization? What makes a prospective student qualified and desirable? What do we hope our graduates leave our programs with? How might any of these assumptions hinder and/or support our justice and equity goals? To what extent is our organization regularly assessing our assumptions and expectations about who our students are and should be? To what extent is the diversity of our student population, as well as the capacity of our graduates to advance justice and equity, a central part of our organization's mission and strategic plan?
	b. STAGES: What is the student experience through all stages of recruitment, admission, orientation, academic engagement and success, retention, and completion/graduation? How are our students experiencing these stages differently, depending on their race, gender, ability, and other dimensions of diversity, and how do we know this? Are relevant instructors and staff receiving guidance, support, and feedback as they engage in any of these stages?
	c. PIPELINES AND PATHWAYS: What are (and what should be) the pipelines into the organizations' programs from our partner and community organizations? Who are our target populations? To what extent are we partnering with organizations and other stakeholders in strengthening these pipelines? To what extent is our organization working collaboratively with other organizations to approach pipelines strategically rather than simply competitively?
	d. FINANCIAL BURDENS AND SUPPORT: Through any or all stages of the student experience, what are the expenses placed on students that make our program(s) financially inaccessible, particularly for students of limited income and resources? Examples include application fees, fees for various tests and assessments, expenses related to attendance, field work or internships, and cost of course materials, housing and transportation, health care, child care, and even aspects that are not explicitly financial in nature but have economic consequence, such as the inability to transfer previous experiences/course credits from previous work/educational institutions, loss of actual or potential income when participating in programmatic experiences or doing field work during school or business hours, limited availability of courses and instructors/staff after work hours, etc. How is our organization addressing such financial burdens?

(Continued)

Priority Areas of Work	Questions for Assessing & Action Planning
	e. ACADEMIC SUPPORT: To what extent does our organization support the academic preparation and success of students who were not well-served by their previous educational systems, as with support for passing high-stakes assessments, support for developing academic or social skills needed to succeed in coursework/program, etc.?
	f. ASSESSMENT AND ACCOUNTABILITY FOR EDUCATION WORK: How does our organization assess that our students align with our mission?
	g. POST-GRADUATION: How is our organization supporting and re-engaging our alumni to advance our justice and equity goals?
7. Increasing the Racial Diversity of Our Instructors	a. IDEOLOGIES: Why has the adult education profession historically been so overwhelmingly white and female, why is the teacher profession similar, and why has this been so hard to change? Why are so many of our more highly compensated and elite positions (administrators, etc.) occupied by white males? Which of these elements/factors are present in our organization?
	b. WHAT DO WE DESIRE: What are typical definitions of and assumptions about staff "fit," being "qualified," or exhibiting "success" or "excellence," and how might these reinforce white privilege or demand assimilation? Are we searching for staff who challenge? Or question? and expand what we do as an organization (versus, say, merely replicating or sustaining)? To what extent are we searching for hires who increase the racial diversity of our instructors, as well as hires who expand the expertise of our staff on issues of diversity, justice, and equity (recognizing that these two groups are not always the same)?
	c. STAGES: What are (and what should be) our strategies for diversifying our staff at each key stage: recruitment, hiring, induction, retention, professional success, and promotion? Where are the exemplars of justice-oriented staff-of-color recruitment & retention plans and initiatives at other organizations?
	d. PIPELINES AND PATHWAYS: Similar to "grow your own" programs as a way to build pipelines for a more diverse teaching force that is from and committed to the communities in which they will teach, what would it mean for any organization to "grow our own" staff? Are there exemplars of how to accomplish this while also honoring concerns about insularity? Might there be opportunities for multiple institutions to "cross-fertilize" grow-your-own programs?
	e. JOB POSTINGS AND OUTREACH: Do we ensure that our job postings and job descriptions include expertise on diversity and equity? How do we involve our partners in our searches? Where are we recruiting? Do we require that there be racial diversity (as can be determined legally) in the applicant pool and/or in the list of finalists before proceeding to interviews? Are we recruiting from non-traditional career pathways?

(Continued)

Priority Areas of Work	Questions for Assessing & Action Planning
	f. SEARCH COMMITTEES: How do we constitute the membership of search committees? Do we require participation from other departments and/or the office of the chief diversity officer? What happens during job interviews (i.e., what the schedule consists of) that might reinforce white or male privilege? Are search committees required to explain why any/all qualified applicants of color were not advanced to the next stage of review? How are the search committee and the larger organization held accountable for checking their own biases throughout the search process? What training is required of search committees?
	g. HIRING: What are the strategies that other organizations have used successfully to recruit staff of color? Three examples include: (a) incentives for hiring two instructors when one search culminates in identifying two strong candidates that can meet various needs of the organization; (b) partner hiring, and accommodating staff needs; and (c) cluster hiring.
	h. INDUCTION: What is the climate for new staff, particularly individuals of color? How are new staff welcomed, onboarded, oriented, mentored, etc.? When can good intentions (particularly of white staff) be counterproductive?
	i. WORKLOAD: Are newly hired staff given a workload that sets them up for success? Are staff of color being asked to do more work because of their identities and/or areas of expertise (as when asked to work on diversity-related initiatives, or when approached by students of color for mentoring), and how is this work supported and credited?
	j. RETENTION: What patterns are discernable for why instructors of color do not stay at our organization? Are we using intersectional lenses (intersections of race with gender, sexuality, religion, disability, etc.) to understand the problems and the patterns? What resources is the organization allocating for instructors' retention and success?
8. Supporting Our Instructors	a. IDEOLOGIES: What are current controversies surrounding the work of instructor, and how do they operate in contradictory ways? For example, "academic freedom" can protect those who speak out against injustice, but also can protect those who do not wish to self-examine, so how do we protect academic freedom even as we challenge each of us to critically self-reflect? Or creating a common curriculum can allow instructors to work collaboratively to develop common activities for students while helping those instructors come to common understandings of outcomes; however, that can also be used to suppress innovation and limit an instructor's ability to modify activities to address students' needs.

(Continued)

Priority Areas of Work	Questions for Assessing & Action Planning
	b. POLICIES: How have existing ideologies about the roles and responsibilities of instructors been normalized in our profession and institutionalized in our policies, and to what extent do these norms and policies inhibit and/or support work by instructors that explicitly names justice and equity? How does (and how should) our organization define and operationalize justice and equity? (See, for example, Step 2 in the Recommendations below this chart.) Where and when are our instructors asked to assess the extent to which all significant aspects of their work advance justice and equity goals?
	c. EVALUATION: To what extent does the increasing reliance on certain forms of evaluation and ranking (like standardized testing and rigid instructor performance standards) hinder and/or facilitate justice-oriented instruction? To what extent does our organization support activist or impact-oriented scholarship (including scholarship that is community-engaged, public-facing, practitioner-focused, open-access, and/or in collaboration with partner organizations)?
	d. TEACHING: To what extent does our organization approach teaching as a collective act, such as by talking about the goals, content, and approaches of our programs and our advising of students (versus, say, each instructor teaching as a solo act with no sharing or oversight)? To what extent is a collective approach to teaching inclusive of all instructors, regardless of their status in the organization?
	e. SERVICE: To what extent does our organization address workload inequities and differentiated service within the organization?
	f. PROFESSIONAL DEVELOPMENT AND SUPPORT: To what extent is the PD for instructors offered by our organization aligned with its justice and equity goals, and are other supports for instructors (including funding and mentoring) similarly aligned? Does our organization support affinity groups around marginalized identities and/or activist topics? Does our organization acknowledge, and challenge discrimination based on discipline, type of course taught, and so on? To what extent does our organization recognize the long-term and emotionally taxing nature of justice work, and work-life balance in general, and then support instructors in doing justice work?
9. **Supporting Our Staff**	a. SUPERVISION: What are common models for organizing staff work and reporting lines, as well as for supervising and managing staff, and taking "disciplinary" action? How do these hinder and/or support our justice and equity goals? How often are we assessing our supervision policies and procedures? How can our organization better train and support staff supervisors to "supervise" in ways that align with our mission and strategic plan?

(Continued)

Priority Areas of Work	Questions for Assessing & Action Planning

b. HIERARCHIES: What hierarchical structures and related cultures of elitism (especially between instructors and staff, and between different racial/gender/etc. groups) typically pervade organizations like ours? How do these institutional structures/cultures connect to issues of diversity, justice, and equity? How do these institutional structures/cultures affect staff and their work, and how do we know this (e.g., are we gathering data from staff)? When are reporting lines and divisions of duties needed, and when are they counterproductive?

c. INTEGRATION: What are alternative models for structuring the work and groupings of staff to be more egalitarian, democratic, and collective? How can staff be more connected with the organization (as with frequent all-organization or board meetings that substantively include staff) and more involved in organizational governance (as with committees and task forces that include staff, and other ways for staff to interact directly with leaders)? How do staff unions and collective bargaining processes affect staff relations and integration; on what aspects of the union structure can we build to improve staff integration; and what aspects should be revised in order to better support our justice and equity goals?

d. RELATIONS WITH INSTRUCTORS: To what extent are instructor-staff divisions existing in our organization, and what are strategies to change them to better reflect our mission and values? What are strategies for instructors and staff to get to know one another better on a personal and professional level (i.e., both who we are and what exactly we do)? How can our organization better draw on community-organizing and movement-building strategies by making relationship building and community building a more central and intentional part of what we do and who we are? How do we benefit from having colleagues with advance education who are not instructors? What distinction do we make between these two categories and why?

e. DIVERSITY: What knowledge, skills, and dispositions do we look for in our staff, and to what extent do these align with our organizational mission and values? How diverse (by race, gender, social class, etc.) is the staff, and how can the organization increase and support this diversity? How are we tracking conflicts and other problems related to diversity in the workplace, and how are we addressing both individual incidents and larger patterns? What does it mean for our organization to be a place where staff of all backgrounds feel welcomed, valued, seen and heard, connected, a sense of belonging, a sense of ownership and responsibility, and an ability to thrive? What are the different job categories of staff that exist in our organization? What kinds of different expertise and training do each bring? Why do we need a staff population that is diverse in several ways (by race, professional expertise, etc.)?

(Continued)

Priority Areas of Work	Questions for Assessing & Action Planning
	f. PERFORMANCE REVIEWS: To what extent does our organization consider the diverse backgrounds of staff in their evaluation processes? To what extent do we engage staff in performance reviews that explicitly address our organizational mission, and that involve them in collaboratively establishing goals for themselves and reflecting on their progress? To what extent are performance reviews formalized and transparent so people can grow and learn, and in contrast, to what extent are informal processes allowing people with privilege to become more privileged? What are the mechanisms for staff to learn and grow and receive feedback?
	g. PROFESSIONAL DEVELOPMENT AND SUPPORT: To what extent are staff receiving opportunities for professional development that parallel those of instructors, including funding, PD offerings, mentoring, retreats, incentives and rewards, promotions or advances, time for such activities, and so on, in order to increase staff capacity to advance our justice and equity goals?
10. Improving the Institutional Climate within Our Organization	a. RELATION TO DIVERSITY: In what ways is institutional climate related to or affected by diversity? How well does everyone in the organization understand the nature of and difference between microaggressions, harassment, bullying, and discrimination? In what ways is climate experienced differently by different groups in our organization?
	b. ADDRESSING CLIMATE COLLECTIVELY: How does the organization's mission and strategic plan address institutional climate? To what extent does our organization engage in conversations about what we mean by institutional "climate," what research has shown to positively and negatively impact climate, how to assess climate, and how organization-wide or unit-wide (e.g., department-level) climate affects well-being, productivity, and feelings of belonging at the level of individual instructors, staff, and students?
	c. POLICIES AND PROCEDURES: What policies and procedures are in place to document problems (safety, exclusion, harassment, discrimination, etc.) and seek support, protection, and justice? How do we know that these policies and procedures are working effectively?
	d. RESOURCES: What trainings, supports, and resources can the organizational allocate to improve institutional climate and the factors that impact it?

(Continued)

Priority Areas of Work	Questions for Assessing & Action Planning
11. Deepening Our External Partnerships	a. REPUTATIONS AND MODELS: What is the reputation of organization regarding our partnerships in the region? What typically are the benefits and burdens for each side of the partnership, and how are both parties assessing these? What are different models and/or frameworks (regarding different purposes, different levels of interaction and investment, different outcomes, etc.) for what our external partnerships can and should look like? How can a holistic and strategic approach to partnerships help us to meet our range of needs and goals? What are (and who should be) the types of partnerships that best align with our justice and equity goals? b. PARTNERS: Who are our external partners, and why are they our partners? Who else should we partnering with, and why? Examples of partners include schools and school districts, community-based organizations, professional associations, service providers, businesses, foundations, allies, public officials, colleges and universities, other similar organizations, professional networks, and so on. Examples of purposes include fund-raising, evaluation, program development, scholarship, teaching, service, advocacy, and so on. c. BARRIERS: What external issues (like the pressure around testing in basic skills) and internal issues (like our internal graduation requirements) are making it difficult to find common ground with partners and/or to find creative solutions to problems or needs that we all agree exist? d. CURRICULUM THAT IS DEEPLY EMBEDDED IN OUR COMMUNITIES: Where and with whom have we connected where our students might engage in placed-based learning, complete any field work, scholarship, and service projects, etc.? To what extent is our organization identifying and cultivating community partnerships, field sites, and field-based instructors that explicitly align with our mission and strategic plan? Is the impact of our relationship with these partners/sites/staff helping to build their (i.e., not only our) capacity to do justice and equity work? While at their placement sites and while working with field staff, are our students building their (students') own capacity to advance justice and equity goals during their time as students and after they graduate as well? e. EVALUATION, SCHOLASRHIP OR RESEARCH THAT IS ACCOUNTABLE TO OUR COMMUNITIES: In what ways do we intentionally seek out feedback from community members about what research would be most helpful in advancing justice and equity in education, or how best to leverage our scholarship to meet their needs?

(Continued)

Priority Areas of Work	Questions for Assessing & Action Planning
12. Managing Crises within and Beyond Our Organization	a. MACRO-LEVEL: What are the macro-level crises facing our organization and similar organizations today? Are any of these "manufactured," and from what other problems are these manufactured crises meant to distract?
	b. MICRO-LEVEL: What are the micro-level crises typically confronting organizational managers in our day-to-day work? What characterizes a crisis at the individual level vs. institutional level vs. ideological level? In what ways could our responses to crises detract from our justice and equity goals?
	c. POLICIES AND PROCEDURES: What are (and what should be) our policies and procedures for: (a) assessing the nature of any crisis as macro/micro, as individual/institutional/ideological, etc.; (b) responding to crises and communicating during and after to all involved or impacted; and (c) assessing how our responses might be exacerbating and/or challenging injustices and inequities?
13. Developing Our Public Voice	a. IDEOLOGICAL AND INSTITUTIONAL CONSTRAINTS: What historically has been the role of organizations like ours in influencing public debates and public policies related to justice and equity in education, especially in our region? What are we telling ourselves is "supposed" to be the work of organizations like ours regarding public debates? What policies (from the state; within our institutions), professional and cultural norms, and other constraints are in place to prohibit, regulate, censor, and/or discourage inserting our organization into the public debate?
	b. REFRAMING THE DEBATE: What is the public policy that we wish to tackle right now, and what is the underlying ideology that we need to reframe? What would be our intended outcome of speaking publicly?
	c. STRATEGIES: Whom should we prioritize as our target audiences right now? What are the venues for doing so (e.g., media; social media; lobby days)? Who are the potential partners for such educational efforts (e.g., advocacy groups; media)?
	d. RESOURCES: What training, supports, and resources can our organization provide for such work to be successful? Where are examples of other organizations speaking publicly and/or of collectives of scholars/leaders speaking publicly?

INDEX

Note: *Italicised* folios refers figures and **bold** tables.